CALLED TO FREEDOM
Reformation 1517–2017 in an Irish context

edited by
Gesa E. Thiessen
on behalf of the Lutheran Church in Ireland

Wordwell

First published in 2019
Wordwell Ltd
in association with the Lutheran Church in Ireland
Unit 9, 78 Furze Road, Sandyford Industrial Estate, Dublin 18
www.wordwellbooks.com

© Copyright text: the authors 2019
© Copyright design and layout: Wordwell Ltd

Front cover image—*Martin Luther* by Lucas Cranach the Elder, (1520).

All rights reserved. No part of this book may be reprinted or reproduced or utilised in any electronic, mechanical or other means, now known or hereafter invented, including photocopying and recording, or otherwise without either the prior written consent of the publishers or a licence permitting restricted copying in Ireland issued by the Irish Copyright Licensing Agency Ltd, 63 Patrick Street, Dún Laoghaire, Co. Dublin, A96 WF25.

ISBN 978-1-9164922-5-7

British Library Cataloguing-in-Publication Data.
A catalogue record for this book is available from the British Library.

Typeset in Ireland by Wordwell Ltd
Copy-editor: Emer Condit
Cover design and artwork: Wordwell Ltd
Printed by Digital Print Dynamics

Contents

Foreword   vii
Stephan Arras and Markus Grimmeisen

Greetings   ix
Patrick Prendergast

Introduction   1
Gesa E. Thiessen

Opening of the Symposium—
Ecumenical Perspectives on Reformation 1517–2017
Michael Jackson   6
Brendan Leahy   13
Stephanie Springer   16
Donald Watts   17

I. Luther, Reforms and the Freedom of the Christian

1. The whole of life ought to be penance—penance in the early Reformation   21
Volker Leppin

2. The idea of reform in the sermons and pamphlets of Martin Luther, 1517–1522   32
Helga Robinson-Hammerstein

3. Luther and Cranach—spreading the Reformation through images   47
Gesa E. Thiessen

4. Love, freedom and guilt—differences between Christian traditions in the conception of the relationship between divine and human freedom   66
Gunda Werner

5. Luther in a Dublin library—reflections on the 500th   78
anniversary of the Reformation
Graeme Murdock

II. Legacies of the Reformation

6. Luther's legacy for Pauline studies in modern debate   91
Martin Meiser

7. Challenging memories—the Reformation in France   104
and the Huguenots in Ireland
Ruth Whelan

8. 'They also appointed bishops for themselves'—religious   126
change in sixteenth- and seventeenth-century Ireland
John McCafferty

9. The Lutheran rectory in German culture and literature   140
Jürgen Barkhoff

10. Marking the Reformation 500 years on—   158
Quo vadis ecclesia semper reformanda?
Martin Sauter

The next 500 years have begun

Epilogue 1   165
Stephan Arras

Epilogue 2   171
Martin Sauter

Contributors   179

Index   184

CALLED TO FREEDOM

Foreword

'Stories on the Road'—this was the title of an exhibition on wheels, a project of the Evangelische Kirche in Deutschland (EKD), which travelled through Europe between 3 November 2016 and 20 May 2017. Sixty-seven cities in nineteen European countries were marked on the road-map of the truck. Visitors were invited to share personal stories about Reformation and ecumenism. On 17/18 February 2017 the truck visited Dublin. The Church Council of the Lutheran Church in Ireland decided to combine the visit of the travelling exhibition with a theological symposium in Trinity College. The symposium was planned and realised together with colleagues from Trinity College Dublin and the German Embassy.

Five hundred years after the Reformation, this, then, might be its most considerable fruit: different Christian denominations and secular institutions are able to celebrate and to study the past and present challenges together. Yet today we witness new borders and populist nationalism increasing in Europe. As a sign of hope, this symposium took a broad European approach. You will find reflections in this volume on the Reformation in Germany, Sweden, Ireland and France, and its impact on the Enlightenment and modern times, including biblical studies, religion, literature, contemporary society and culture.

The Lutheran Church has been deeply moved and is grateful to all those who contributed to making our theological symposium happen. We were delighted with the high standard of the lectures and speeches. They also include the sermon on Reformation Day, 31 October 2017, by Roman Catholic Archbishop Diarmuid Martin in the Lutheran Church in Dublin, and the contributions on Remembrance Day in November 2017 by the German Military Bishop, Dr Sigurd Rink, as well as several speakers from Germany, Ireland, France and Northern Ireland, organised through fine teamwork between the German Embassy, the Lutheran Church and the Glencree Centre for Peace and Reconciliation.

Half a millennium has passed since Luther's times. Today we appreciate and value the rich diversity of the church worldwide. We are able to share our knowledge and our 'stories' of Reformation as an ongoing process in an increasingly secularised world. This book hopes to be a contribution to the ongoing quest of the *ecclesia semper reformanda*.

We wish to thank the following people and institutions. While we have done our best to be comprehensive, we apologise if we have inadvertently omitted any names: Peter Adams, German Embassy, Dublin; Kajsa Ahlstrand, University of Uppsala; Hans Ulrich Anke, EKD; Jürgen Barkhoff, Trinity College; Werner Blau, Trinity College; Con Casey, Trinity College; John Dexter, Goethe Institut Choir; Susanne Erlecke, EKD; Archbishop Michael Jackson, Church of Ireland, Dublin; Maureen Junker-Kenny, Trinity College; Bishop Brendan Leahy, Roman Catholic Church, Limerick; Volker Leppin, Tübingen University; John McCafferty, University College Dublin; Archbishop Diarmuid Martin, Roman Catholic Church, Dublin; Wolfgang Marx, University College Dublin; Martin Meiser, University of Saarbrücken; Graeme Murdock, Trinity College; Andrew Pierce, Trinity College; Provost Patrick Prendergast, Trinity College; Helga Robinson-Hammerstein, Trinity College/Lutheran Church in Ireland; Ian Stuart Robinson, Trinity College; Martin Sauter, Lutheran Church in Ireland; Stephanie Springer, EKD; Revd Donald Watts, Presbyterian Church, Ireland; Gunda Werner, University of Graz; Ruth Whelan, Maynooth University; Trinity College Dublin; Trinity College Library; German Embassy, Dublin; Goethe Institut, Dublin; Goethe Institut Choir; Evangelische Kirche in Deutschland (EKD); the staff of the EKD Reformation Exhibition Truck; the Church Council of the Lutheran Church in Ireland; all helpers, especially those who worked behind the scenes; and Gesa Thiessen, Lutheran Church in Ireland/Trinity College, for tirelessly working on the Symposium and for editing this book.

Finally, we want to express our special gratitude and appreciation for the life and work of the late Dr Helga Robinson-Hammerstein, who taught Reformation History in Trinity College Dublin over decades. She was an excellent *Prädikantin* (non-stipendiary minister) who significantly contributed to shaping the Lutheran Church in Ireland, rooted deeply in Martin Luther's theology and much involved in ecumenical exchange and friendship.

Stephan Arras and Markus Grimmeisen

Greetings

Your Excellency, Distinguished Guests,

Good afternoon. It's a great pleasure to welcome you all to Trinity College Dublin for this wonderful commemorative event: the Reformation at 500. It's an honour for Trinity to be hosting this travelling exhibition, or *Reformation Roadmap*, which—as most of you are aware—is an initiative of the German government together with the Lutheran Church and is visiting 67 places in nineteen European countries.

Trinity College is the only Irish stop for the exhibition, and to anyone who knows Irish history this makes sense: our university owes its very foundation to the Reformation. We don't always like to remember this because religion has often been a cause of conflict on this island. But we should recall that Trinity was founded by royal charter granted by the great Reformation queen, Elizabeth I, a mere 75 years after Martin Luther nailed his theses to the door of All Saints Church in Wittenberg—the event that started it all and which this exhibition is commemorating.

Few have had a greater impact than Martin Luther: before he died, he had founded a new church, translated the Bible into German and converted to his thinking key electors and princes of Europe—including, of course, Henry VIII of England. And he had changed the way that universities teach.

Trinity began as a college of theology for students studying the doctrines of Luther, Calvin and other luminaries of the Reformation. Archbishop James Ussher—often called 'Trinity's first scholar'—was a product of this education and a stalwart defender of it. His achievements were exceptional, including publishing in 1639 the most substantial history of Christianity in Britain and Ireland to date, and building up the library here in this College.

When Ussher arrived as a student in 1594, Trinity had just 30 books and ten manuscripts. To bulk this up, Ussher, as vice-provost, made book-buying visits to England every three years and set the pattern of valuable acquisitions for the library. He was motivated to do this to build up scholarship in the new college, of course, but also out of Protestant zeal—he wanted to 'spread the word' to Ireland.

It's important to remember and commemorate our foundations, and it's interesting that this most significant anniversary for the Reformation and for Trinity should occur during the Decade of Commemorations, when Ireland is remembering the events that led to the foundation of the State.

On behalf of the College, I thank the German government and the Lutheran Church for bringing this most imaginative exhibition to Trinity and providing the occasion for us to explore our heritage. As well as this *Reformation Roadmap*, we are hosting a symposium, which is starting shortly and continuing tomorrow, with distinguished speakers from Germany, Europe and Ireland.

And the Library, in conjunction with the Schools of English and of History and Humanities, is running an exhibition in the Long Room till the end of the month. Entitled 'Power and Belief', it draws on the astonishing collections held in our Library, including most notably a very rare volume by the Czech reformer Jan Hus, published in 1537 and originally housed in the library of Thomas Cranmer, archbishop of Canterbury. Cranmer was burned as a heretic in 1556, during the reign of Queen Mary, and his books were confiscated. Fortunately this volume found its way to Trinity, where it has been preserved.

The exhibition also includes a 1523 edition of Martin Luther's translation of the Old Testament and William Bedell's 1685 work *Leabhuir na Seintiomna*, the first translation into Irish of the Old Testament.

Continuing the celebration, our chapel is holding three concerts this week, celebrating the musical legacy of the chorales of Martin Luther; two of them were held on Saturday and Wednesday past, and the third and final will take place tomorrow at 7pm. This is presented by the Goethe Institut.

The extent of the celebration means that many Trinity colleagues are involved—librarians, chaplains, theologians, historians and more. I would like to thank all of you for the work and effort you have put in.

I hope that not only staff and students in the college but also visitors, local and international, will get the chance to see these exhibitions and reflect on the extraordinary changes brought about by Martin Luther 500 years ago, and their continuing impact.

Thank you.

Patrick Prendergast, Provost, Trinity College

Introduction

Gesa E. Thiessen

The year 2017 marked the 500th anniversary of the Reformation.[1] On 31 October 1517 Augustinian monk Martin Luther sent his *Ninety-Five Theses* to bishops and clergy for discussion; these theses concerned good works and the widespread abuse of the selling of indulgences in the church. Indulgences, used for financing the building of St Peter's in Rome, promised the uneducated laity the remittance of punishment in purgatory and thus functioned as a 'fast track' to heaven. In Thesis 45, Luther contended in no uncertain terms: 'Christians are to be taught that someone who sees a human being in need, and passes them by, and gives [money] for pardons, purchases not the indulgences of the pope, but the indignation of God'.

Reading St Paul and translating the New Testament into German brought about a tidal change in Luther's contemplations and personal quest for God. His central concern would be how humans develop a right relationship with God. It came to be known as the doctrine of justification. In St Paul Luther found answers to his question, 'How do I find a gracious God?' Not by procuring indulgences but by faith in the God of grace. As Paul writes: 'But now, irrespective of law, the righteousness of God has been disclosed … the righteousness of God through faith in Jesus Christ for all who believe' (Rom 3: 21). Humans cannot assure their own salvation through countless indulgences and good works. It is God's love and grace and our faith that save. Faith, Luther stated, 'is a living, bold trust in God's grace, so certain of God's favour that it would risk death a thousand times trusting in it'. Faith is the proper response to *God's* initiative. For Luther the search for the God of love was not only theological but existential, not a matter of scholastic speculation but real. In this search, St Paul, St Augustine and the German mystics Johannes Tauler and Meister Eckhart were formative in Luther's thought.

At the heart of Luther's theology, then, was the notion that the human being is, and always must be, in a free, direct relationship with God, without coercive practices on the part of the institutional church. In one of his central reformatory writings, *The Freedom of a Christian* (1520), he declared: 'A Christian is the most free lord of all, and subject to none; a Christian is the most dutiful servant of all and subject to everyone'. Far from rejecting good works, as he has often been misunderstood to do, he asserted that for a Christian, 'free lord' *and* 'dutiful servant', it is a given that good works will flow freely out of one's faith.

Luther's reformatory aims concerned the church and the education system in Germany. Christians should be taught to read the Bible and be informed about their faith. Masses were to be held in the vernacular and the Eucharist to be distributed under both species. Luther's polemics against the decadent pope and hierarchy were sharp. He did not recant and was declared a heretic and outlaw in 1521. Despite efforts to the contrary, the split with Rome became inevitable, a consequence which Luther never intended nor could have foreseen in 1517.

Thankfully, 500 years on, false perceptions and mutual condemnations have been overcome by the ecumenical movement and the *rapprochement* between churches. Theologians from all denominations now agree that on *theological* grounds church division need never have happened. The legacy of the Reformation is vast and reaches into our own times, most especially in relation to notions of grace and salvation, ecclesiology, human and religious freedom, individual conscience, and the importance of religious and secular education.

To mark the Quincentenary, our symposium took place on 17–18 February 2017 in Trinity College Dublin and focused on the central notion of freedom in Luther's thought and in Christian life, as well as on some of the post-Reformation legacies and developments, including the Reformation's impact on Ireland. With the resounding success of the symposium, which was attended by an unexpectedly large number of people, the idea then arose to publish the proceedings and to invite some extra articles. While not all invited academics were able to contribute—especially on the Reformation's legacy in the development of music, philosophy and the natural sciences—we are delighted to include five extra articles and two ample epilogues from our pastors. Moreover, we are grateful to Nick Maxwell and Wordwell for kindly agreeing to publish this book.

Part I, 'Luther, Reforms and the Freedom of the Christian', begins with Volker Leppin's chapter, introducing the reader to Martin Luther's background in the mystical thought of the late Middle Ages. Mystical theology and spirituality has oftentimes been associated with Catholic theology. Hence the mystical dimension in Luther's theology and faith life has received comparatively little attention in Protestant scholarship. Leppin shows how Luther's thinking was not radically new but deeply embedded in prevailing mystical ideas, notably Meister Eckhart, Johannes Tauler and even Bernard of Clairvaux, yet also developed on from these leading medieval theologians.

In a careful examination of Luther, Helga Robinson-Hammerstein focuses on ideas of reform in his sermons and pamphlets between 1517 and 1522. Paying tribute to Luther's pastoral side, as he understood himself first of all as a 'preacher' and 'man of the word', even as a university professor, she notes how Luther was slow to encourage the faithful to rush into changes, emphasising that faith is and always must grow in a free decision grounded in the Scriptures and recognising the conscience of the believer.

A striking example of Luther's advocacy of restraint becomes apparent in his reaction to the outburst of iconoclasm in Wittenberg in 1521, which in turn led him to comment on the role of images and other material religion in his Invocavit Sermons and elsewhere. I discuss Luther's views on religious images in Chapter 3, including an analysis of some central works of art and a selection of polemic woodcuts in pamphlets by the painters of the Reformation, Lucas Cranach and his son, Lucas Cranach the Younger.

In Chapter 4, Gunda Werner investigates the relationship between divine and human freedom in Luther's and Roman Catholic Tridentine theology and in current theological scholarship, beginning with an analysis of mercy as a theological category and its relationship with justice. She examines key concepts of love, freedom, sin, guilt and divine action, taking in Erasmus's and Luther's differing views on human freedom of the will.

'Luther in a Dublin library' offers a look into the rich collection of early printed books in Trinity College Library from the time of the Reformation. Graeme Murdock was not only instrumental in organising the exhibition 'Power and Belief: the Reformation at 500', coinciding with the symposium, but also contributes Chapter 5, which traces the fascinating history of some of these books, notably the *Epistolae quaedam piissimae et eruditissimae Iohannis Hus, quae solae satis declarant Papistarum pietates, esse Satanae furias* ('Some very godly and erudite letters of Jan Hus, sufficient in themselves to show that the piety of the papists is satanic madness'), prefaced by Luther and published in 1537.

In Part II, 'Legacies of the Reformation', perspectives emerge on various developments—biblical, ecclesial, political, social and cultural—after the Reformation, extending historically into the Enlightenment and to the present day and geographically into France and Ireland. Martin Meiser, in Chapter 6, examines and critically reflects on Luther's influence on modern Pauline studies. Given that Luther came to be known, and is remembered today, as the great church reformer, it is sometimes forgotten that he was a biblical scholar and wrote extensive commentaries on central Scripture texts. Meiser assesses in particular the new perspective on Paul in modern Pauline studies and whether it does justice to Luther's writings. Further, he considers both the legacy and non-legacy of Luther in contemporary biblical scholarship.

In Chapter 7 Ruth Whelan sheds light on a topic that may not immediately come to mind when one thinks of the Reformation, i.e. its developments in France, centring on the Protestant Huguenots, who in the seventeenth century were persecuted, excluded and suffered greatly, forced to leave France for Germany, Switzerland and England. Some thousand even settled in Ireland. Whelan thus shows that our general perceptions of the Reformation as continuously and straightforwardly leading to freedom and democracy are clearly challenged—some of the Reformation's legacy is rather more complex, violent and painful.

In Ireland the situation was equally complex. As John McCafferty shows, Henry VIII hated Luther, and the Reformation in Britain, looking more to Geneva than to Wittenberg, was *sui generis*, a 'British thing'. The sixteenth and seventeenth centuries saw British imperial rule ever expanding in Ireland and the country received 'a minimally glossed English reformation'. Luther's idea of educating the people in matters of faith and freedom through the vernacular was not much undertaken by Anglican clergy; it was the Catholic clergy who spoke Gaelic, and Protestants of Irish birth were 'vanishingly rare'. As McCafferty notes: 'The story of Ireland's experience of Martin Luther's reformation and all that radiated out from it is not one of a call to interior freedom. It is a story of statecraft.'

Turning back to Germany, Jürgen Barkhoff examines the Lutheran pastorate in German culture and literature. While post-Reformation Lutheran clergy often lived from modest financial means, they were, along with the doctor and the lawyer, the educated men in the parish. They studied the biblical languages and were aware of cultural, artistic and scientific developments. Their children received a good education and many would step into their fathers' shoes, while others would become academics, scientists and even critics of religion. The list of names of leading thinkers, artists and scientists who descended from Protestant clergy is indeed one of the most remarkable legacies of the Reformation.

The second part finishes with Martin Sauter's 'Marking the Reformation 500 years on—*Quo vadis ecclesia semper reformanda?*'. Sauter looks back into the sixteenth century and outlines central concerns in Luther's teaching and work, and then asks whether inspiration is to be gained from the legacy of the Reformation in our own times. This he affirms with a clear 'yes', noting in particular the importance of education, freedom of expression in daily life, in arts and culture, and most especially the ecumenical movement, which has steadfastly moved the churches towards reconciliation.

The conclusion to our publication is presented in two epilogues. Stephan Arras reflects on the current state of the Christian church in relation to the commemorative year 2017 both in Ireland and in the wider church. In particular, he outlines some of 'the fruits' of the Reformation that might contribute towards shaping the future of Christianity—listening to the Word, our notion of freedom, the realms of church and politics, and church unity.

Martin Sauter, who worked as pastor-in-residence at University Lutheran Chapel, Berkeley, in 2017/18 experienced first-hand the enormous impact of two issues which concern not only the church but the whole of humankind: climate change through massive, unprecedented wildfires and migration from Latin America towards California. He points out how the churches, including the Lutheran Church, need to address and take a clear, Gospel-inspired stand on these issues and 'start moving'. Reformation in how we view and treat the Earth, our planet home, its natural resources and our fellow human beings, so in need of homes, food, freedom, justice and redemption, will certainly offer challenges for the universal church into the future.

Note
[1] The first part of the 'Introduction' is a slightly adapted version of my article on Luther published in the *Irish Times*, 7 February 2017, ten days ahead of the symposium at Trinity College Dublin.

Opening of the Symposium—
Ecumenical Perspectives on
Reformation 1517–2017

The Most Revd Dr Michael Jackson, Archbishop of Dublin, Church of Ireland

Introduction
I take you on a journey at the outset to a field close to the railway station in the city of Oxford. You might wander through it and notice little, or your eye might be drawn to four large stones which give you the outline shape of a rectangle. This is all that remains today of Osney Abbey, a medieval monastery, the second-largest in England in its day, dissolved as part of the Reformation. Its stones were carted away to help to build the modern and secular university further up the hill, a university which today is synonymous internationally with academic endeavour and excellence. This is what history does to us. This is how history plays its hand. This is all that remains of a glorious past that once was present. This is one of the ways also in which what was past is invested afresh in a changed future.

To speak generically of the Reformation is both *important* and *problematic*: *important* because something on the big canvas of Europe religiously and politically did in fact happen, however sporadically and scattered across time and place; *problematic* because the use of the term 'reformation' can tend to freeze in time a concept that is in and of itself elastic, dynamic, organic and repetitive and was life-giving in its day, and which has subsequently been taken up by a range of expressions of Christianity as life-giving still. It will be fairer and fuller to speak of the Reformations.

In sixteenth-century Europe, certain principles and concepts, many of which had already taken a critical toll on the church catholic before then, found their voice and changed the face of ecclesiastical, civic and economic life. This has resulted in both freedoms and disharmonies with which we continue to live today. It has further resulted in transporting and transplanting European religious polemics into the whole of the known world, as the missionary arm of the churches sought to win for Christ souls anywhere and everywhere, locking them into the particularities of 'the one side' or 'the other side'. Ireland is an example of how this structured religious antipathy is part of the weave of two communities, forged in the furnace of history and now trying to be one community in a post-colonial world. Ironically, but honourably, it could further be argued that it was Protestant religious toleration that enabled Roman Catholicism, in a new expansionist phase of its own life, to undertake missionary work afresh in the Protestant empires of the new, emerging world. Reformation is complex and versatile and transformative.

God and empire
Reformation and its own aftermath were all done in the name of a God who must ever stand above the exclusivities of religious denominationalism as the primary starting point and goal of human striving for any of us in the mature understanding of religious identity. But it has not always been seen like this. The contemporary near-powerlessness of Christianity in European democratic self-understanding and engaged citizenship combined is a distorting filter for us today in understanding what was happening and why it was happening as it was. Religion and identity once marched together more naturally in Christianity, as they do in other World Faiths today. 'Go and make disciples of all nations …' in the right hands is an invitation to share the person of Jesus Christ with all you meet as a way of expanding the breadth of human encounter; in the wrong hands it is an invitation to dominate and to distort even more than it is an invitation to serve and to save. Such expansionism was not the rolling out of piety alone; it marched hand in hand with aggressive colonialism, power and money. Religious superiority carries always with it the temptation to obliterate local inheritance, with which it can often have only an uneasy traded relationship of suspicion. It came with an inversion of power that is only heightened by internal competitiveness for dominance and territory. Reformation, in and of itself, brings an element of theological and religious cannibalism to the battlefield of change. Colonisation and civilisation, the latter being a self-explanatory paradigm from the perspective of the conqueror, regularly ride roughshod over the culture and the religion of the host nation. Imperialism, as ancient Rome had long ago shown, has mouths to feed and borders to patrol. Drawing together earth and heaven 'in little space', as the Christmas carol expresses it, by means of defined and exclusive religious affiliations helps wonderfully to concentrate the mind around territorial belonging and the great obsession of all empires: land.

Luther and the church
It would be wrong to anaesthetise or shackle the principle that lies within and behind the theological work of reformation. Its theological rationale is one of

salvation by Scripture, grace and faith alone. The corollary of this is that sanctification in and of itself owes nothing intrinsic to good and penitential works on our part. The issue at the heart of reformation, then as now, is the classic conflict over the question of the integrity and the range of human free will within an understanding of operational and interventionist divine providence. The conclusion of the exploration of the Reformation period is that sanctification is a product, not a condition, of an instant justification by God. On one level, this was a small adjustment of Pauline and Augustinian doctrine, critical and original on the part of Luther himself nonetheless. Luther had freedom and used his freedom to develop this style of theology in his home territory of Saxony while being condemned in Rome. The combination of support and condemnation fuelled his tireless expression and exposition of this simple message: *sola scriptura, sola gratia, sola fide*. For Luther, therefore, striking at doctrinal roots in this way makes his reformation very different from earlier attempts at reforming the church; in fact, it offers a radically different picture of church, in which all believers are simultaneously sinners and justified, all are equally priests. It also claims high moral ground in being an original brand of Christianity through its claim not to be novel and modist but primitive and biblical. This is the root of its radicalness. This theological recipe went on to develop an anti-ecclesiology such as to deny the papacy any effective authority in the church most widely understood along with challenging transubstantiation, compulsory celibacy and monasticism.

Faith and power
Politically and ingeniously, Luther combined the accrual of patronage with his espousal of princely authoritarianism during the Peasants' War. Power and piety were set to march hand in hand not only in Germany but also in Denmark and Sweden and, as things progressed, in other Scandinvian countries, where church life was reorganised and regulated in such a way that the Lutheran Reformation underwrote the validity of, and lay in the hands of, the godly prince. England and Ireland, in their own particular way, followed suit in their own idiosyncratic manner. Other Reformers, and alternative Reformations, followed with Zwingli in Zürich, especially with Zwinglianism's combination of uncompromising biblicism, severe iconoclasm and denial of the real presence of Christ in the Eucharist. This engendered two conflicting confessional traditions, and with Bucer in Strasbourg and Calvin in Geneva, the second, Calvinism (originally, of course, a term of opprobrium), was a complex interaction of political, religious and social forces. This created a new tension and balance between ecclesiastical and civil authority, with the result that the church authorities exercised

a more independent rule in civic life than in any Lutheran manifestation of reformation thus far.

Theologically, Calvin named explicitly the role of predestination in salvation. This marks a significant parting of the ways in that Lutheranism, under the pen of Melanchthon, became wary of something, namely divine predestination, that has become characteristic of this branch of Reformed thought, even though its roots could be traced in part to Luther's anxieties about the sufficiency of human freedom over against divine freedom. Such Calvinism became the driving force of reformation in parts of Germany, France, Hungary, the Netherlands, England (and Ireland) and Scotland. The Scottish Reformation was made by its reformers, especially Knox, its nobility and its people and followed Jean Calvin. The English Reformation was primarily political and an accommodation between Calvinism and Catholicism—somewhat witheringly referred to by one scholar, Peter Lake, as 'avant-garde conformism'—brought about by the ricochet and domino effect of, successively, Henry VIII's overthrow of papal supremacy and dissolution of the monasteries, Edward VI's implementation of a widespread introduction of doctrinal and liturgical alterations in a Calvinising direction resulting in the Prayer Book of 1552 and the Forty-Two Articles of 1553, and Elizabeth I's re-imposition of the Protestant Formularies that had obtained in the time before Mary, her immediate predecessor in the Roman Catholic tradition, who sought to reverse a generation of ecclesiastical change. This combined Elizabeth's instinct for worship based on a traditional church structure with the guiding, if by then departed, hand of the subtle and liturgical Thomas Cranmer, who has turned out in so many ways to be the salvation of us Anglicans through the Book of Common Prayer. It is the Anglican conviction to this day that our doctrine is to be found in our liturgy and vice versa. This gives us today, after the further impact on our polity of not quite an internal Anglican reformation but of what is called the Oxford Movement, the particularities of Anglicanism as Catholic and Reformed, grateful for continuities, however muddled, which serve us well in a contemporary generation, not least for their honesties of origin internally and externally but even more for their open untidiness and rescuing of compromise as a positive work of God and humankind. It also gives us another contemporary honesty about Anglicanism as ultimately non-confessional and as 'that messy contested tradition whose great virtue is that it cannot pretend to any great virtues' (*The Tablet*, 6 August 2016, p. 16).

The Church of Ireland
However confusing we are to others and to ourselves, we now seek to live

Christ first, church second, as a contribution to community and communion in a world where we ourselves have for long been too happy with polemics over against eirenics. Because of politics and plantation, the Reformation in Ireland followed the English approach, with the Anglican tradition long holding what now seems to be an incredible position of ecclesio-political dominance, or Establishment. Only in 1870 did it move out of a realm of political dominance into the much more ecclesiastically confined and defined level democratic structure of internal Synodical Disestablishment, with no overt political influence by virtue of faith or denomination. But Ireland also contains—independent of Anglicanism but to this day significantly influencing Irish Anglicanism—strong elements of influence from the Scottish Reformation, along with the arrival of a significant number of people from the Radical Reformation in England to Ireland during the seventeenth century.

In 2017 we should not forget that in contemporary Ireland there are people of more than 200 nationalities and of a wide range of World Faiths. The seventeenth-century immigrants to Ireland were Non-Conformists to an English Reformation that was seeking to salvage itself and to reinvent itself through stitching together its history and its monarchy, and one which until the nineteenth century used the sacrament of Holy Communion as a test for the holding of public office in the life of the state. As Irish Anglicans and as historical carriers of the inheritance outlined above, as well as being exponents of our own fractious relationships with what is often referred to as 'Catholic and Dissenter', we need to be realistic and contrite that our good relationships with Roman Catholics in Ireland are something of very recent and gracious giving on their part to us as much as of our giving to them. Without mutual forbearance on many sides, a relationship at all levels of society and church life, such as we now take for granted and enjoy with tolerant openness, simply would not have been possible, nor would we be in a position to live lives of ecumenical exploration, interaction and adventure as we currently are.

Two further reformations
The rise and the dominance of institutions, along with the capacity for change they regularly bring to bear on the individuals who either belong to them or are subjected to their ways of working, is not, of course, new to the Reformation. However, the introduction of the open competition of religious free enterprise which is now a commonplace in ecclesiastical life owes its origin in terms of authoritative church bodies and families to the Reformation. The Reformation opened the windows to particular types of religious opportunity. Scholars are well aware that reformation of this character has engendered at

least two further streams of development. The first is generically named the Radical Reformation and is associated in the first instance with the Anabaptists. Not only is this a direct challenge to the enforced and assumed combination of baptism and citizenship which had obtained for 1,000 years, it is also by extension a radical separation of Church and State. It can further be argued that this movement, not least as a result of and as a response to its own persecution, is one of the origins of the pluralistic, tolerant religious world of modern western democracies. This understanding has continued to influence political life worldwide as we cope with the death of institutionalised Christendom, the rise of secularism and the movement of people of World Faiths, originally derivative of, and notionally confined to, one geographical area, to any and every part of the globe and bringing with them their culture and their religion as part of their identity. This in and of itself is a shock to the system of a generic Western Christianity that has long been beating the drum of its own victimhood, bereavement and obsolescence. The second is named the Counter-Reformation or the Catholic Reformation. The significant question to be asked is this: was this movement a reaction against the Reformation movement itself or was it a movement which drew on its own independent sources for renewal and which shared the fundamental concerns of Protestantism to evangelise, to instruct, to create a new moral framework and to make society more actively Christian? Among such Reformed within the obedience to Rome we can name the Society of Jesus, which, with an amazing turn of fortune, today has its Loyola Institute at the heart of Archbishop Ussher's Dublin University while the original Protestant professorships have sunk beyond trace. The Jesuit Order, with its independent voice critical of centripetal institutionalisation and its characteristic of compassionate justice, is reformed but expressed differently, of course, from any self-consciously Protestant Reformation. Today, for the first time, it finds itself as the source, the *fons et origo*, of the bishop of Rome in the person of Pope Francis. A reformed priest is bishop of Rome.

Lund and Malmö 2016
Before the Reformation, the default setting of Christian religious establishments, East and West, to novelty in theology or religious community was to apply the test of heresy. This was the only real file on the shelf for dealing with your religious neighbour with whom you disagreed or whose flourishing you wished to truncate or obliterate. The Reformation has changed all of that, however violent and tortured the process. Its longevity and its 500 Years commemoration in 2017 attest to a level of operational courtesy—after warfare, incrimination, anathematisation—that makes it important for us to see it as an

event—indeed, a series of events—with continuing impact and importance. It changed things. Things are different. In Lund in Sweden on 31 October 2016 we saw what we perhaps thought we would never see in our lifetime: Pope Francis, bishop of Rome, and Bishop Munib Younan, president of the Lutheran World Federation, signed in Lund cathedral a theological agreement, *From conflict to communion—Lutheran–Catholic common commemoration of the Reformation in 2017*, and in Malmö Arena a practical concordat between Caritas Internationalis and the Lutheran World Federation in aid of Syrian refugees in the Middle East. They were accompanied by Kurt Cardinal Koch and the Revd Dr Martin Junge, general secretary of the LWF. Their message was as simple as the earliest Christianity itself: what unites us is stronger than what divides us. This was a public commitment to common witness and service and in so many ways brings us full circle and out of darkness into understanding. We will continue to be different. We will, however, travel together rather than walking apart.

Reformation and choice
The Reformation is rightly lauded for offering choice in the public expression of faith in God. The contemporary world has shown us that choice can and does foment competition and cause chaos. The ecclesiastical world now has the opportunity to embrace choice with the pivotal recognition that the Other is essential to our setting our agenda, individually and corporately, and that your margin is the centre of my world. Connecting Others and margins is the calling of all churches together. The Reformation took place in a world where Christianity had no option but to rub shoulders with World Faiths other than itself. Some things it got spectacularly and disastrously wrong. We, too, in our day have no other option than to rub shoulders and to shake hands with those of World Faiths other than our own. Ecumenism simply is no longer sufficient. Reconciliation, in which Ireland, North and South, has sought to specialise and to which the Irish School of Ecumenics has contributed so significantly, demands of us as responsible citizens inter-faith dialogue, understanding and respect.

I return to my opening illustration of Oxford University and Osney Abbey. In the setting of the University of Dublin 2017, perhaps the challenge to the universities is this: is it still really necessary to be anti-religious in a world where mature humanity has long been calling all of us, religious and irreligious people and religious and irreligious institutions alike, to engage with the secular in a reconfigured humanism? And the question could extend to the wider educational establishment also. Is it still really necessary to find faith in God so problematic a concept, even if it is 'not for you', when today it seeks not to dominate and to indoctrinate but to contribute values of altruism and adventure to the human experiment, and is open to criticism and to contradiction in a spirit of tolerance which goes beyond toleration? Do we all not need the freedom of reformation at some level of our operational existence even if we resist it at the pit of our stomach? Do we not live in a world where things have to continue to 'give' if we are all to do at least what Samuel Beckett, alumnus of this university, once invited us to do with chilling realism:

> *Fail again*
> *Fail better?*

Revd Dr Brendan Leahy, Bishop of Limerick, Roman Catholic Church

Look how good and how pleasant it is when brothers and sisters live together in unity! This line from Psalm 133 is one we can savour today at the official opening of the Reformation Quincentenary Theological Symposium. In a country that has known various strands of Reformation, I am pleased to be standing today alongside Provost Prof. Patrick Prendergast, Archbishop Michael Jackson (Church of Ireland), Revd Dr Donald Watts, ICC (Presbyterian Church in Ireland), and other ecumenical representatives to bring you the greetings of the Catholic Church in Ireland and also as the Co-Chair of the Irish Inter-Church Meeting.

On 31 October 2016 I had the privilege to be in Lund, Sweden, for the ecumenical commemoration of the Reformation by the Lutheran World Federation (LWF) and the Roman Catholic Church. As Pope Francis and Bishop Munib Yunan, president of the LWF, signed the joint declaration that stated 'what unites us is greater than what divides us', I was struck by the simplicity and humility of the occasion. How far we have all travelled in 500 years!

As we commemorate Martin Luther's reforming zeal, Catholics get a chance to correct some of the bad images that we inherited about him. We appreciate today that the era in which he was living was extremely complex, socially, politically and religiously. It is also acknowledged today that for many centuries our view of Luther was shaped by the commentaries of Johannes Cochlaeus, a contemporary opponent of Luther. In the heat of the polemics of the time, Cochlaeus characterised Luther as 'an apostatized monk, a destroyer of Christendom, a corrupter of morals, and a heretic'.

We know that Luther had his defects. His writings about the Jews were terrible. He was polemical and could have entered more into dialogue—but then, too, so could many on the Catholic side. Despite limitations, we appreciate that it is important to recall that Luther's aim was to *renew* the Church, not divide her.

The liturgy at the Lund ceremony last year referred to the image of the Vine and the Branches. It reminded us that we are one body and it is as members of that body, walking together in Christ, that we witness to Him. The secretary of the LWF, Martin Junge, referred to the pioneers of ecumenism and commented that 'as they lived and witnessed together they began to see one another no longer as separated branches but as branches united to Jesus Christ. Even more, they began to see Christ in their midst.' And that gave them new eyes to see past, present and future through eyes of mercy and hope.

For his part, Pope Francis emphasises again and again that it is by walking together, serving our neighbour together, especially those on the margins, that we grow in unity with one another. In his homily at Lund he made a number of important points, reminding us that 'we too must look with love and honesty at our past, recognizing error and seeking forgiveness, for God alone is our judge'. He continued: 'We ought to recognize with the same honesty and love that our division distanced us from the primordial intuition of God's people who naturally yearn to be one'. He observed how too often in the past 'we closed in on ourselves out of fear or bias with regard to the faith which others profess with a different accent and language'.

One of the prayers during the Lund liturgy contained a sobering statement: 'In the sixteenth century, Catholics and Lutherans frequently not only misunderstood but also exaggerated and caricatured their opponents in order to make them look ridiculous. Lutherans and Catholics often focused on what separated them from each other rather than looking for what united them ... They accepted that the Gospel was mixed with the political and economic interests of those in power. Their failures resulted in the deaths of hundreds of thousands of people.'

Today we are in a different place. The second imperative proposed by the document *From conflict to communion—the Lutheran–Catholic common commemoration of the Reformation in 2017*, elaborated by the Lutheran–Catholic Commission for Unity, working on behalf of the Lutheran World Federation and the Pontifical Council for the Promotion of Christian Unity, proposes that 'Lutherans and Catholics must let themselves continuously be transformed by the encounter with the other and by the mutual witness of faith'.

In his homily, Pope Francis reminded us that when we see each other with new eyes we can learn from one another. In striking fashion, he underlined what Catholics have learned: 'with gratitude we acknowledge that the Reformation helped give greater centrality to sacred Scripture in the Church's life ... The spiritual experience of Martin Luther challenges us to remember that apart from God we can do nothing ... With the concept "by grace alone", he reminds us that God always takes the initiative, prior to any human response, even as He seeks to awaken that response. Here we can recall Thesis 28 of the *Heidelberg Disputation,* where we read: "The love of God does not find what is already loveable, but it creates it".'

When people meet in a conference such as this one commemorating the Reformation, it is not merely an occasion to commemorate or celebrate past events but rather an opportunity to rediscover the deep and vital insights underlying the theology, spirituality and pastoral praxis so strongly united in Luther. The theology Luther proposes is of immediate existential relevance. It calls out to us and wants to transform us to be true Christians.

As one scholar commenting on Luther's works notes, 'a deeper and more exact understanding of the central intentions of Luther's theology may serve as a light in this time when the churches, perhaps more than in other times, are struggling with the challenge of the *ecclesia semper reformanda*. For Luther, church reform did not mean simply changing or adapting to the tendencies or mentalities of an epoch but *re-formatio* in the sense of a *return to the original form* of Christianity, which appears in the clearest way in Christ crucified.'[1]

After all, truly Gospel-engendered reform is an event that never really comes to an end but one that needs to occur in every present moment. Neither in the Protestant nor in the Catholic world can there be a 'Reformed' church that can consider itself as having arrived at the perfect form, as if reformation were something that can be achieved once and for all, as if it might become a kind of possession. We are and must always be *ecclesia reformanda*. This was very much underlined at the Second Vatican Council and is a theme of Pope Francis's pontificate.

The protagonists of a true reformation in the final analysis are not 'reformers' who put themselves forward as such but those who allow the call of the Gospel to conversion to be heard in an ever new way.

Authentic reformation is built on Christ, and it brings us to live in Christ and in our neighbours, becoming 'Christ for the other'—and, indeed, 'Christ also for the other church'!

I'd like to give the last word to Luther. As a young district vicar of his order, he wrote to one of his brothers, Georg Spenlein, in a letter of 1516: 'Just as Christ welcomed you and made your sins His own, and made His justice yours … so too you should … welcome your brothers and sustain them with patience and make their sins your own and, if you have anything good to offer, make that theirs' (see WA BR 1, 35).

May your seminar be animated by all that is best in Martin Luther, offering one another all that is best of your scholarship and insight.

Dr Stephanie Springer, Evangelische Kirche Deutschland (EKD)

We are very pleased that Dublin is a way station on the European Road Map. Many thanks for the invitation and for the hospitality we are enjoying. We are celebrating the 500th anniversary of the Reformation differently from earlier generations in various respects. (1) We celebrate in a huge community, not only nationwide but also in a fellowship of 47 churches of different denominations with a Reformation tradition—Reformed, Lutheran and United Protestant Churches. Despite different traditions and histories of Reformation, they have all accepted the year 1517 as a symbolic date. We are marking this Quincentenary from Wittenberg to Rome, from Dublin to Riga and from Bergen to Ljubljana. The Church of England is hosting a stopover in Cambridge and ecumenical partners are generally involved. (2) Unlike former centenaries, we don't celebrate a *Luther* year—it has to be a *Reformation* anniversary. After all, the Reformation was an event that brought together driving forces from different places. Consequently, the other Reformers, too, are appreciated: Huldrych Zwingli in Zürich, Jean Calvin in Geneva, Matthew Zell in Strasbourg, Tamás Nádasdy in Hungary, among others. We are also rediscovering the role of women in the Reformation—Katharina von Bora, Katharina Zell and Anna of Denmark, to name but a few. (3) It may be seen as a slight sensation that we are not setting ourselves apart from the *Catholic* Church. We were able to reach a joyful consensus that we are celebrating a common *Christusfest* (festival of Christ). In Germany we are marking the Reformation Year together in several places. On 11 March the German Bishops' Conference and the Evangelical Church in Germany will hold a joint Healing of Memories service in Hildesheim. At this service we will remember the wounds that the separated churches inflicted on one another during the Reformation period. Both sides will ask God for forgiveness, give thanks for what the two churches mean to one another and express what they value about each other.

The European Road Map and its sky-blue show-truck, touring Europe since November 2016, are a symbol for overcoming borders—and not only geographical and denominational ones—and yet we are marking the Reformation anniversary year at a time when the international community is under threat. This already casts its shadow over our celebrations. Despite the festivities, we cannot forget the increasing emphasis being laid on national identity. Indeed, we are witnessing horrifying examples of isolationism.

The European Road Map sends a strong signal of another kind: that we are united by more than what separates us. Through our common faith in Christ as the Lord of the world, we seek the kingdom of God together. Together we are called to work for justice, peace and the integrity of creation. Thus we can become supporters of a united and human Europe that shows solidarity beyond its own borders with the whole world.

Dublin is one of 67 way stations forging a bond between places of Protestant life throughout Europe. Many thanks for being part of it and for organising this ambitious and sophisticated conference at Trinity College.

Revd Dr Donald Watts, Presbyterian Church, Ireland

Good afternoon. It's a great pleasure and privilege for me to represent the Irish Council of Churches at this significant event in a year set aside to commemorate the Reformation in Europe. I know that the present president of the Irish Council of Churches, Bishop John McDowell, would have liked to be here but had commitments elsewhere. I'm particularly pleased to be standing alongside my friend Bishop Brendan Leahy. For the previous two years we represented the two elements of the Irish Inter-Church Meeting—the Roman Catholic bishops and the Protestant, Orthodox and Reformed branches of the churches in Ireland who are members of the ICC.

I suppose it could be argued historically that Ireland was an island on the western fringe of Europe, not greatly troubled by the tumultuous events of Reformation elsewhere. When Christians of the Protestant or dissenting traditions arrived, they might have had considerable political influence but they didn't greatly disturb the dominant position within society of the Roman Catholic Church. Indeed, they could often be written off as 'outsiders'. If that was once the case, and I realise that it's a fairly superficial view, it certainly is not the case today. Ireland is becoming a much more diverse and multicultural society, and the churches together are realising that the Christian tradition is one element in the mix—still a very important element but nevertheless one alongside others. A Christian viewpoint is best heard if it is expressed by the churches together. That is what the Irish Inter-Church Meeting seeks to do. It has been in existence since about 1973, initially as a response to the deepening crisis for society in the North, but in recent years it has been redefining its ambition to respond, from a Christian perspective, to political and societal change both North and South.

The Irish Council of Churches has a longer history, having been founded in 1923 by broadly Protestant churches; the first Orthodox tradition joined in 1997. The Lutheran Church has been a member since 1972, and I must say a valued and active member. For as long as I have been a member of the ICC executive, the Lutheran Church in Ireland has been at the forefront of ecumenical discussion. I would pay tribute to the role of the previous pastors; in particular, it was a privilege to work alongside Corinna Diestelkamp, and now Pastor Stephan. Supporting them over many years has been Martin Sauter, and it was a great delight for me to take part, a couple of years ago, in his ordination service. The Lutheran Church here has a very genuine interest in ecumenical affairs and in developing strong relationships between church, society and State.

This is why we welcome the exhibition on the Reformation and the seminal, overarching contribution of Martin Luther. I am not a Reformation historian but as an amateur observer I would venture two comments. Luther's work was at a time when throughout Europe the accepted relationship of church to society was changing, probably more rapidly than most people could handle. Luther's genius was to focus the church's attention on the question of what it meant to be the church. In a study of some years ago, Rowan Williams pointed to the way, as he put it, 'a theological revolution had reopened the whole question of how and why the Church was different'. That surely is a question that we must continue to probe today in the changing nature of our society.

Secondly, however, I suggest that it is important to recognise that Luther was not suggesting the privatisation of faith, a position that some would be very happy with if the church adopted it today. While he emphasised the importance of an individual's response to the saving act of God in Jesus Christ, that response must then be lived out in the challenging context of a changing world-view.

This exhibition is timely in reminding us of the struggles and insights of the reformers, particularly Martin Luther. If I can end with a principle of my own Presbyterian tradition—Reformed, always reforming.

Note

[1] Hubertus Blaumeiser, '"Re-formatio": the Reformation of the sixteenth century and church reform today', *Claritas: Journal of Dialogue and Culture* **5** (2) (2016), 20–32, at p. 31.

I.
LUTHER, REFORMS AND THE FREEDOM OF THE CHRISTIAN

1
The whole of life ought to be penance—penance in the early Reformation

Volker Leppin

'Our Lord and Master in saying "do penance" meant that the whole life of the believer ought to be penance.'[1] This is the first thesis in *The Ninety-Five Theses* against indulgences and somehow the starting point for the Reformation movement. As will be shown, however, this thesis is not the result of a radical renewal of theology by a sudden Reformation breakthrough but of late medieval mysticism. In 1517 Martin Luther, monk and professor, did not intend anything other than a reform of piety and theology in the horizon of mystical theology.

The development of Luther's understanding of penance

In the light of recent research, the key figure for understanding Luther's development concerning penance is John Tauler (d. 1361), a Dominican monk of the fourteenth century.[2] Tauler may be referred to as a student of the more famous mystic Meister Eckhart, although it is uncertain whether they ever met in person. Tauler was greatly influenced, however, by Eckhart's sermons and writings, which he probably came to know as he lived in the same place, Strasbourg, where Eckhart had been for some years. Both were Dominicans and both helped to integrate nuns in the spirituality of their order. The most noteworthy difference between the two was the fact that Tauler heard of Eckhart's condemnation as a heretic in 1329 through the bull *In agro dominico*. From then on he had to be cautious not to be accused of heresy, too. Thus in his sermons Tauler avoided all that might rouse the ecclesiastical hierarchies. Nevertheless, his sermons contained something explosive that Luther, almost two centuries later, detected in his reading of them. Tauler's sermons were collected in his lifetime and arranged around the liturgical year. Thus a handbook emerged with sermons for the whole liturgical year, useful for preachers and even more for readers who wanted to follow the liturgical year with spiritual guidance.

The first sermon served to introduce the whole collection and presented its central tenets. It was a Christmas sermon, explaining the three Masses of Christmas night. These three Masses, as Tauler interpreted them, represented three dimensions of the birth of God: the first was the Trinitarian self-distinction of the Father and the Son in eternity; the second was the birth in Bethlehem as the centre of God's history with humankind; and the goal of both was the third dimension, the birth of God in the soul of the believer. This concept of the birth of God in the soul was not newly invented by Tauler. Here he followed Eckhart, and some sermons by Eckhart on the same issue were integrated under Tauler's name into the Tauler collection. In this way the sermons of a 'heretic' could be preserved in a non-suspicious context. Tauler's sermons were copied in many manuscripts. They were first published in Leipzig in 1498. Ten years later a further edition followed in Augsburg.

The Augsburg edition of 1508 was widely used in Wittenberg, presumably under the cautious recommendation of Johannes Staupitz. Among the readers was Martin Luther, a young professor at the university. In Tauler he would find a new understanding of penance and this, in fact, was the starting point for reformation in several respects. The central issue in *The Ninety-Five Theses* was nothing other than penance, as, in medieval thinking, indulgences were a consequence of penance. Following contrition and confession, indulgences were part of the third step, i.e. the satisfaction of penance.

Indeed, Luther himself described his coming to a new understanding of penance in a manner that reminds us of his recounting of his reformation breakthrough. In a letter to Staupitz in 1518, accompanying his explanation of *The Ninety-Five Theses*, the *Resolutiones*, he wrote:

> 'I remember, venerable Father, that sometimes in your salutary talks in which Jesus Christ used to give me comfort, the word "penance" occurred ... There, we accepted you as if you spoke from Heaven: that real penance starts only with love of justice and God. What [usual confessors] depicted as the goal and perfection of penance should be just the beginning.'[3]

Here it becomes obvious that the first decisive issue for Luther was penance and not yet justification. For Luther at that time, penance was something compared to which there could be 'nothing sweeter or more gracious'.[4] In terms of chronology, it can actually be proven that this new understanding of penance developed in Luther not only through Staupitz but also by his reading of Johannes Tauler.[5] We are fortunate in knowing how Luther read this late medieval mystic; the edition he used in 1515 or 1516 has been preserved. Modern scholarship has been able to identify the notes on the margins as Luther's. Concerning our discussion here, the most interesting note refers to a text where Tauler debates the necessity of confession and appears fairly sceptical about it:

'You might fall seventy times a day, but whenever you do, you shall come back to God. And penetrate God so intensively that you might forget your sins when you come with them to confession and you are not able to tell them. You should not be terrified by this, it does not happen to your harm, but to give you insight into your nothingness and to despise yourself in relaxation, not in gloom … Saint Paul says: "For those who love God, everything is of use", and the glossa adds: "even the sin". But be quiet and flee to God and be aware of your nothingness. Stay with yourself, do not run with this to the confessor!'[6]

Luther seems to have been delighted with these sentences. Referring to the first section, he wrote on the margin: 'Remember this!'[7] Some lines further on, when Tauler speaks about avoiding the confessor, Luther notes: 'very useful advice!'[8]

From these observations one concludes that by listening to Staupitz and reading Tauler Luther developed a new understanding of penance. Later on, he would find further relevant material for his new understanding in reading the New Testament which had been edited and annotated by Erasmus and published in 1516. Here he discovered the philological argument. The Greek word for penance, *metanoia*, originally meant something like 'beyond the mind' or 'after the mind', which Luther understood in the sense of a total change of the mind.[9] Thus in 1516 we see how Luther came to a new understanding of penance, including two aspects. Firstly, penance in its biblical sense is not a single act but a lifelong habit of the believer. Secondly, this implies that penance in its biblical sense cannot be what is performed by the priests in the sacrament.

These are the fundamental issues of Luther's protest against indulgences as discussed in *The Ninety-Five Theses*, but they are not new; they are based on mystical and humanistic insights. Luther was a late medieval theologian, making his own points in some regards but all still within the late medieval context.

What would make this monk famous, just a few months later, was his sharpened critique of indulgences arising from this understanding of penance. Indeed, we can trace this development. In a sermon in May 1517, he even appears to quote Staupitz himself and the advice Staupitz had given him: true penance is that which 'hates the sin, loving justice and punishment'.[10] Love of justice—this exactly was the starting point for penance according to Staupitz and recalled here by Martin Luther.

We have to understand Luther's whole development regarding his thought on penance in the years 1516/17 in the context of Staupitz's advice and lectures on Tauler. While Luther was quite cautious in his lectures, open critique against church practices of his time are evident in his sermons. As early as 21 September 1516, Luther explained that true believers should not trust in their own penitential efforts but only in *God's* redemption from sin.[11] What was required of humans was only true contrition.[12] He continued this line of thought in a sermon given on 24 February 1517, attacking indulgences:

> 'In addition, the diffusion of indulgences perfects a kind of servant justice. They do not achieve any other than that the people learn to be afraid of the punishment of sins, but not in the same way of the sins themselves and to flee them and be terrified about them. So, the fruit of indulgences cannot be felt, but instead great safety and the admission to sin, so that no one, if he would not fear the punishment for sins, would try to achieve the indulgences for nothing.'[13]

With this, Luther's critique reaches the point where the whole sacrament is affected and indulgences do not appear to be denied but are principally questioned. Again, this does not reveal any fundamental shift from what Luther had read and learned from Tauler, but it shows that the Wittenberg monk had started to draw consequences concerning the piety of the people in his parish—and he added some polemics, mocking the 'snoring priests'.[14] Of course, he was a priest, too, but this did not prevent him blaming his colleagues.

His arguments here make apparent, however, that in his *Ninety-Five Theses* Luther followed Tauler's understanding of penance. Indeed, Luther himself wanted to be understood in this way. In March 1518 he wrote to Staupitz: 'I myself merely followed the theology of Tauler, as well as the booklet you gave to be printed to Christian Goldschmied a short while ago'.[15] The booklet mentioned was the so-called *Theologia deutsch*, another mystical treatise from the late Middle Ages which Luther, obviously with the help of Staupitz, had published in 1516 and thought of as a text quite close to Tauler's style.[16] Thus Luther's letter to Staupitz demonstrates that six months after having completed *The Ninety-Five Theses* Luther still saw himself entirely in the line of John Tauler. This, however, was the time when suspicion against him had already begun in Rome; he was already in serious conflict, but these were conflicts *within* the late medieval church, not against it, as the traditional narrative of Reformation history has held.

The late Middle Ages in modern view

This leads us to wider reflections on our understanding of late medieval times and the Reformation from a contemporary perspective. In fact, perceptions of the Middle Ages in modern research have always been influenced by perceptions of the Reformation. Modern research initially did nothing but outline early modern concepts. For centuries, Protestants had seen the late Middle Ages solely through the eyes of Luther and his fellow reformers. To them, the late Middle Ages had been the time of a religion of achievement and merits. Human beings had to work for their own salvation by means of good works. At worst, good works were nothing more than certain amounts of money that were paid for indulgences. This image of the late Middle Ages made it almost imperative for Luther to critique this type of piety as one which, instead of leading to God, was steering people away from God.

Not surprisingly, the Catholic view was completely contrary; their early narrative established Luther to be a heretic who had fought against a principally good and well-ordained medieval church, causing damage to the whole of Christianity by splitting the western church. It was Heinrich Suso Denifle who, at the beginning of the twentieth century, transformed this traditional Catholic view into a scholarly position.[17] According to him, the Reformation was the result of a person with a 'problematic character': Martin Luther had not understood all the gifts of salvation offered to him in the late medieval church but had interpreted them in a scrupulous, almost insane, manner. The problem, then, was not the problem of an epoch but of just one person, who had to be blamed for what he had caused. Karl Holl made a powerful response to Denifle with his famous Berlin speech on 31 October 1917.[18] Holl depicted Luther as someone who created a completely new type of religion, the religion of conscience (*Gewissensreligion*), which ended the medieval ecclesiastical oppression of the individual. In quite a learned manner both Holl and Denifle rekindled the traditional narratives of their respective confessions and reiterated long-held prejudices against Luther, on the one side, and against the Middle Ages, on the other.

After the Second World War this situation changed remarkably, with beginnings even before that, and a new Catholic view on the Reformation emerged with the dawn of Vatican II and the spring of ecumenism. Joseph Lortz[19] and Erwin Iserloh[20] drew a completely new picture of the late Middle Ages and the Reformation. Now the Middle Ages were no longer perceived as an intact epoch but as quite the opposite. Both scholars were able to identify that a decline had begun as early as the fourteenth century, generating disorder and irrationality. Luther was given a new place in history. He was no longer accused of having been the destroyer of Catholicism. Rather it was asserted that he fought against something in himself that he had been taught was Catholic but in fact was not Catholic in a strict sense. While, according to Lortz and Iserloh, this did not make Luther Catholic, it made his protest understandable, even somehow legitimate.

In comparison to Denifle, this was obviously a considerable and positive step in ecumenical research and interchange. Yet immediately such argumentation posed a crucial problem: what had made Luther legitimate had been the grievances of the late medieval church. Understood correctly, however, this implied that when these grievances were corrected—and for Lortz and Iserloh they were corrected by the Council of Trent—there was no remaining legitimation for Protestant churches. The Reformation had served the Catholic Church in identifying problems, but it had no legitimacy in itself to continue with the setting up of new churches. It did not take much time to provoke a Protestant answer. It came from church historian Bernd Moeller. He depicted the late Middle Ages as one of the most pious epochs in Christendom,[21] whatever this superlative might mean. The image drawn by Moeller was something of a narrative about the change from a quantitative increase in piety to a more qualitative one. While piety in the late Middle Ages in all its intensity had been ecclesiastical, Luther opened the way for a freer, more individual type of piety.[22] Obviously, one might think at first glance that this model seemed to be relatively close to Holl's. The difference between Luther and the Middle Ages was still perceived in terms of the categories of individuality and conscience. Even if formally the Middle Ages were described by Moeller in a more positive way, the fundamental difference was upheld. Thus, just as with Lortz and Iserloh, we see in Moeller the persistence of confessional patterns informing an elaborate and learned model of historiography.

The situation in the 1960s was, at least on the surface, that the perceptions about the late Middle Ages had completely changed between the confessions. Catholic theology no longer regarded the Middle Ages as an unbroken epoch destroyed by the Reformation, but rather the other way round. On the other hand, Protestant views understood the Middle Ages as an intensive religious time but, obviously, without a negative view of the Reformation.

The surprising shift in the evaluation of the late Middle Ages raises another question, however. If it is possible to view the late Middle Ages in totally black or white colours, the truth may be somewhere in the middle. Newer approaches do not tend to perceive the Middle Ages any more homogeneously than the models presented above. Rather, this epoch was a dynamic time of tensions or polarities.[23] Three of these tensions are of particular importance for an understanding of reformation: a tension between centrality and polycentrism, a tension between lay culture and clergy and, last but not least, a tension between outer piety and inner piety. Here I just want to provide a brief sketch of these tensions.

The polarity of centrality and polycentrism refers to the simple fact that in the late Middle Ages we can see, on the one hand, an ever-growing tendency to strengthen papal powers in juridical as well as ceremonial terms. Theologically we talk about this phenomenon in terms of late medieval papalism. On the other hand, many authorities in the universal church at this time sought to appropriate powers to themselves, for example in introducing bishops or reforming orders into their territories, such as in Saxony or Württemberg. The medieval church, therefore, was not only a papal church but also a decentralised church in which many actors played a role.

A further polarity was between clergy and laity. Obviously clergy were of great importance in the late medieval church and society. People needed the clergy for their salvation by means of the sacraments. The clergy accompanied people's lives from baptism to last rites and were present in daily life through distributing the sacrament of the altar, which in turn was important for upholding the common wealth in territories and cities. On the other hand, lay people were all too aware that priests and monks did not always live as they should. Anti-clericalism was a widespread phenomenon in late medieval Europe, even if lay people still needed the clerics not only to offer the Mass but also to preach. One of the most significant developments in the fifteenth century was the increase of special positions for preachers at big city churches, i.e. priests who did not have the duty to offer the weekly Mass but who served in special services centred around the sermon. This provided the opportunity for lay people not only to be objects of sacramental provision but also to be presented with coherent explications of biblical texts. Therefore more and more lay people, also by reading spiritual treatises, became competent figures in the church, in obvious tension to the leading role still occupied by the clergy.

This leads us to the third and, in the context of this essay, decisive polarity: the tension between outer and inner piety. Briefly, outer piety is evidently expressed in the practice of indulgences, i.e. a kind of conduct where quantities and measures are more important than the believer's cast of mind. Inner piety, in marked contrast, is concerned with the believer's spiritual habits and trusting faith—her or his way of relating to, and standing before, God. Here, then, we return to the beginning of this chapter. The most excellent shape that inner piety took was mysticism, as outlined above. What we find in Tauler shows precisely what inner piety means: an altering of mind and spirit instead of merely outward practices of penance. This is where we approach Luther. Luther's background and formation was in this inner kind of piety, and his protest against indulgences was, indeed, a protest against outer piety.

What makes all of this fascinating are the complex developments in the ensuing years. When Luther began to write on the concept of the priesthood of all believers, at the very latest in his treatise *To the Christian Nobility of the German Nation* in 1520, he linked the ideals of inner piety with the social tensions between lay people and clergy. He emphasised that the difference between the two states, lay and ordained, was no longer to be seen as being of any moral value. This enabled him to create a further link: in the treatise to the nobility he argued that, precisely because there is no essential difference between clergy and laity, temporal authorities were able, empowered and even commissioned to reform the church. Here, then, we have the very core of the Reformation, deriving as it did from the Middle Ages and also starting a new development: inner piety, a new emphasis on the role of the laity and a strengthening of the polycentric powers. These together made possible the development of church renewal, even though its roots and various dimensions all derived from the Middle Ages.

The lasting legacy of mysticism

One might ask whether Luther's mystical roots, however obvious they might be, remained important to him once he had come to a clearer understanding of reformation theology. Many Protestants do ask this question, as since the end of the nineteenth century there had been a sense that mysticism and the Reformation had little to do with one another.[24] It has become clear, however, that the mystical dimension in Luther is strong and decisive. The best known use that Luther made of mystical theology within the Reformation framework is the *Treatise on the Freedom of a Christian* (1520). Here he described the encounter between Christ and the believer using the mystical imagery of bride and bridegroom, with faith as the spousal ring.[25] Obviously, the bridal metaphor derived from Bernard of Clairvaux, and was also used by Staupitz. Luther's application of this metaphor shows that for him there was no contradiction between mysticism and the doctrine of justification. Both taught the same: God comes to save the Christian believer without any human presupposition.

Less well known is the fact that Luther made use of mystical thought later on, too, in different contexts. In his Wartburg *Church Postil* (1522), which had great impact on the culture of Lutheran preaching, we encounter a passage clearly informed by Eckhart's/Tauler's idea of the birth of God in the soul:

'Here, the Evangelist has given us a sign in that he is quiet about the names of Joseph and Mary, calling them just father and mother, to give us reason to think about the spiritual meaning. Who now is Christ's spiritual father and mother? ... Thus, it is clear, that the Christian church, which means all human beings believing in Christ, are the spiritual mother of Christ, and all apostles and teachers among the people, whenever they preach the Gospel, are his spiritual father. So whenever a human being comes to faith, Christ is born by them.'[26]

Here we find the mystical idea of the birth of Christ in the soul of the believer in the midst of Reformation preaching. Nevertheless, there can be no doubt that mystical language and content decreased in Luther's preaching owing to his conflict with the so-called 'Schwärmer'. With them, he noted, there was a use of mystical ideas leading to an uncontrolled theology with tendencies of uproar and unrest. However fair or unfair his judgement might have been concerning Karlstadt and Müntzer, it led Luther to reduce his use of mysticism. Yet it did not diminish completely but initiated a transformation that can be called a special kind of sacramental mysticism in the mature Luther. In a sermon for Maundy Thursday in 1523, we find an image that became decisive for Luther's mystical interpretation. In the Lord's Supper, he said, we become one cake with Christ and among us.[27] The image he uses here resembles the idea of bride and bridegroom which he outlined in his treatise on liberty. In fact, while in this text the mystical encounter is just bound to the faith, in the sermon of 1523 mysticism includes both faith and reception of the sacrament of Holy Communion. So while in the 'Schwärmer' mysticism might be more moderate than Luther feared it to be, through all its transformation it still remained mysticism.

Notes

[1] Martin Luther, *Weimarer Ausgabe* (Weimar edition, henceforth WA) 1, 233, 1–2: 'Dominus et magister noster Iesus Christus dicendo "Penitentiam agite &c." omnem vitam fidelium penitentiam esse voluit'.

[2] Volker Leppin, *Die fremde Reformation. Luthers mystische Wurzeln* (Munich, 2nd edn 2017).

[3] WA 1, 525, 4–14: 'Memini, Reverende pater, inter iucundissimas et salutares fabulas tuas, quibus me solet dominus Ihesus mirifice consolari, incidisse aliquando mentionem huius nominis "poenitentia", ... te velut e caelo sonantem excepimus, quod poenitentia vera non est, nisi quae ab amore iusticiae et dei incipit. Et hoc esse potius principium poenitentiae, quod illis finis et consummatio censetur.'

[4] WA 1, 525, 20–1: 'nunc nihil dulcius aut gratius ... sonet quam "poenitentia".'

⁵ '[O]mnem vitam fidelium penitentiam esse voluit'. V. Leppin, 'Zur Aufnahme mystischer Traditionen in Luthers erster Ablassthese', in V. Leppin, *Transformationen. Studien zu den Wandlungsprozessen in Theologie und Frömmigkeit zwischen Spätmittelalter und Reformation*, Spätmittelalter, Humanismus, Reformation, vol. 86 (Tübingen, 2015), 261–77.

⁶ Sermones: des hoch| geleerten in gnaden erleüchten do|ctoris Johannis Thaulerii sannt | dominici ordens die da weißend | auff den nächesten waren weg im | gaist zů wanderen durch überswe| bendenn syn. Von latein in teütsch | gewendt manchem menschenn zů | såliger fruchtbarkaitt, Augsburg: Hans Otmar 1508, fol. 192^V.: 'ob du des tags zů sibentzig mal fallest als offt soltu wiederkeren vnd kommen wider zů got. vnd dring dich wider in got also schwindiglichen dz dir dein sunde zů mal entpfallen. so du da mit zů der beicht kommest. das du jt nitt wissest zů sagen. Dis sol dich nit entsetzen. es ist dir nit aufgefallen zů schaden. sunder zů ainer bekentnuß deines nichtes. vnd zů ainer verschmehunge dein selber mitt ayner gelassenhayt. nicht mitt ainer schwärmůtikait (….) Sant paulus spricht. Alle die got lieben den kommpt alle ding zů gůt. Nu di gloß spricht. Auch dy sünd. Sunder schweig vnd fleühe zů got vnd sihe auf dein nicht. Vnd bleib innen. nit lauf zů hant da mit zů dem beichtiger'.

⁷ WA 9, 104, 11: 'Hoc nota tibi'.

⁸ WA 9, 104, 12: 'Utilissimum consilium'.

⁹ WA 1, 525, 24–30; cf. NOVVM IN-| strumentum omne, dilgienter ab ERASMO ROTERDAMO| recognitum et emendatum non solum ad græcam ueritatem, ue-| rumetiam ad multorum utriusque linguæ codicum, eorumque ue-| terum simul et emendatorum fidem […] (Basel, 1516), [Annotationes] 241: 'μετάνοεῖτε. […] At nostrum uulgus putat esse pœnitentiam agere, præscripta pœna quapiam luere commissa. […] Alioqui μετάνοια dicta est a μετάνοεῖν, hoc est, a posterius intelligendo, ubi quis lapsus, re peracta, tum demum animadvertit erratum suum. […] Meo iudicio commode uerti poterat, Respicite, siue ad mentem reddite.'

¹⁰ WA 1, 99, 10–11: 'amore iustitiae et poenarum odit peccatum'.

¹¹ WA 1, 86, 31–2: 'Hi non sua poenitentia sed Dei gratia peccatum sanari confidunt'.

¹² WA 1, 98, 26–9.

¹³ WA 1, 141, 22–6: 'Adhuc servilem iustitiam mire perficiunt ipsae effusiones indulgentiarum, quibus nihil agitur quam ut populus discat timere, fugere, horrere poenam peccatorun, non autem ita et peccata. Ideo parum sentitur fructus indulgentiarum, sed magna securitas et licentia peccandi, Ita sane ut, nisi timerent poenam peccatorum, nullus vellet optare gratis istas indulgentias.'

¹⁴ WA 1, 141, 37: 'O stertentes Sacerdotes'.

¹⁵ WA.B 1, 160, 8p.: 'Ego sane secutus theologiam Tauleri et eius libelli, quem tu nuper dedisti imprimendum Aurifabro nostro Christianno'.

¹⁶ WA 1, 153: 'ist die matery faßt nach der art des erleuchten doctors Tauleri, prediger ordens'.

¹⁷ Heinrich Denifle, *Luther und Luthertum in der ersten Entwicklung. Quellenmäßig dargestellt* (Mainz, 1904/1909).

¹⁸ Reformation Commemoration at Friedrich-Wilhelms-Universität, Berlin, 31 October 1917. Speech by Prof. Dr. Holl: 'Luthers Auffassung der Religion'. Published in an extended version: Karl Holl, 'Was verstand Luther unter Religion?', in K. Holl, *Gesammelte Aufsätze zur Kirchengeschichte*, vol. 1: *Luther* (Tübingen, 1932), 1–110. The

latter version was the basis for Holl's immense influence on Luther research.

[19] Joseph Lortz, *Die Reformation in Deutschland* (Freiburg, 1939/40).

[20] Erwin Iserloh, 'Martin Luther und der Aufbruch der Reformation (1517–1525)', in Hubert Jedin (ed.), *Handbuch für Kirchengeschichte*, vol. 4 (Freiburg, 1967), 3–114, at 3–10.

[21] Bernd Moeller, *Spätmittelalter* (Göttingen, 1966), 40.

[22] B. Moeller, *Die Reformation und das Mittelalter. Kirchenhistorische Aufsätze* (ed. Johannes Schilling) (Göttingen, 1991), 93.

[23] For this understanding see my programmatic essay, 'Die Wittenberger Reformation und der Prozess der Transformation kultureller zu institutionellen Polaritäten', in V. Leppin, *Transformationen*, 31–68.

[24] See V. Leppin and Marco A. Sorace, 'Mystik im ökumenischen Horizont. Schwierigkeiten und Chancen in katholischer und evangelischer Theologie', *Catholica* (Münster) 63 (2009), 262–83.

[25] WA 7, 25, 26–34.

[26] WA 10/I/1, 387, 3–15: 'Da hatt der Euangelist aber eyn maltzeychen gesteckt, das er hie schweygt der namen Joseph und Maria, nennet sie vatter und mutter, uns ursach tzu geben an die geystliche bedeuttung. Wer ist nu Christus geystlicher vatter unnd mutter? […] So ists nu klar, das die Christliche kirche, das ist: alle glewbige menschen sind Christus geystliche mutter, und alle Apostel und lerer ym volck, ßo sie das Euangelium predigen, sind seyn geystlicher vatter. Und ßo offt eyn mensch von new glawbig wirt, ßo offt wirt Christus geporn von yhnen.'

[27] WA 12, 486.

2
The idea of reform in the sermons and pamphlets of Martin Luther, 1517–22

Helga Robinson-Hammerstein

That Martin Luther considered himself first and foremost a man of the spoken word, as preacher and even as university professor, is not a controversial statement. It is now also generally accepted that his popular pamphlets follow the style and sentence structure of the spoken word. Late fifteenth-century and early sixteenth-century vernacular literature never discarded its essentially oral function, even when it was written down and printed so as to reach a wider audience. The majority of the audience, being illiterate, had to have the printed word read out to them.

When Luther discovered in the printing press the gracious gift of God that could achieve the more extensive proclamation of His Word, this did not involve a momentous switch from spontaneous oral to recondite literary modes of expression. Certainly in his extremely productive early career as a preacher and writer, a great deal of what was printed had actually first been delivered as sermons and then only slightly reworked for publication. His concise and popular preaching style, as well as the matching style of his numerous devotional pamphlets, Luther claimed to have derived straight from his personal encounter with the Bible. He was, however, supremely anxious to have his printers produce carefully proofread books. Johann Rhau-Grunenberg, whom Luther entrusted with many of his early works, was not above reproach in this respect, and Luther told him so on many occasions.[1] At the same time Luther was deeply conscious that the quality of the human voice in the spoken word could not be adequately substituted in print. He objected very vehemently to his sermons being rushed into print by some scribe who had simply sat under his pulpit and noted down the words as they poured forth. He complained bitterly in the preface to the revised printing of a previously surreptitiously published sermon: 'Even though someone may wish to capture my sermon, let him moderate his haste and allow me to advise on the promulgation of my words. There is a great difference between bringing something to the light of day by means of the living voice and doing so by means of the dead script.'[2]

In the university environment Luther's task of teaching and working out his scriptural theology was greatly facilitated by the use of printing as a welcome device for duplicating essential information: for instance, the printed texts for his lectures on the Psalms, which provided for interlinear glosses.[3] Printing was crucial in his successful fight against the dominant influence of Aristotle on Christian theology. The unique broadsheet edition of the *One Hundred Theses against Scholastic Theology*, discovered by Dr Maria von Katte in the Herzog-August-Bibliothek in Wolfenbüttel, refocuses attention on Luther's vital activity as a university reformer. Luther drew up the theses for the theological disputation of the respondent Franz Günther of Nordhausen, which took place on 4 September 1517, with Luther himself presiding. The theses represent the high point in the struggle against medieval Aristotelianism.[4] Scholars in Luther's former university, Erfurt, were highly offended by Luther's courageous effrontery in challenging the whole of medieval scholarship by attacking age-old traditions. Luther's correspondent in Nuremberg, Christoph Scheurl, however, to whom he sent a copy of the theses after the disputation had taken place, exclaimed jubilantly that Luther had paved the way for the restoration of true Christian theology.[5] Certainly, within a few years of his appointment as professor of theology, Luther, with the help of the young Greek scholar Philip Melanchthon, had overhauled university studies in Wittenberg. The stated aim, as far as studies in the Theological Faculty were concerned, was not simply what had been advocated for so long by the Church councils—to turn out better-educated priests. It was rather to equip students to discover the truth for themselves by investigating the original sources in the humanist philological manner.[6]

The reformation of the university made Wittenberg the leading academic institution in Germany. A massive influx of students from all regions of Germany and further afield responded favourably to the changes. Many of these students were to become the preachers of the Lutheran Reformation. It can therefore be said that Wittenberg University was the essential powerhouse of the Lutheran Reformation. Had Wittenberg been an old institution of learning, the long-established scholastic tradition might have presented an insuperable obstacle to reform, but the university was a recent creation and the reforms were speedily introduced. This was the decisive factor in the progress of Luther's reformation of religion. The Lutheran Reformation originated in the university and it retained its academic framework throughout. Luther himself was a university professor throughout his public career.

This reformation of an institution energetically undertaken by Martin Luther is of striking significance for his whole career. This was the only kind of reformation that he recognised as feasible. In his estimation, the university was the one institution that could and must be reformed by active human planning and effort. All other institutions could and would be reformed in 'God's own time'. Matters could, however, only be helped along by pastors preaching the 'pure Word of God' and laymen listening to and heeding it, without rushing headlong into changes. Luther's message is apparent, for example, in his sermon 'on prayer and procession in Rogation Week', published as a pamphlet in 1519. During the spring and summer of 1519 he was carefully reshaping popular piety, particularly on the occasion of Church festivals into which popular customs had intruded.[7] Rogation Week (the weekdays before Ascension Day) had been set aside by the medieval Church for special prayers and processions in the fields. Luther was well aware of the importance that his parishioners attached to participation in such long-established, reassuring rituals, intended to avert plague and bad harvests, but he sought to demonstrate that a public blasphemy was perpetrated when worshippers indulged in excessive drinking. Luther disapproved of processions—indeed, he was in general suspicious of all extramural religious activities—but he realised that a long-established tradition could not be abolished overnight.

The emphasis in the Rogation Week sermon of 1519 is on the acceptance of God's assurance as a precondition of all effective prayer—an important step in the development of Luther's prayer theology. He appealed to the common sense of his hearers, which he believed could be trained to perceive that long-established customs might have been infiltrated by the Devil.[8] A similar theme appears in the sermon 'on the most revered sacrament of the holy, true body of Christ and of the brotherhoods', preached and printed in 1519. This was the first detailed exposition of Luther's teaching on the sacrament of the altar. The second part of the sermon deals with the *Bruderschafften*, the 'brotherhoods', the professional associations that were originally devotional in character but had retained only their outward ritualistic trappings without any deeper religious significance. Luther condemned their communal life, characterised now by gluttony, but, as in the case of other expressions of late medieval piety, he did not advocate their forcible dissolution or suppression. The sermon maintains that they should be allowed to die out naturally, as their members gained better insights into the true, scripturally authenticated religious observances.[9]

It is possible, therefore, to argue that at the beginning of his public career in the empire Martin Luther had completed the one vital reforming task that he believed human endeavour could successfully undertake: the reformation of the University of Wittenberg. It is essential to bear this in mind when looking at the second aspect of Luther's activities in 1517: as parish priest and preacher in daily contact with ordinary people, the 'simple folk'. For the sake of the salvation of his parishioners Luther launched a public attack on the practice of selling indulgences, since by this means people were offered remission of sins for money without repentance. The ensuing indulgence quarrel highlights the recognition by the institutions of the early sixteenth-century Church of a hierarchical social order. To have their sins compounded, kings, princes and bishops were asked to pay 25 Rhenish guilders; barons, lesser prelates and abbots ten; the lesser nobility six; burghers and merchants three; and artisans one. It was suggested that the poor—including peasants—should not be excluded from the benefits of the system. They might be given their remission free of charge if they prayed with due devotion.[10] Luther refused to apply such a differentiating social yardstick in matters of sin and remission. In his view, all men were equally in need of grace, which could not be purchased by paying money to any institution, even if that institution needed it very badly.

Luther's theology of salvation expressed itself in a strongly anti-institutional reaction—and by so doing affected crucial vested interests of the papal curia. He became obsessed with the vision of faceless institutions misleading people and manipulating them for their own materialist ends. This is the tenor of practically all his early pamphlets but particularly of his great Reformation tracts of 1520, his direct challenges to Rome in 1520 and first and foremost in his pamphlets against indulgences. These pamphlets, as a follow-up to the *Ninety-Five Theses*, gained him unprecedented popularity, although it is obvious to the later observer that popular anti-clericalism and Luther's anti-institutional animus were different in origin and scope. It is highly unlikely that popular anti-clericalism would have been more than a fashionable but ineffectual phenomenon without the appearance of Luther. The effect of his sermon preached on the way to the Diet of Worms provides only one example of this, albeit a very dramatic example. This impromptu sermon, on the theme of piety and righteousness, was preached in haste in Erfurt on 7 April 1521 and immediately printed there on the basis of notes taken during the sermon. The title of the printed version reveals that the publication was promoted by a layman. The popular demand for words from Luther's lips was now almost uncontrollable.[11]

One of Luther's early publications was not a work from his own pen but an anonymous medieval mystical text that had been made available to him, in the first instance, in an incomplete manuscript: *Eyn deutsch Theologia*. He published it twice with a preface, firstly in 1516, on the basis of the incomplete manuscript, and secondly on 4 June 1518 in the full version, which had meanwhile been sent to him. What attracted him to this treatise was the essential Christian paradox exemplified in the figures of Adam and Christ. Hence the interpretative subtitle that he gave to his edition of the tract: 'A noble little book of the right understanding of the figures of Adam and Christ, that Adam

The 1518 version of one of Luther's early publications, an anonymous mystical text of the fourteenth century that had been made available to him in an incomplete manuscript: *Eyn deutsch Theologia*. He published it twice with a preface, firstly in 1516, on the basis of the incomplete manuscript, and secondly on 4 June 1518 in the full version pictured left.

must die in us and Christ must rise'. Significantly, his preface counters two major accusations that were to remain permanent features of his public career. He stated, firstly, that the little book provided him with an opportunity to demonstrate that his teaching was no innovation and, secondly, that the German language was a proper vehicle for the Word of God.[12]

Luther's own first little book published in German was his interpretation of the seven penitential psalms, which appeared in 1518. Here he states expressly that the little book is intended for his rough Saxons and not for the sophisticated Nurembergers, who, however, applauded the work after it was recommended to them by Johann von Staupitz, Wittenberg's first professor of biblical theology and Luther's mentor. The work is not an adaptation of his lectures on the Psalms of 1513–15, although careful research had gone into its preparation. In his preface Luther mentioned as his sources the Vulgate, the commentary of St Jerome and Johannes Reuchlin's *Septene*: that is, Reuchlin's examination of the seven penitential psalms on the basis of his Hebrew scholarship, published in 1512. Luther's work offers translations and interpretations of the penitential psalms (Psalms 6, 32, 38, 51, 102, 130 and 142). Again the text shows that he was fully aware that he would be accused of innovation and of revealing too much of the mysteries of God to the simple folk in their own language, but he was clearly prepared to take that risk.[13] Significantly, the title of the work announces that this is an interpretation *nach dem schrifftlichen synne*, 'according to the literal sense'. Patristic and medieval exegesis of the Scriptures traditionally used all 'the four senses' of Scripture: the 'tropological' (moral) sense, the 'allegorical' (ecclesiological) sense and the 'anagogical' (eschatalogical) sense as well as the 'literal' sense. As a young scholar, Luther had used the traditional 'four senses' in his exegesis but from the time of his lectures on the Epistle to the Romans in 1515 he came increasingly to believe that Scripture had only a single, 'literal' sense.[14]

Two whole ranges of popular but non-polemical pamphlets—which amount to a conscious transformation of every aspect of popular piety and a review of the traditional sacraments—were written by Luther, either in response to requests from friends who wished to be better instructed or as a result of the requirement to preach sermons on canonically prescribed biblical texts.

A highly significant early publication is his Latin treatise on the Ten Commandments. While Lucas Cranach was painting a fairly traditional and iconographically conventional illustration of the Ten Commandments for the Wittenberg Town Hall, Luther transcended conventionality in his extraordinarily popular sermons on the same theme, preached between 2 July 1516 and 24 February 1517. When he published the substance of the sermons as a book on 20 July 1518, he had, according to one contemporary, pulled the veil from the face of Moses and, in the opinion of another observer, elicited the effective Christian meaning from the Law. The treatise was intended to act as a mirror held up to the sinner for self-examination. The image of the mirror was not, of course, a new departure: it was a medieval teaching device that was continued by humanist writers of the early sixteenth century, notably in their 'mirrors for princes'. Luther, however, provided much more than a catalogue of demands, the non-fulfilment of which entailed ecclesiastical punishments. It is interesting to see that—by contrast with the distorting mirror of polemic, which was consciously and consistently elaborated in the service of the Reformation of the Word—this first instance of the use of the mirror imagery is found in the proclamation of the literal, Christological sense of the Word, applied to everyday issues as they arose. Luther used the treatise as an opportunity to subject popular aberrations to a comprehensive critique. Popular superstitions like witchcraft, magic and astrology are castigated in the treatise. All aspects of popular religious practices are criticised: the worshipping of saints, the zest for pilgrimages, holidays and all the excesses, like over-eating and drunkenness, that were associated with them.[15]

The general advice to 'throw your sins on Christ and have faith' is subsequently developed in a series of printed sermons of 1519. It appears, for instance, in the sermon on the contemplation of Christ's suffering and on preparation for facing death in faith in God's Word.[16] The theme is the uselessness of rituals that are not Word-centred.[17] These sermons of 1519 link positive, consoling, reassuring observations about God's promise with a rejection of popular practices such as carrying letters, crosses or images about one's person in an attempt to avert danger. Luther's conviction was that through the development of all these little placebos the essence of the Word had been changed into a mere fiction.

In January 1519 Luther preached a sermon on marriage, of which he himself issued a printed version in May, after the appearance of an unauthorised printing. In his discussion of the role of marriage he emphasised three issues. In the first instance the sacramental nature of marriage was still retained: 'a holy sign of the unity between God and man'. Secondly, he was anxious to re-evaluate the words of the promise, which initiated a bond of trust between earthly partners and should not be treated in a cavalier fashion. A third issue, however, was the most important to him. The purpose of the union was to bear fruit, and the Christian education of children is represented in the sermon as 'the highest indulgence'.[18] To emphasise the household as the mainstay of the Christian community was not in itself new, but Luther's advocacy involved a significant shift of emphasis. Eventually he was to deny that celibacy should be considered more holy than marriage and he removed sexual intercourse between married folk from the list of sins.[19] The theme of marriage was one of the most frequently treated in Reformation pamphlets, from the early 1520s onwards always with the stress on the divine but non-sacramental institution of the union, which had been established in the Garden of Eden. (This was also the main pictorial representation in pamphlets on marriage.)[20]

The printing in 1519 of a series of individual sermons dealing with the traditional sacraments was stimulated by 'the thirst for scriptural instruction' of the dowager Duchess Margarethe of Braunschweig-Lüneburg. The first of these, 'on the sacrament of penance', distinguishes between remission by the Church and forgiveness by God. Only the latter is represented as conferring consolation on the sinner. The primacy of faith is postulated, without any attack on the sacrament itself.[21] The practice of auricular confession was bound, however, to come under review, since, according to Luther, every Christian had, in principle, authority to grant absolution—although, for the sake of the maintenance of order, official absolution is reserved to the clergy. He returned to the subject of penance in a treatise written in 1521 during his exile in the Wartburg and dedicated to the knight Franz von Sickingen. Here Luther criticised the power of the Church to manipulate the sacrament. He rejected the traditional practice of auricular confession as false and misleading.[22] In the other two works of 1519 for the instruction of the duchess of Braunschweig-Lüneburg, baptism[23] and Holy Communion (in the first of Luther's works on that sacrament)[24] are given full scriptural status as sacraments. These three printed sermons on the traditional sacraments were followed by a short work entitled 'A Sermon of the New Testament, that is, of the holy mass'. The theme is Christ's vicarious death, which constitutes the true community of Christians. The sermon, which rejects the sacrificial character of the Mass, caused a storm of protest. Johannes Cochlaeus, an early and unrelenting opponent of Luther, called it 'heretical, hussitic and an incitement to rebellion by the lowly'.[25]

Yet more controversial were the three great Reformation tracts of 1520. The first of these, the *Address to the German Nobility*, was conceived as a comprehensive statement of the fundamental demands of a necessary Reformation, set down by Luther when he was faced with a heresy trial. The first part of the *Address* develops a new ecclesiology on the basis, firstly, of the idea of the priesthood of all believers against the papal tradition of postulating the superiority of its own spiritual authority. It was based, secondly, on the statement that every Christian has immediate access to God, thus rejecting the exclusive papal authority to interpret Scripture. Thirdly, it posited the idea that secular princes, in their capacity as Christians, ought to summon Church councils when bishops and the pope failed to fulfil their obligation to the Word. The second part of the *Address* contains 28 practical proposals about the issues with which a reform council should concern itself.[26] The second tract, *On the Babylonian Captivity of the Church* (published by Luther in Latin for the exclusive use of scholars), constitutes a wholesale attack on the sacramental system created by Rome, as an elaborate means of deception and financial exploitation. Only baptism, Holy Communion and penance (the last primarily as a pious custom) are retained as the scripturally instituted sacraments.[27] The third tract, *Of the Freedom of the Christian Man*, elaborates the paradox of Christian freedom and servitude, on the basis of the Pauline Epistles. It is preceded by an abject dedication to Pope Leo X—a last attempt at reconciliation with the papal curia.[28]

Confrontation with Rome, however, became inevitable. It was accompanied by increasingly immoderate language on the part of Luther after the issuing of the first papal bull against him, *Exsurge Domine*, threatening excommunication. A series of pamphlets in 1520 begins by arguing that the pope was being kept in the dark by false counsellors (a customary device used by opponents of established authority), asserts that the papal bull was a forgery by Johann Eck (the chancellor of the University of Ingolstadt, who had drafted the bull at the request of Pope Leo X) and ends by calling the pope 'Antichrist'. The pamphlet entitled in the German version *Against the Bull of the Antichrist* constitutes Luther's selective and fiery rejection of the allegations in the bull *Exsurge Domine*.[29] Luther's complete refutation of all the allegations made against him in the first papal bull appears in the treatise entitled in his own German translation *Ground and Reason for all the Articles wrongly condemned by the Roman Bull*. It was his secular overlord and protector, Frederick the Wise, elector of Saxony, who had urged such a comprehensive treatment of the issues.[30] A third pamphlet, *A letter to Pope Leo X*, is a German version of Luther's Latin letter of apology to the pope for having attacked him so relentlessly. The German text was published before the Latin original was sent to Rome and backdated to 6 September 1520, apparently to avoid the impression that Luther had been intimidated by the arrival of Johann Eck with the second papal bull against Luther, *Decet Romanum Pontificem*, proclaiming his actual excommunication. The apology proves to be, in fact, a much sharper indictment of the pope than before but claims to be following a well-established tradition. Luther stated that his advice to the pope conformed to the model of the treatise *De consideratione* of St Bernard of Clairvaux (c. 1150), addressed to Pope Eugenius III, 'which', wrote Luther, 'every pope ought to know by heart'.[31]

In this crisis Luther decided to take the ordinary Christian into his confidence. The spoken word of the sermons and the printed word of the pamphlets and broadsheets were consciously used by Luther and his helpers to uncover the evils that existed in the Church, transforming the practice of moralising revelations into direct attack. Preaching and print must support the Word against these evils in the knowledge, and even the hope, that the result must be *seliger unfrid, auffruhr unnd rumor*, 'blessed restlessness, agitation and rumbling discontent'.[32] In his *Great Sermon on Usury* in 1520 Luther had stated that he had no intention of retracting any of his previous allegations, even if it caused offence. In fact, he intensified his allegations, so that 'Christ's teaching should be an even greater stumbling block'.[33] Christ's bringing the sword and causing discord among people was, of course, announced in Scripture (Mt 10:34) and Luther often referred to this passage, but he was far from interpreting this discord as encouragement of social unrest. That he wished to unsettle people in their attitude to the Church through his preaching and pamphleteering is evident—for instance, in the polemical impromptu sermon that he preached in Erfurt on his way to the Diet of Worms. Invectives against the Aristotelian philosophy that shored up the Roman Church and against 'fables' that were uttered from its pulpits form the background to his proclamation of the faith in Christ that removes all need for so-called 'good works' to assist salvation. Many objected to the violent style of the Erfurt sermon and it was apparently so distorted by rumours that a lay supporter of Luther felt compelled to release it in print.[34] While Luther was preaching, part of the overcrowded church seemed in danger of collapse, but Luther was able to reassure the congregation, blaming the disturbance on 'the Devil, who groans and frets in the presence of the pure Word'. After Luther left the scene of the sermon, however, anti-clerical attacks caused immense confusion in Erfurt.[35]

Luther had no fear for his own life in all this turmoil. In the face of the assembled empire at the Diet of Worms in April 1521, he was quite aware that he was in the weak position of a 'lone monk' with the backing merely of his university colleagues and with only volatile popular support for his teaching. All human consideration for law and order suggested the need for a new Church order for those communities willing to follow the Word after Luther's excommunication had been given force by the imperial ban. Luther, however, rejected such considerations. A short pamphlet of 1522, *On the avoidance of human teachings*, encapsulated his attitude. The faithful were warned not to rush into changes. The Word must be preached and a natural consensus established so as to avoid a new kind of legalism, worse than that of the Roman Church.[36] The people must be instructed consistently in the faith by all possible means, including the long-term beneficial work of schools. Hence Luther's urgent appeal to the councilmen of the cities and towns of Germany to set up, finance and maintain Christian schools. His pamphlet of 1524 sets out to prove that this would be in the interest not only of the spiritual but also of the secular welfare of the community.[37]

Nowhere is the warning against over-hasty change and the risk of legalism more strident than in the sermons and letters in which Luther responded to the 'Wittenberg Movement'. During the enforced absence of Luther in the Wartburg in 1521 and early 1522 Wittenberg experienced reform agitation, culminating in the imposition by the town council of a new civic constitution. Luther's senior university colleague and collaborator Andreas Bodenstein von Karlstadt wished to introduce immediately all the necessary reforms that Luther had advocated in his pamphlets, notably the abolition of the Mass, the dissolution of the monasteries and the permitting of clerical marriage. He assumed that these measures would turn Wittenberg into a community 'without abomination' and therefore pleasing to God.[38] In the spring of 1522 Luther himself rushed to Wittenberg to stop these innovations by preaching against them. He preached a series of eight sermons, beginning on *Invocavit* Sunday (9 March) and ending on *Reminiscere* Sunday (16 March). The eight *Invocavit* Sermons, preached before the whole community of Wittenberg, explained why the changes introduced in that community by means of the Wittenberg Ordinance (January 1522) must be rescinded and the previous order, although corrupt, must be restored, at least for the time being.

The *Invocavit* Sermons reviewed all aspects of late medieval sacramental piety and reiterated Luther's former criticism of abuses. He nevertheless emphasised the need for a different response from that of the Wittenberg Ordinance, and most certainly a more measured process of implementation of the truth of the Gospel. He argued that it would be damaging to the authority of the rediscovered Gospel and the exclusive salvific truth contained in it to force the consciences of the people through new laws—particularly people whose faith was as yet too weak to grasp the true meaning and significance of the liberating Gospel. The Word must be preached purely and consciences must be strengthened through this pure preaching so that the majority of the faithful could, given time, accept the spiritual freedom for which the Word had permanently freed them. Luther demanded due consideration for the weak for the sake of their consciences. Faith must be grounded in the Scriptures; a weak faith would be suffocated by legal constraints; faith could never be forced by laws. As for the reforms introduced in the 'Wittenberg Movement', priests may indeed marry, and nuns and monks may leave the cloisters if they wish. Forbidding such freedom is against God's will, but freedom must not be made a law: no one should attempt to protect this freedom by devising a new ordinance. Even those who have already been enlightened by the Gospel must temporarily suspend the use of their freedom in order to encourage the weak to become obedient to the Word alone.[39]

Luther summarised his attitude to the recent developments in Wittenberg in a letter of 17 March 1522 to his friend Nikolaus Hausmann, pastor of Zwickau, and contrasted with these 'tumults' his own idea of reformation. Hausmann was not to allow any innovations either by a decision of the congregation or by force: 'what our people tried to destroy by force and violence are only to be destroyed by the Word'. 'I condemn the fact that masses are held to be sacrifices and good works', wrote Luther, 'but I refuse to lay hands on the unwilling or on unbelievers or use violence against them.' No one is to be forced into the faith but must be drawn by the Word. Luther condemned 'the laws of the pope concerning confession, communion, prayer, fasting', but these practices must continue for the time being for the sake of the weak who are still entangled by them. When the weak have become strong, these laws may be discontinued. This was Luther's way of teaching (*forma docendi*): he asked Hausmann to proceed in the same way. 'Hearts must be driven gradually, like the flocks of Jacob (Genesis 33:13), so that they first take up the Word of God of their own accord and when at last they are strengthened, they may do all things.'[40]

Notes

[1] Josef Benzing, *Buchdrucker-Lexikon des 16. Jahrhunderts (Deutsches Sprachgebiet)* (Frankfurt, 1952), 181; Elizabeth L. Eisenstein, *The Printing Press as an Agent of Change* (Cambridge, 1979), 307 n. 17; Andrew Pettegree, *Brand Luther: 1517, Printing and the Making of the Reformation* (New York, 2015), 42, 44, 51–2, 100, 104, 109–10, 112, 114, 139–40, 145, 147.

[2] *Eyn Sermon von dem Elichen standt vorendert vnd corrigiret durch D. Martinum Luther Augustiner tzu Wittenbergk*, first edition (Johann Rhau-Grunenberg, Wittenberg, 1519). Luther had felt obliged to issue this corrected authorised version in May 1519 after this sermon on marriage had been printed in an annoyingly distorted form by the Leipzig printer Wolfgang Stöckel. Luther's works are cited in this article according to the Weimar edition: *D. Martin Luthers Werke. Kritische Gesamtausgabe, Abteilung Werke*, vols 1–61 (Weimar, 1883ff), hereafter *WA*. The reference here is to *WA* 2, 163. See also Josef Benzing, *Lutherbibliographie* (Baden-Baden, 1966), no. 363.

[3] In his own copy of this work, the *Dictata super Psalterium*, Luther entered in his own hand a short summary of each psalm and brief interlinear and marginal glosses. The autograph survives in the Herzog-August-Bibliothek in Wolfenbüttel. See Hans-Ulrich Delius (ed.), *Martin Luther Studienausgabe*, 1 (Berlin, 1979), 29–30. See also J. Benzing, *Lutherbibliographie*, no. 68a; Maria Grossmann, *Wittenberger Drucke 1502–1517: Ein bibliographischer Beitrag zur Geschichte des Humanismus in Deutschland* (Vienna, 1971), 90; Pettegree, *Brand Luther*, 43, 48.

[4] *Ad Subscriptas conclusiones Respondebit Magister Franciscus Guntherus Nordhusensis pro Biblia. Presidente Reverendo patre Martino Luder Augustinen. Sacrae Theologiae Vuittenburgen. decano loco & tempore statuendis* (Johann Rhau-Grunenberg, Wittenberg, 1517). See *WA* 1, 221–8; Delius, *Martin Luther Studienausgabe*, 1, 165–72; Pettegree, *Brand Luther*, 51. This unique copy of the broadside (Herzog-August-Bibliothek, Wolfenbüttel, shelf mark 434.11 Theol. 2º) was found by Dr von Katte pasted into a copy of the collection of Luther's works printed by Adam Petri of Basel in July 1520.

[5] Christoph Scheurl, letter to Luther, 3 November 1517: *Christi theologiam restaurare et in illius lege ambulare*, in *D. Martin Luthers Werke. Kritische Gesamtausgabe, Abteilung Briefwechsel*, vols 1–15 (Weimar, 1930ff), hereafter *WA Br*. The reference here is to *WA Br* 1, 115–16. See Martin Brecht, *Martin Luther: his road to Reformation 1483–1521* (Minneapolis, 1985), 120, 160–1.

[6] Brecht, *Martin Luther*, 161–74, 279–81; Heiko A. Oberman, *Luther: Man between God and the Devil* (New Haven/London, 1989), 158–74; Heinz Schilling, *Martin Luther, Rebell in einer Zeit des Umbruchs* (Munich, 2012), 134–43; Pettegree, *Brand Luther*, 46–52.

7 Brecht, *Martin Luther*, 351–5.
8 *Ein Sermon von dem gebeet vnd procession. yn der Creützwochen. Auch sunst von allem gebet durch dz gantz Jar wie sich der mensch dar in halten sol, allen cristen menschen nützlich vnd selig zu wissen* (Johann Knoblouch, Strasbourg, 1519). See *WA* 2, 172–9; Benzing, *Lutherbibliographie*, 385. See the translation and commentary by Helga Robinson-Hammerstein, *Martin Luther: On Prayer and Procession in Rogation Week (1519)*, rev. edn (Dublin, 1997). The pamphlet became very popular with printers throughout Germany: thirteen reprints are extant. It was later incorporated in composite devotional works by Luther.
9 *Eyn Sermon von dem Hochwirdigen Sacrament, des heyligen waren Leychnams Christi. Vnd von den Bruderschafften. D.M.L.A. Fur die Leyen* (Johann Rhau-Grunenberg, Wittenberg, 1519). See *WA* 2, 739, and *WA* 9, 791; Benzing, *Lutherbibliographie*, no. 497. See also Delius, *Martin Luther Studienausgabe*, 1, 270–87; Brecht, *Martin Luther*, 361–3.
10 Brecht, *Martin Luther*, 180–2.
11 *Eyn Sermon D. Martini Luthers so er auff dem hyneweg zu K.M. gen Wormbß zu zyhen, auß bit vortreflicher vnd vil gelarter, ane vorgehende fleyß, ader suenderliche studirung in der eyle zu Erffurdt gethan, von eynem leyhen ... in druck bevoln vnd v'schaft* (Mathes Maler, Erfurt, 1521). See *WA* 7, 804; Benzing, *Lutherbibliographie*, no. 896. See also Brecht, *Martin Luther*, 449.
12 *Eyn deutsch Theologia. das ist Eyn edles Buchleyn, von rechtem vorstand, was Adam vnd Christus sey, vund wie Adam yn vns sterben, vnd Christus ersteen sall* (Johann Rhau-Grunenberg, Wittenberg, 1518). See *WA* 1, 376; Benzing, *Lutherbibliographie*, no. 160. The woodcut on the title-page is one of the earliest examples of Luther's collaboration with Lucas Cranach. It illustrates the message of the subtitle rather incongruously: Adam is being buried by *putti* with little shovels and hoes, while Christ in glory dominates the upper half of the scene.
13 *Die Sieben buszpsalm mit deutscher auszlegung nach dem schrifftlichen synne tzu Christi vnd gottes gnaden, neben seyns selben, ware erkentniß, grundlich gerichtet* (Jacob Thanner, Leipzig, 1518). See *WA* 1, 156; Benzing, *Lutherbibliographie*, no. 76.
14 On Luther's use of the term *schrifftlich* see Moriz Heyne (ed.), *Deutsches Wörterbuch von Jacob Grimm und Wilhelm Grimm*, 9 (Leipzig, 1899), col. 1746: the editor notes, 'wir würden *wörtlich* brauchen'. See also Brecht, *Martin Luther*, 89: 'In the course of his interpretive activity, Luther recognized the inadequacy of the traditional method. Beginning with the lectures on Romans, the scheme of the fourfold sense of the Scriptures recedes more and more ...'. On 'the four senses' see G.W.H. Lampe (ed.), *The Cambridge History of the Bible*, 2 (Cambridge, 1969), 196, 214.
15 *Decem Praecepta wittenbergensi predicata populo per P. Martinvm Luther Avgvstinianum* (Johann Rhau-Grunenberg, Wittenberg, 1518). See *WA* 1, 395; Benzing, *Lutherbibliographie*, no. 192. In 1518 and 1519 shorter German versions were published, together with brief expositions of the Creed and the Lord's Prayer. See Brecht, *Martin Luther*, 352–3. On Cranach's illustration see Elfriede Starke, *Lukas Cranach d. Ä. Die Zehn-Gebote-Tafel* (Leipzig, 1982).
16 *Eyn Sermon von der betrachtung des heyligen leydens Christi D. Martini Luther zu Wittenberg* (Johann Rhau-Grunenberg, Wittenberg, 1519). See *WA* 2, 131; Benzing, *Lutherbibliographie*, no. 313. *Eyn Sermon von der Bereytung zum Sterbenn. M.L.A.* (Johann Rhau-Grunenberg, Wittenberg, 1519). See *WA* 2, 680; Benzing, *Lutherbibliographie*, no. 435.

See also Delius, *Martin Luther Studienausgabe*, 1, 230–43.
[17] As also in *Ein Sermon von dem gebeet vnd procession* (see note 8).
[18] *Eyn Sermon von dem Elichen standt vorendert vnd corrigiret durch D. Martinum Luther Augustiner tzu Wittenbergk* (Johann Rhau-Grunenberg, Wittenberg, 1519). See *WA* 2, 163; Benzing, *Lutherbibliographie*, no. 363. A version of the sermon on marriage had been printed in an annoyingly distorted form by the Leipzig printer Wolfgang Stöckel.
[19] *Uom Eelichen Leben. Martinus Lut. Wittemberg. M.D.xxij.* (Johann Rhau-Grunenberg, Wittenberg, 1522). See *WA* 10/2, 268; Benzing, *Lutherbibliographie*, no. 1239. See Lyndal Roper, *Martin Luther, Renegade and Prophet* (London, 2016), 294–5.
[20] E.g. Thomas Stör, *Der Ehelich standt vonn got mit gebenedeyung auffgesetzt, soll vmb schwaerheyt wegen der seltzamen gaben der Junckfrawschafft yederman frey seyn, vnd nyemant verboten werden* (Wolfgang Stürmer I, Erfurt, 1524).
[21] *Eyn Sermon von dem Sacrament der pusz D.M.L.* (Johann Rhau-Grunenberg, Wittenberg, 1519). See *WA* 2, 710; Benzing, *Lutherbibliographie*, no. 462. See also Delius, *Martin Luther Studienausgabe*, 1, 244–57.
[22] *Von der Beicht ob die der Bapst macht habe zu gepieten. Doctor Martinus Luther. Wittenbergk* (Johann Rhau-Grunenberg, Wittenberg, 1521). See *WA* 8, 133; Benzing, *Lutherbibliographie*, no. 947.
[23] *Eyn Sermon von dem heyligen hochwirdigen Sacrament der Tauffe. D.M.L.* (Johann Rhau-Grunenberg, Wittenberg, 1519). See *WA* 2, 724; Benzing, *Lutherbibliographie*, no. 479. See also Delius, *Martin Luther Studienausgabe*, 1, 258–69.
[24] *Eyn Sermon von dem Hochwirdigen Sacrament, des heyligen waren Leychnams Christi* (see note 9).
[25] *Eyn Sermon von dem newen Testament, das ist von der heyligen Messe Doct. Mar. L. Aug. Wittenbergk* (Johann Rhau-Grunenberg, Wittenberg, 1520). See *WA* 6, 349; Benzing, *Lutherbibliographie*, no. 669. See also Delius, *Martin Luther Studienausgabe*, 1, 288–311; David V.N. Bagchi, *Luther's earliest opponents. Catholic controversialists, 1518–1525* (Minneapolis, 1991), 123 and fn. 19.
[26] *An den Christlichen Adel deutscher Nation: von des Christlichen standes besserung: D. Martinus Luther. Vuittenberg* (Melchior Lotter Jnr, Wittenberg, 1520). See *WA* 6, 397; Benzing, *Lutherbibliographie*, no. 683. See also Delius, *Martin Luther Studienausgabe*, 2, 89–167. This first edition of 4,000 copies was sold within five days of its publication in August 1520. The second and third editions followed rapidly and were purchased with equal avidity.
[27] *De Captivitate Babylonica Ecclesiae, Praeludium Martini Lutheri. Vuittembergae* (Melchior Lotter Jnr, Wittenberg, 1520). See *WA* 6, 489; Benzing, *Lutherbibliographie*, no. 704. See also Delius, *Martin Luther Studienausgabe*, 2, 168–259. This great Reformation tract was first translated into the vernacular—with many errors—by Luther's opponent Thomas Murner. Even the corrected form, printed by Johannes Schott of Strasbourg in 1520, did not satisfy Luther. He objected to these scholarly theological issues being dragged into the public arena in a racy and undifferentiating polemical translation. The corrected German version contains the famous woodcut portrait of Luther by Hans Baldung Grien, showing him as the man of faith, grounded in the Scriptures.
[28] *Von der Frayheyt eynisz Christen menschen. Martinus Luther. Vuittembergae. Anno Domini 1520* (Johann Rhau-Grunenberg, Wittenberg, 1520). See *WA* 7, 15; Benzing, *Lutherbibliographie*, no. 734. See also Delius, *Martin Luther Studienausgabe*, 2, 260–309.

[29] *Widder die Bullen des Endchrists: Doctor Martinus Luther. VUittembergk. Jm Jar. MDXX* (Melchior Lotter Jnr, Wittenberg, 1520). The Latin text is entitled *Adversus execrabilem Antichristi bullam*. See *WA* 6, 613; Benzing, *Lutherbibliographie*, no. 728.

[30] *Assertio omnivm articvlorvm M. Lutheri, per Bullam Leonis X. nouissimam damnatorum. Vvittembergae. Anno M.D.XX.* (Melchior Lotter Jnr, Wittenberg, 1520). See *WA* 7, 92; Benzing, *Lutherbibliographie*, 779. Luther's German translation: *Grund vnnd vrsach aller Artickel D.Marti. Luther: szo durch Romische Bulle vnrechtlich vordampt seyn. Vuittemberg.* See *WA* 7, 308; Benzing, *Lutherbibliographie*, no. 846. See also Delius, *Martin Luther Studienausgabe*, 2, 310–404.

[31] *Eyn sendbrieff an den Bapst Leo den czehenden. D. Martinus Luther auss dem lateyn ynsz deutsch vorwandelt. Wittembergk. 1520* (Johann Rhau-Grunenberg, Wittenberg, 1520). See *WA* 7, 2; Benzing, *Lutherbibliographie*, no. 731.

[32] *Auff des bocks zu Leypczick Antwort D.M. Luther. Wittenberg. 1521* (Johann Rhau-Grunenberg, Wittenberg, 1521), a polemic against his opponent Jerome Emser, *WA* 7, 281: *es ist ein seliger unfrid, auffruhr unnd rumor, den gottes wort erweckt, da geht an rechte glaub unnd streytt widder den falschen glauben*. Luther also wrote of the *seligen auffruhr* that was caused by the Word of God in 1522 in *Eyn trew vormannung Martini Luther tzu allen Christen, sich tzu vorhuten für auffruhr und emporung*, *WA* 8, 654.

[33] *Eyn Sermon von dem Wucher. Doctoris Martini Luther Augustiner zu Wittenbergk* (Johann Rhau-Grunenberg, Wittenberg, 1520). See *WA* 6, 33; Benzing, *Lutherbibliographie*, no. 559.

[34] *Eyn Sermon D. Martini Luthers so er auff dem hyneweg zu K.M. gen Wormbß zu zyhen* (see note 11).

[35] Brecht, *Martin Luther*, 448–9.

[36] *Uon menschen leren tzu meyden D. Marti. Luther. Wittenberg. MDXXII* (Nickel Schirlentz, Wittenberg, 1522). See *WA* 10/2, 63; Benzing, *Lutherbibliographie*, no. 1172.

[37] *An die Radherrn aller stedte deutsches lands: das sie Christliche schulen auffrichten vnd hallten sollen. Martinus Luther. Wittenberg. MDxxiiij.* (publisher unknown, Wittenberg, 1524). See *WA* 15, 15; Benzing, *Lutherbibliographie*, no. 1875.

[38] Andreas Bodenstein von Karlstadt, *Predig oder Homiliien uber den Propheten Malachiam genannt* (S. Grimm and M. Wirsung, Augsburg, 1522): a printed sermon dated 18 February 1522, referring to Wittenberg as 'the Christian town', whose inhabitants show great fervour for the pure Word of God. On Karlstadt's theological and social views see Ulrich Bubenheimer, 'Scandalum et ius divinum. Theologische und rechtstheologische Probleme der ersten reformatorischen Innovationen in Wittenberg 1521/22', *Zeitschrift der Savigny-Stiftung für Rechtsgeschichte, Kanonistische Abteilung* 90 (1973), 263–342. See also Helmar Junghans, *Wittenberg als Lutherstadt* (Berlin, 1979), 110–16.

[39] *Acht Sermone D.M. Luthers von ihm gepredigt zu Wittenberg in der fasten* (Wittenberg, 1523). See *WA* 10/3, 1–64; Benzing, *Lutherbibliographie*, no. 1320. See also Delius, *Martin Luther Studienausgabe*, 2, 520–58; Martin Brecht, *Martin Luther: Shaping and Defining the Reformation, 1521–1532* (Minneapolis, 1990), 59–66; Helmar Junghans, 'Freiheit und Ordnung bei Luther während der Wittenberger Bewegung und der Visitationen', *Theologische Literatur-Zeitung* 97 (1972), 95–104.

[40] Martin Luther, Letter 459, to Nikolaus Hausmann, *WA Br* 2, 474–5.uh

3
Luther and Cranach—spreading the Reformation through images

Gesa E. Thiessen

The decisive changes that affected the universal Church and theology during the sixteenth century included the second great occurrence of iconoclasm in Christian history, but while each of the major Reformers commented on this subject their views were far from univocal. Even just a brief glance at older as well as contemporary Lutheran and Calvinist/Presbyterian church buildings provides an immediate idea of the differing views adopted by Luther on the one hand and Zwingli and Calvin on the other. Indeed, to this day, a visit to places of worship of the Catholic, Lutheran, Anglican and Reformed traditions provides pointers to the central tenets of their respective theologies of the image and the liturgical concerns of each denomination.

In places where the Lutheran Church was to establish itself as the major denomination, i.e. in the north and some other parts of Germany and in Scandinavia, iconoclasm had little or no impact, apart from the removal of multiple side altars in the alcoves of larger churches. Lutherans continued to worship in pre-Reformation churches with few alterations of the interiors. Thus many beautiful pieces of medieval art and architecture survived. Paintings and sculpture were and still are liberally displayed, frequently including an imposing crucifix in the sanctuary, a clear reference to Luther's concern with the *theologia crucis*. Luther's recommendation that priests were to stand behind the altar facing the congregation was generally adopted. Yet many older churches contain altars and high altars towards the back of the sanctuary and are still in use today. The Augsburg Confession Article XXI says: 'Our churches teach that the history of saints may be set before us so that we may follow the example of their faith and good works, according to our calling'. Lutheran churches therefore include images and sculptures not only of Christ but also of biblical and occasionally even of extra-biblical saints, as well as stained-glass windows, ornate interior reliefs and architecture, beautifully carved or otherwise embellished high altarpieces, liberal use of candles on the altar and elsewhere, and a special emphasis on the prominence of pulpits, which can also be highly ornate in older churches with didactic depictions of central biblical stories. In older churches numerous images and altarpieces of Mary are present. Compared to a Roman Catholic church interior, usually the only striking difference is the absence of the tabernacle and the sanctuary lamp, the Stations of the Cross and a small holy water font at the church portal. Nevertheless, in a few Lutheran high churches tabernacles and sanctuary lamps have been kept or reintroduced and the adoration of the sacrament continued.

Luther wrote a treatise, 'The Adoration of the Sacrament', in 1523 in which he defended Eucharistic adoration—an aspect of devotion which in most Lutheran churches was not retained after Luther's death owing to the influence of Melanchthon, who did not favour it.

Regarding images and the Eucharist, a similar scenario is evident in Anglican churches, even if, of course, there, too, are significant differences between high and low church interiors. In low Anglican churches, owing to the Calvinist influences, sculptures and images are less prevalent than in Lutheran or Roman Catholic places of worship.

Reformed Calvinist and non-conformist churches are generally quite different. These often strike one as rather bare and sometimes lacking in aesthetic expression. They contain only a small altar or none but usually have a prominent pulpit, as everything centres on the preached word. A baptismal font is present, while pictures and statues are largely absent, candles few or none, and crucifixes or crosses also usually absent. While the buildings, especially older ones, may convey an atmosphere of austere grandeur, the stark—one might say 'puritan'—interiors usually have little aesthetic appeal. It must be said, however, that at times the austerity can convey its own sense of a calm aesthetic free of clutter and distraction.

This is, of course, a very brief and therefore generalised account within the scope of this chapter. That there have been notable exceptions and developments, especially in the last 50 years, whether in Lutheran, post-Vatican II Roman Catholic, Anglican or Reformed churches, will not be disputed or denied. The intention is merely to create something of a brief visual introduction to the various kinds of liturgical interiors in the respective traditions before focusing on Luther and Cranach.

Luther on the role of images

The Reformation concerns included, among other far more pressing issues, the role of images, relics and saints in the church. Given that the veneration of these was so much part of church life in the Middle Ages—at times in an exaggerated and even idolatrous fashion—Luther and other reformers saw the need to tackle this issue. If one reads and compares the reformers in this context, one is immediately struck by the noticeably balanced approach that Luther adopted.

While he was aware of the danger of images and cautioned against their use, he valued their didactic and evangelical role in spreading the biblical message as well as his theological-reformatory aims, and he acknowledged their importance in remembering the Trinity and the saints.

As on so many occasions in his life, Luther did not set out to write a systematic treatise on the theology of the image but rather events propelled him to take a stance. In late 1521 he secretly returned to Wittenberg from the Wartburg owing to the turmoil and iconoclasm that had broken out under his former teacher and fellow reformer Andreas von Bodenstein Karlstadt and his followers.

We find Luther's most important comments on images and relics in two of his fulminant *Invocavit* Sermons, which he preached between 9 and 16 March 1522 to restore order in Wittenberg, as well as in a piece entitled *Against the Heavenly Prophets in the Matter of Images and Sacraments* (1525), which was an attack on Karlstadt, who had rushed into implementing radical liturgical reforms in Luther's absence.

Luther's all-consuming preoccupation was, of course, justification by grace through faith, as well as the abuse of indulgences. These issues and the possession of relics and use of images were related, however. The buying and selling of relics was a widespread custom at the time. Luther's protector, Frederick the Wise, for example, owned over 19,000 relics. This business was similar to the whole question of indulgences. To own such relics or to donate images to churches came into the realm of good works; they were thus considered a means of accumulating grace and earning salvation.

For Luther, then, fundamentally images were adiaphora. They were a minor issue. He considered it a matter of Christian liberty to have images and crucifixes or not. In his own words, images are a 'small matter'; they 'are neither good nor bad'; they are 'unnecessary and we are free to have them or not, although it would be much better if we did not have them at all'. 'If I were asked, I should have to admit that images do not anger me [as such]. If there were only one human being on earth who used images rightly, the devil would immediately urge against me: Why, oh why do you condemn that which may be used rightly? He would then have achieved his triumph and I would have to concede it.'[1]

Luther's central concern was the freedom of the Christian justified before God by faith, and this he applied to most spheres of life. For example, as with images, Luther would point out that to marry or to remain in the monastery was a matter of liberty. It is not the presence of religious images in churches that Luther attacks, but the reasons why they are installed. He points out that among his opponents the worst misuse regarding images is that they believe that thereby they are doing good works, serving God. This connects with his overall concern that the Christian, as Paul had emphasised, is saved through grace.

Luther in his sermons in March 1522 develops his argument as to why images should be allowed and he does so in relation to his opponents, who, as he concedes, have reasons to oppose the use of images. He asserts that images may be of considerable benefit in preaching and teaching the Good News. He notes: 'It is true that they are dangerous, and I wish there were none of them on the altars. But we cannot prove it right to mutilate and burn them instead of tolerating them … We must permit the images to remain, but preach vigorously against the wrong use of them.'[2] Images and crucifixes thus should be allowed as long as they are not worshipped but used 'for memorial and witness'. Works of art, Luther comments, can also be used for pleasure and decoration. Karlstadt and the radical reformers, on the other hand, wanted to have statues and images destroyed, to abandon the use of music in worship and hold services in civil clothes.

In 1525, three years after the iconoclastic events in Wittenberg, Luther wrote a refutation of Karlstadt's position in a more systematic discussion of images. He asserts that he does not want to defend religious images but that no one is obligated to destroy them, as long as one puts one's trust not in them but in God alone. The fundamental issue here for Luther is the distinction between external material images in churches and the internal idols worshipped in the human heart. If images of Christ, Mary and the saints are used in proper fashion for helping us remember and give witness to these they have a positive role. Further, as a means of proclaiming the Gospel and for aims of reform, images are welcome and even powerful. Luther points out that Karlstadt, in his obsession with material images, failed to attack and reject the far more dangerous and *real* idols, the *idols of the heart*. This is one of the most important arguments in his whole discussion on images and it remains pertinent to this day: the danger *not* of material religious images but the ever-present proneness to idolatry *within the human being*. The temptation of mammon and greed, the misuse of power—these are the truly dangerous idols that we need to destroy. Material religious images are not the issue but rather the false images and idols that occupy the human being. Luther concludes with a resounding endorsement of images:

> 'Yes, would to God that I could persuade the rich and the mighty that they would permit the whole Bible to be painted on houses,

on the inside and outside, so that all can see it. That would be a Christian work. Of this I am certain, that God desires to have his works heard and read, especially the passion of our Lord. But it is impossible for me to hear and bear it in mind without forming mental images of it in my heart. For whether I will or not, when I hear of Christ, an image of a man hanging on a cross takes form in my heart, just as the reflection of my face naturally appears in the water when I look into it. If it is not a sin but good to have the image of Christ in my heart, why should it be a sin to have it in my eyes? This is especially true since the heart is more important than the eyes, and should be less stained by sin because it is the true abode and dwelling place of God.'[3]

It is noteworthy that Luther here recognised that the sense of seeing, just like the sense of hearing, is intrinsic to the human being. The visual should not be denied, because it is simply part of the human being to have and create mental and material images. We can have images and even need them but we must not worship them. All that the believer ought to be aware of is to make use of such images in a healthy fashion, conducive to educating people in the faith and aiding them in remembering Christ, the saints and the Gospel stories.

Lucas Cranach—painting the Reformation

Luther's and Melanchthon's aims of reform were significantly supported by the painter Lucas Cranach the Elder (1472–1553), and later by his son Lucas (1515–86).[4] A leading German Renaissance painter and printmaker in woodcut and engraving, Cranach became court painter to Frederick the Wise, elector of Saxony, in 1504 and became *the* painter of the Reformation. Lucas Cranach the Younger, somewhat in his father's shadow, should in fact also be remembered as such. Cranach developed a close friendship with Luther and his family. He became wealthy, had a pharmacy and a large workshop in Wittenberg and, as a shrewd businessman, despite his firm support for the reformers, he continued with commissions for the Catholic Church, including commissions for some of Luther's fiercest opponents. Cranach painted portraits of the reformers and large works containing the central theological teachings of Luther and his followers.

It is well known that the Reformation succeeded largely owing to the invention of the printing press in 1450 and thus the new possibilities of spreading ideas fast. As Eamon Duffy points out, Cranach's mass-produced images made Luther's the most familiar face in the sixteenth century.[5] With Luther and

Melanchthon, Cranach produced a number of highly polemical prints in the comic-book-like pamphlets current at the time, satirising the pope, clerics and corrupt church practices. Such pamphlets, forerunners of today's newspapers, were used by both reformers and Catholics to spread crude propaganda against each other, but those produced on the reformers' side proved far more effective than those of their opponents. Propaganda from the reformers had four main themes—anti-popery, individual salvation, social morality and scriptural stories—while Catholics focused on anti-Luther agendas, morality, veneration of the saints and scriptural stories.[6]

Having read St Paul, Luther's central insight and concern involved the human being justified by faith through grace. He thereby drew attention to the distinction between Law and Gospel/grace (*Gesetz und Gnade*). This distinction became the fundamental hermeneutical principle in Lutheran biblical exegesis of Scripture. Article 4 of the Apology of the Augsburg Confession (1531) reads: 'All Scripture ought to be distributed into these two principal topics, the Law and the promises. For in some places it presents the Law, and in others the promise concerning Christ ...'. Luther did not understand the Law as belonging solely to the Old Testament and the Gospel to the New Testament. Rather, those who believe in Christ will continue having to obey the Law; they must live according to God's will. Ultimately, however, they live in the promise of salvation in and through Christ's abundant gracious love. Thus the Law prepares the way to the Gospel, and faith in the Gospel of Christ grants justification and salvation.

Cranach was to depict this fundamental idea in pictorial form in several works, titled 'Law and Grace'. The image of 1529 (Gotha Schlossmuseum), the most famous example, served as the prototype for later images of the same theme.[7] The painting is divided by a tree with a crown which on the left bears no leaves while on the right leaves are clearly visible. On the left side, the Old Testament motifs essentially convey that the Law alone will not grant salvation and get us into heaven. In the distance we see Christ in Judgement in heaven, while Adam and Eve are placed underneath with the snake and the tree of knowledge, indicating the fall from grace. To their right is the story of Moses and the brazen serpent from the Book of Numbers (21: 4–9). In the foreground, a skeleton and a demon, reminiscent of the monstrous monk calf used by Luther in his anti-Catholic polemic pamphlets, pursue a desperate man into eternal damnation. Moses on the bottom right gazes on these events. The white tablets with God's Law stand out against the orange and black robes. These scenes show that the Law will inescapably lead to hell if mistaken as a path to salvation, as demonstrated in the damned naked man.[8] On the right side of the image, in

Lucas Cranach the Elder, *Law and Gospel*, c. 1529 (Schlossmuseum, Gotha, Germany).

contrast, the central message is that it is faith in Christ, the crucified God, which will lead to salvation. The naked man here is not damned but stands before, prays to, adores and looks upon Christ on the Cross, aided by John the Baptist, pointing towards Jesus. St John writes in his Gospel: 'Just as Moses lifted up the snake in the wilderness, so the Son of Man must be lifted up' (Jn 3: 14). The naked man on the right side of the image does not come with a record of his good deeds and he does not vainly follow the Law. He is stripped bare and knows that salvation is dependent on faith in Christ's grace. The risen Christ is standing in a large, bright, sun-like halo above the empty tomb, triumphant with the flag of the Resurrection, the saviour of those who believe in Him. The whole image conveys that God is both judge and saviour and that the Law alone will not save but should lead us to faith in Christ and his Gospel, to the promise of forgiveness of sin and eternal life.

Another image, begun by Cranach the Elder shortly before his death and completed much later by Cranach the Younger in 1555, is located in the Peter and Paul Church in Weimar. It is a variation of the same theme on Law and Gospel. Here Jesus occupies centre stage and the Old Testament scenes have moved into the background. The figure of Christ is repeated on the left; he is conquering death and an evil demon, similar in appearance to the work from 1529. In the background we see the Expulsion from the Garden of Eden, re-

CALLED TO FREEDOM

Lucas Cranach the Younger, *Christ on the Cross*, centre panel of a triptych, 1555 (Peter und Paul Kirche, Weimar).

minding us of the reality of sin and our need for salvation. Moses is again shown with the tablets, while the tale of Moses and the Brazen Serpent and the New Testament story of the Annunciation to the Shepherds are depicted as examples of God's grace. John the Baptist, to the right of Christ, points one of his fingers at Christ and with the index and middle finger of his left hand to the *Agnus Dei*, the Lamb of God. Next to him stands Lucas Cranach. Striking is the stream of blood issuing from Christ's side and flowing directly onto Cranach's forehead, implying the direct access of the believer to the triune God with no need of a priest as intercessor. Luther, stately and confident, on the far right, points to passages (1 Jn 1: 7; Hebr 4: 16 and Jn 3: 14–15) from his German Bible concerning the redemptive blood of Christ freeing all believers from sin. In this much later work there is a heightened focus on the Gospel, i.e. on Christ, and a pronounced didactic and ecclesiastical emphasis, pointing to Luther and his followers as those who have the correct understanding of the Gospel, the ones who in the tradition of the biblical saints and the early Church are spreading the good news of Christ. This concentration on the figure of Christ was a new

Lucas Cranach, *Passional Christi und Antichristi*, woodcuts, 1521.

development in Reformation and post-Reformation art, and is visible to this day in Lutheran churches through the frequent presence of large crucifixes in places of worship. It is also interesting to note that Luther and Cranach the Elder had died at this stage and are here, and also in other images, put into the picture in strikingly similar fashion to depictions of saints or donors in Renaissance art.[9] Nevertheless, the emphasis is different: Luther and his followers are shown as defenders and teachers of the true faith in a merciful Christ, while the donors in Renaissance art had their images included like plaques presenting themselves as pious believers, doing a good work by financing the production of ecclesiastical art.[10]

In 1521 Cranach produced the *Passional Christi und Antichristi*, the most devastating of polemic pamphlets in the sixteenth century, with thirteen pairs of woodcuts illustrating texts by Philip Melanchthon. Blatant and easily understood by all, this little picture-book compares the passion of Christ with that of the pope, the anti-Christ. In visual antitheses, these woodcuts powerfully juxtapose the truth of Christ's life and passion with the pope's wholly corrupt practices.

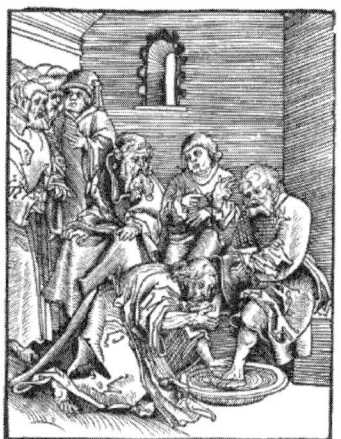 

Lucas Cranach, *Passional Christi and Antichristi,* woodcuts, 1521.

In one image Christ is driving the money-changers out of the temple (Mt 21). The image opposite shows the pope, enthroned like God in a temple, who sells to a subservient people indulgences and dispensations, and to the clergy bishoprics and other Church offices. Another set of images juxtaposes Jesus in simple clothes and washing the feet of His disciples with a depiction of political leaders and people arriving to kiss the pope's feet. A further pair of pages shows Christ, on the left, taking up His cross to die for the salvation of humankind and implying that those who follow Christ must, like Jesus, be ready to take up their cross (Mt 16), while, on the right, the pope is carried around by the clergy in the pomp and splendour of a divine-like emperor.

Luther's opponents, however, were not slow to respond. A woodcut on the cover of a pamphlet in 1529 by Johann Cochlaeus, a leading German humanist and adversary of Luther, shows Luther as the seven-headed beast mentioned in the Book of Revelation. Luther is shown as a scholar, monk, priest, turban-wearing Turk, a fanatic goaded by hornets, a Church Visitor correcting abuses and a wild man, identified as Barabbas. This monster is the Anti-Christ, the arch-enemy of the true Church and the herald of the terrible trials before Christ's Second Coming. A year later the Lutheran side hit back with the seven-

Spreading the Reformation through Images

Seven-headed Martin Luther, from a pamphlet by Johannes Cochlaeus (Valentin Schumann, Leipzig, 1529); title-page woodcut attributed to Hans Brosamer.

Seven-headed papal beast, c. 1530, anonymous woodcut (Staatliche Museen zu Berlin, Kupferstichkabinett).

headed pope animal, the '*regnum diaboli*' of the pope, the anti-Christ.

Monstrous births were seen as bad omens in the Middles Ages. Luther, still a medieval man, firmly believed that unusual natural phenomena, such as comets and 'monstrous prodigies', were God-willed and signs of impending disaster. The 'most notorious' and best-known monstrous births in his time were two creatures that came to be known as the 'papal ass', 'washed up on the banks of the Tiber in Rome in 1496', and the 'monk calf', born in Freiberg, Germany, in 1522.[11] Luther and Melanchthon wrote a polemical pamphlet in 1523 titled 'The Meaning of Two Gruesome Figures, the Papal Ass of Rome and the Monk Calf of Freiberg found in Meissen' (*Deuttung der czwo grewlichen Figuren, Bapstesels czu Rom und Munchkalbs zu Friberg ijnn Meijszen funden*). It contained two woodcuts produced by Cranach. The papal ass was based on an engraving by Wenzel von Olmutz. Representing the pope and a monk, these two images were used to show that the Day of Judgement was near. They were regarded as illustrations of the degeneracy of the Church. Jennifer Spinks has argued that, while monstrous births before Luther and Melanchthon could be interpreted both in negative and in positive terms, with this publication there was a decisive shift whereby such images not only became more polemical and anti-papal but also took on a notably 'apocalyptic' and 'eschatological' aspect, as is also evident in the seven-headed anti-Christ in reference to the Book of Revelation. The papal ass is a female figure with an ass's head, woman's breasts, belly and vagina, an elephant's foot in place of the right hand, fish scales on the neck, arms and legs, a face of an old man protruding from its back and a dragon's head on its tail, with one foot of an ox and the other of the legendary figure of the griffin. Melanchthon noted that God considered the donkey a lowly figure, hence the papal ass's head, while the female breasts and belly represented 'the body of the papacy: that is Cardinals, bishops, clerics, monks … their life is simply guzzling food, boozing, unchaste lechery, and leading "the good life" on earth'.[12] The right foot represents 'the servants of the church: priests, papal teachers, and in particular, scholastic theologians'. One hand, 'like an elephant's foot', represents the forceful spiritual regime of the pope, which 'tramples and grinds down', while the human hand signifies 'the pope's worldly regiment of secular rulers' who support the pope.[13] Luther's interpretation of the monk calf is no less damning. He alludes to the golden calf, the false idol. He says that God has dressed this calf in monks' habits and so, in Luther's words, the calf shows that 'monks and nuns are nothing other than false liars who externally lead a spiritual life'. Individual body parts are symbolic of their failings: the creature's blindness shows the monk's and nun's ignorance of the true nature of God; the donkey's ears refer to the 'intolerable tyranny' of the forced practice of confes-

'The Meaning of Two Gruesome Figures, the Papal Ass of Rome and the Monk Calf of Freiberg found in Meissen' (*Deuttung der czwo grewlichen Figuren, Bapstesels czu Rom und Munchkalbs zu Friberg ijnn Meijszen funden*): 1523 pamphlet by Martin Luther and Philip Melanchthon, woodcuts by Lucas Cranach.

sion. The tight cowl conveys the monk's stubbornness; the mouth, half human jaw, half bestial, indicates that instead of preaching God's word they preach for their own good. The papal ass thus represented the pope and the monk calf his followers, two powerfully repulsive figures that aided the reformers' polemics.

The pope and abuses in the Catholic Church were not, however, the only subjects of Lutheran polemics. Theological differences between Lutherans and Calvinists brought about growing conflict in the latter part of the sixteenth century. In 1591 Zacharias 'Rivander' Bachmann, a Lutheran pastor, wrote *Lupus excoriatus* ('the wolf stripped of its skin'). The book's title is clear evidence of what orthodox Lutherans thought of Zwinglians and Calvinists. The book contains an image entitled the 'Calvinist wolves of discord'. The wolves are dressed in monks' habits and devour a sheep named 'concordia'. The sheep refer to the *Concordia Wittenbergensis*, a failed attempt at reconciling Lutherans and Zwinglians in 1536. The caption underneath the illustration reads: 'Beware the false prophets coming in sheepskins to you, but inside they are rapacious wolves (Matth. 7)'.

Having considered a few of the most gruesome polemical images in Christian history, one's theological and aesthetic sensibilities will find relief in the famous Reformation altarpiece located in the city church in Wittenberg. It bears testimony to the central Lutheran understanding of being church as mentioned in Article 7 of the Augsburg Confession of 1530: 'Also they teach that one holy Church is to continue forever. The Church is the congregation of saints, in which the Gospel is rightly taught and the Sacraments are rightly administered.' On the left Melanchthon, aided by Luther and Cranach, baptises a child. In the central panel Luther distributes Holy Communion in a Last Supper scene, and on the right-hand panel the reformer of the north of Germany, Johannes Bugenhagen, with the keys, hears confession. It is interesting to note that in this altarpiece confession features as the third sacrament, alluding to the fact that Luther did not want to abolish its practice, even though he would harshly criticise the papal abuse of coercing people to confession instead of it being encouraged as a voluntary act. Article 11 of the Augsburg Confession states that private absolution should remain in the church. Private confession is not, however, generally practised in Lutheran churches. On the predella underneath we see Luther on the right with the open Bible, preaching the Gospel and pointing to the small figure of Christ on the cross, set in the centre against a bare church wall, and the people of Wittenberg as the congregation, including Cranach, on the left. Joseph Leo Koerner, in his magisterial *The Reformation of the Image*, begins with an expansive analysis of this predella image and compares it with Caspar David Friedrich's *The Cross in the Mountain* (1807/8), painted in the context of Romanticism and the Enlightenment.[14] Friedrich, the foremost German Romantic painter, an ardent Lutheran who appears to have had contact with Schleiermacher, painted this first altarpiece dominated by landscape, i.e. Christian faith expressed in the context of transcendence in nature. Embedded in an image of rocks and fir trees one sees a thin, tall cross and the small, slight figure of Christ turned away from the viewer and towards the sun, symbolised through three rays, implying the Trinity. It is at once an expression of Luther's *deus absconditus* and *deus revelatus*, with a stress on the hidden God, yet a God Who, despite modernity's growing doubts and questioning, is still *there*. In his analysis of Cranach and Friedrich, Koerner writes that Cranach had

> 'deliberately detached his crucifix from the scene of preaching in which it rises. This was neither the historical, flesh-and-blood Crucifixion, nor a miraculous vision, nor a crafted effigy of Christ on the cross. Markedly removed from the physical world, yet still also visibly *there*, this quintessential Lutheran image marked a first step

toward the pure facticity of Friedrich's landscape view: where the Reformation located the sacred in a separate realm of inner faith, Romanticism made do with the residual void. The modern age dawned within the Protestant altarpiece at the place where, in Luther's own church, painting endeavoured to show divinity's detachment from the world ... Friedrich and Cranach, it seemed, addressed the same question: How visually to represent a hidden God?'[15]

It seems, indeed, that Friedrich, about 250 years later, in the context of the Enlightenment, not only found himself trying to render the hidden God but was also painting in an era in which faith itself became increasingly privatised, hidden and no longer quite as much taken for granted as it once was—hence the Romantic tendency to transpose religious sensibility into feeling and nature. Koerner comments that, 'at first glance', Cranach's and Friedrich's works appear to be 'paradigmatic instruments of a disenchantment of the world', the process in which, according to Max Weber, 'magic was eliminated from salvation'.[16] Koerner asserts, however, that Cranach's works actually replaced both the Catholic retable and the 'iconoclastic blank that gave the new painting space'.[17] He thus concludes that the Lutheran crucifix is 'an icon and an iconoclasm. It does not simply restore, reactively, sacred pictures to a cleansed church. It maintains itself in a state of remove, asserting by visual means that what it shows is elsewhere and invisible. Yet, it also stubbornly stands *there*.'[18] Koerner calls this having and not having of images 'iconoclash' and points out that Lutheran art renewed rather than removed church art. He also notes, however, that works like Cranach's in fact evidence a 'decline in the craft of painting', the portrayal of Christ on the Wittenberg altarpiece 'being aesthetically unengaging'.[19] What came to matter was the didactic, communicative dimension in art, rather than the emphasis on 'superior craftsmanship' and the aesthetic that would celebrate that a 'sacred likeness was humanly made' and which thus might 'advertise its kinship with an idol'.[20]

Having considered some works by Cranach the Elder and Younger, ranging from outstanding altarpieces to crude polemic pamphlets, one is made aware how both powerfully contributed to the spread of the ideas of Luther and his followers, thereby aiding the Reformation in conceptual-artistic fashion. Despite the decline in the aesthetic quality of art noted by Koerner and other art historians, the reputation of Cranach as belonging to the leading painters in early sixteenth-century Europe and his and his son's legacy as the artists of the Reformation remain undisputed.

Lucas Cranach the Elder and Younger, *Reformationsaltar*, c. 1547 (St Marien Kirche, Wittenberg).

Conclusion: from Wittenberg to the worldwide web

The Council of Trent, in its response to the reformers, reiterated mainly what the Second Council of Nicaea had affirmed about 800 years earlier. It stressed that those responsible for teaching the Catholic faith were to 'instruct the faithful diligently' regarding the saints, relics and images. Luther essentially commended the educational, evangelical and memorial role of images and abundantly used them for his reformatory aims. He fundamentally considered images in religious contexts a minor issue, a matter of Christian liberty. In this way Luther lowered the status of images. They were no longer to be regarded as means of good works by those who commissioned them and they were no longer to be venerated but used primarily for teaching, witness and memorial. In this way Luther's approach assuaged any danger of associating such objects with 'magic' powers, i.e. the danger of idolatry was removed. At the same time, Luther did not go down the iconoclastic route of image destruction but nuanced its use. The Council of Trent, however, encouraged the continued invocation of saints and a proper honouring of relics and images. Those who deny the honour due to relics of the saints should be 'condemned absolutely'. Nevertheless, in order to distance themselves from accusations of idolatry, the Council clearly pointed out that veneration is understood to be paid to the 'original subjects', not to the material image.[21]

Luther, as demonstrated in our discussion, took a balanced approach to the question of images and crucifixes in places of worship. While he was critical of the possibility of their idolatrous abuses, he (unlike Zwingli's and Calvin's vehement iconoclasm) advocated moderate changes in the use of images, noting that it is essentially a matter of Christian liberty to have images or not. While Lutherans interpreted this liberty as a mandate to keep and value images, Calvin, Zwingli and their followers took it to be their freedom and even imperative to destroy them.[22] Luther and the Lutheran Church ever since have stayed thus in much closer proximity to Rome than to Zürich and Geneva regarding the question of religious imagery.

To this day Christian spaces of worship significantly reflect the theological and liturgical aesthetics of their denominations. In the latter half of the twentieth century, however, with the ecumenical movement and Vatican II, and with the unprecedented expansion over the last 25 years of interdisciplinary studies in theology and the arts among theologians of various denominational backgrounds, including even Calvinist and Pentecostal scholars, there is now large agreement on the necessity of developing aesthetic sensibility and art-historical awareness of the wealth of art with Christian subject-matter in those studying for church ministry as well as among the faithful.

Unlike in the Middle Ages, art no longer functions as the *biblia pauperum* for an illiterate Christian laity, but rather it is the gallery which has become the clichéd 'modern temple' for many amongst the educated middle classes, and the art market a promotion of good art at best and of the golden calves of the super-rich at worst. In our intensely visual age, people are bombarded like never before with images through internet and television, including much imagery which is truly idolatrous and harmful, promoting consumerism and violence. In the face of such negative influences, it is all the more important that the role of the visual arts conducive to worship, to faith and the spiritual life, and to education is explored and furthered in theology and ministry.

Lutherans and Catholics willing to learn from, and co-operating with, one another need to give importance to the preached word *and* to the sacrament of Holy Communion, to communal singing *and* to visual art. Christians together must challenge, ask questions and explore how images can play a positive, creative and critical role in the church into the future. Hence, not unlike Luther

500 years ago, one would suggest that Christians today must be both iconodules and iconoclasts, i.e. promoting images that are life-enhancing while not being shy to question images that promote the antithesis of fundamental human and Christian values. If all of these components—word and music, sacramentality and image—are present in worship, communities will be sustained in their faith, in their aesthetic and liturgical sensibilities, and in their search for meaning, truth, beauty and goodness in a suffering and fragmented world.[23]

Notes

[1] Helga Robinson-Hammerstein, *Faith, Force and Freedom. Translation of the Fourth Invocavit Sermon & Introduction. A Navicula publication* (Dublin, 2001).

[2] Martin Luther, 'Receiving both Kinds in the Sacrament' (*Invocavit* Sermon, 1522), in Abdel Ross Wentz (ed. and trans.), *Luther's works, vol. 38. Word and Sacrament II* (general ed. Helmut T. Lehmann) (Philadelphia, 1959), in Gesa Thiessen (ed.), *Theological Aesthetics—A Reader* (London/Grand Rapids, MI, 2004), 130f.

[3] Martin Luther, 'Against the heavenly prophets in the matter of images and sacraments' (1525) (trans. Bernhard Erling and Conrad Bergendoff), in *Luther's works, vol. 40. Church and Ministry II* (general ed. Helmut T. Lehmann) (Philadelphia, 1958), in Thiessen, *Theological Aesthetics*, 132–4.

[4] The year 2015 in the *Luther Dekade* leading up to the feast of the 500th anniversary in 2017 was dedicated to the theme *Bild und Bibel* ('Image and Bible'); 2015 was chosen for this theme as the year was the 500th anniversary of the birth of Lucas Cranach the Younger.

[5] Eamon Duffy, 'Spiritual surrender', *The Guardian*, 1 March 2008 (http://www.theguardian.com/books/2008/mar/01/art.art; accessed 12 December 2017).

[6] John Hartmann, 'The use of propaganda in the Reformation & Counter-Reformation' (http://www.people.vcu.edu/~jahartmann/writings.html; accessed 12 December 2017).

[7] For an analysis of how Law and Gospel found expression not only in paintings but also in richly adorned weaponry, medals and drinking vessels among Lutheran political leaders in the sixteenth century see Jutta Charlotte von Bloh, Yvonne Fritz and Dirk Syndram, *Das Wort im Bild: Biblische Darstellungen an Prunkwaffen und Kunstgegenständen der Kurfürsten von Sachsen zur Reformationszeit* (Dresden, 2014).

[8] Bonnie Noble, 'Cranach's The Law and Gospel' (http://smarthistory.khanacademy.org/cranachs-the-law-and-gospel.html; accessed 12 December 2017).

[9] Philip Stoellger, 'Emanzipation des Bildes, Cranach's Blutstrahl der Gnade als wirksames Zeichen', *Das Magazin zum Themenjahr 2015, Reformation—Bild und Bibel* (Evangelische Kirche Deutschland (EKD), 2015).

[10] The Brera *sacra conversazione* altarpiece by Piero della Francesca, commissioned by Federico III da Montefeltro, duke of Urbino, and portraying him in his armour kneeling at the feet of the Madonna, is a striking example.

[11] Jennifer Spinks, *Monstrous Births and Visual Culture in Sixteenth-Century Germany* (London, 2009), 59. For my discussion of these two images I rely on Spinks's analysis, pp 59–79.

[12] Melanchthon, cited in Spinks, *Monstrous births*, 68.

[13] *Ibid.*, 68.
[14] Joseph Leo Koerner, *The Reformation of the Image* (Chicago, 2004 and 2008).
[15] *Ibid.*, 9–10.
[16] *Ibid.*, 11.
[17] *Ibid.*, 11.
[18] *Ibid.*, 11–12.
[19] *Ibid.*, 13.
[20] *Ibid.*, 13.
[21] On Luther, Zwingli, Calvin and the Council of Trent concerning images and aesthetics see Thiessen, *Theological Aesthetics*, 125–45.
[22] Koerner, *op. cit.*, 157–8.
[23] This chapter is a slightly shortened and revised version of G. Thiessen, 'Luther and the role of images', in Declan Marmion, Salvador Ryan and Gesa E. Thiessen (eds), *Remembering the Reformation: Martin Luther and Catholic Theology* (Minneapolis, 2017), 167–92.

4
Love, freedom and guilt—differences between Christian traditions in the conception of the relationship between divine and human freedom

Gunda Werner

Prelude: mercy as a guiding theological principle and its relationship to justice

The concept of mercy is currently an ever-present element in Catholic discourse, whether with respect to Church politics or to magisterial theology. This concept shaped the discourse in and around the Family Synods of 2014 and 2015, provided the central concept for the Year of Mercy 2015/16 and appears 34 times in *Amoris Laetitia* alone. The concept of mercy is introduced as a powerful theological idea, in reaction to the increasing discrepancy between the Magisterium and the faithful in doctrinal and disciplinary questions. When Pope Francis, in the Bull of Indiction *Misericordiae vultus* of the extraordinary Jubilee of Mercy, presented mercy as the fundamental ecclesiological moment, he emphasised the mandate for the Church to make room for mercy in all aspects of ecclesial activity in concrete form. Evidence of this constitutive ecclesial quality must therefore be visible not only in the preaching office of the Church, the fruits of which include, among other things, the above-mentioned magisterial statements, but must also be identifiable in the sanctifying and leadership offices of the Church.[1]

In few ecclesial fields of activity is the concept of mercy so present as it is in the sacramental activity of the Church in connection with the concept of the forgiveness of sins. How is it possible, however, to make room for mercy without undermining justice? The tension between mercy and justice provides the background for addressing the underlying theological question of how to conceive of the relationship between the sinful individual and the merciful God.[2] While the Bull of Indiction of the so-called Holy Year, which lasted until the end of November 2016, is a pleasant change from other Roman pronouncements, it is similarly marked by the question of the way in which ecclesial activity towards sinful human beings should reflect divine action. This document, and thus the Holy Year of Mercy as a whole, suggests the interpretation of God's action as that of the merciful Father. By means of this encoding, priests are reminded that the sacrament of confession is not an instrument of torture (this theme has also appeared in *Evangelii Gaudium*), that God stretches out His hand to everyone, that divine mercy is immeasurable and that thus priestly activity must be oriented towards this image of God. The interpretation of God's merciful action, which 'will always be greater than any sin', so that 'no one can place limits on the love of God who is ever ready to forgive' (3),[3] is set as the guiding principle of the sanctifying and preaching praxis of the Church. Thus mercy is 'the very foundation of the Church's life' (10), and the credibility of the Church depends upon the mercifulness of its preaching and witness (10). The Church, however, has long since forgotten this and puts the emphasis on justice. Mercy is closely related to forgiveness, and both are the face of love.[4]

Understood in this way, mercy becomes the main category which shapes the behaviour of God towards fallible human beings and which then ought to influence their behaviour towards one another. Thus a guiding category is introduced into a proceeding which has traditionally been developed according to two other perspectives: the interaction between God and sinful humanity is presented in the guise of the court of justice, and as the meeting in court of the sinful human being with the just God to theologically try the freedom of the will as the source of sin. The controversial theological abrasiveness of the arguments about the freedom of the will do not come to the forefront in the case of the category of mercy, but the question of how the free will of human beings relates to their actions is fundamental in theological debate. For this reason I will focus on the dispute concerning the freedom of the will which broke out afresh with Luther's inquiries, putting it in the context of a subject-oriented architecture, as—surprisingly enough!—suggested by the Council of Trent. The Council addresses free will in the context of original sin, justification and penance, and centres on the crucial issue of how responsible human beings are for their actions and for their redemption.

'Love, and do what you will'? Dogmatic-historical reconstructions of the state of sin and God's action

God's mercy for sale—reformed critique of penance and repentance
There seems to be unanimous consensus among researchers that the Reformation found its critical position in the dispute over the contemporary practice of confession and penance.[5] 'By attacking indulgences, Luther put the entire medieval penitential system into question. As he further applied the principle of justification by grace through faith, he considered the sacrament of penance legitimate only to the extent that it proclaimed the gospel's promise of grace and encouraged the sinner to trust fully in divine forgiveness. This, the reformers

concluded, was not the case in penance as they knew it.'[6] The Reformation's main point of critique is the established Catholic practice of confession and penance. Because it systematically turns against the practice of indulgences, it touches upon the fundamental element of conversion. For against the apparently near-automated forgiveness of sins, Martin Luther sets his insight that the entire life of the Christian must be understood as a life of conversion and penance—an insight which will culminate in the critique of the Reformation, and which he bases in Scripture and the early Church. Faith alone is the power which makes possible the forgiveness of sins. 'Thus, if confidence (*fiducia*) in the exonerating Word of the Gospels (*absolutio*) is the deciding element of penance, then true repentance (*contritio*) is the other integral element of penance.'[7] Luther is therefore completely convinced 'that the human being is a sinner before God'.[8] Sinfulness is intrinsic to human nature and not added on to it. Thus it is only because of divine mercy that creation and the human beings who live in it continue to exist. From Luther's perspective, humans can best be described as 'bent' or distorted. Indeed, Luther's own experience of his life of faith and his examination of the experience of faith led him rather to believe that God does not act to save. Nonetheless, in the cross of Jesus God does save and justify the sinner. Because Luther lets himself be led by the question of how it can be that God saves in spite of sin, he comes to the insight that it is God alone who saves. It is this insight which sets Luther's theology apart from scholasticism. In scholastic disputes grace is understood as a quality or habitus of the soul. Luther transforms this concept in such a way that grace is at one and the same time the justice and the mercy of God, unearned and justifying (cf. WA 3, 47, 11–16). For this reason Luther understands human beings as justified and as sinful; they are *simul justus et peccator*. The 'nature of sin [is] defined as unbelief',[9] and thus human beings and their relationship to God are put at the centre of theological reflection, so that theological attempts to deal with related questions must be addressed from this perspective. Initially Luther seeks to determine the nature of sin more exactly: how does unbelief show itself? Here he adopts ideas from Augustine, when he describes the nature of sin as concupiscence. This further qualification entails, however, the intensification of sin, since sin is the cause of the disfigurement of the human being. Cupidity remains even in the baptised person as sin. It is therefore not merely the temptation to sin. Human beings are completely dependent upon the grace of God, in their whole being and in all their possibilities, precisely because sin is so comprehensive.

The problem of sin and cupidity, however, brings to the surface further theological difficulties. First, the interplay between repentance and faith presents itself as a problem for reformatory theology, as with repentance the question arises as to what value subjective feelings have with respect to repentance. How can one be sure that the attested repentance is wholehearted and complete? The paradoxical situation arises that pure faith in the forgiveness of sins can weaken the comprehensive meaning of repentance as much as works of penance can. For this reason Luther insists that penance must be understood as having two parts: *confessio* ('confession' of sins) and *absolutio* ('absolution').[10] Repentance is, however, subsumed into faith; 'contrition [is] no longer enough to free the *homo incurvatus in se* from his deformation, this is done by faith'.[11] The consequence is as clear as it is far-reaching. Any human co-operation with grace and redemption is impossible. Contrary to Erasmus, says Martin Laube, freedom is 'freedom from freedom'.[12]

The internal architecture of sinful activity and merciful salvation in the Council of Trent
In 1524, prior to the Council of Trent (1545–63), Erasmus of Rotterdam published his work *De libero arbitrio diatribe*. Here he reconstructs, on the one hand, biblical and early Church arguments in favour of the freedom of the will, and, on the other hand, he argues against Luther's increasingly radical conception denying the freedom of the will. In this polemical work Erasmus presents a twofold argument. Not only does he find plenty of examples in tradition and Scripture that demonstrate the dignity of human beings in their freedom to do good, he also offers a decidedly theological argument, specifically a moral-theological argument. According to Erasmus, if there were no freedom to act, there would be no responsibility for actions. If there were no responsibility, no one could be held guilty.

If human beings were incapable of doing anything, then there would be no room for merit and guilt; and if there were no room for merit and guilt, there would also be no room for punishment and reward. If, on the other hand, human beings were to do it all, then there would be no room for grace, which Paul so often mentions and emphasises (IIIa.17).

Erasmus clearly holds fast to the idea that God turns in grace towards every single person, and that he or she can hold onto this. If human beings decide for grace, then God continues to offer grace and human beings can freely accept it. They can also, of course, refuse grace! Such refusal, then, is the guilt that destroys human beings. In this theory of freedom, Erasmus distances himself clearly from Pelagius, who puts too much trust in free will. Erasmus prefers a 'both … and' approach, which leaves some room for free will while emphasising grace (IV.16). The argument can be summed up by saying that while Erasmus preserves freedom for the sake of responsibility and grace and holds onto the free will of human beings, Luther understands human beings as so corrupted by original sin that they can only be justified by grace. Erasmus's position can be understood as a counter-concept to the position of Luther, and it was in many respects advanced as the concept of justification at the Council of Trent. Erasmus's interpretation of the Letter to the Romans—that Romans 5 does not mention original sin—was, however, together with Luther's positions, condemned by the Council.

Because of the need to clarify disputed matters, the Council of Trent plays a key role in the debate about the understanding of sin and freedom. The ruinous consequences of the reception of the Council for the lives of individual Catholics, however, has tainted the Council of Trent with a sort of 'unfortunate fame'. For this reason I will follow the more recent research on the Council, which points out the difference between the 'actual Tridentinum',[13] marked by great ambiguity and openness in its teaching, and the post-Tridentine reinterpretation of Trent. Indeed, I am convinced that in view of the relevant theological issues regarding the question of sin and freedom, the Council was the 'turning point to the modern era',[14] because it allowed the crystallisation of genuinely modern themes. These are, in my opinion, most visible in the way that the Council of Trent approaches the theological controversy concerning the praxis of the forgiveness of sins and justification. Here the subjective role of the human person is central, although the theological approach sets it clearly apart from the reformed development. Trent was creative in that it brought together the idea that human beings retain their free will indefinitely, as articulated in the Decree on Justification, with the theological statement of original sin and the concept of sacramental penance by means of penitence as disposition of justification. This penitence does not make the human being either a hypocrite or a sinner, as understood by the reformers; rather, as a free disposition penitence remains the explicit activity of the human being.[15] Furthermore, this disposition is necessary 'for the justification of the human being by the forgiving grace of God'.[16] Thus can the individual points be reconstructed.

The Council of Trent recognised the necessity of approaching individual theologoumena in a differentiated manner and of achieving an original theological position. The sensitive theological issues of this topic all orbit around the theme of sin and grace: the questions concerning original sin, free will and the related theological intersection of penitence and justification. I am convinced that it is only with the convergence of these themes that the real issue, the convergence of God and human beings in view of sin, comes to the surface.

As Pröpper describes the situation,[17] no discussion of the definition of original sin was necessary at the Council of Trent.[18] The participants agreed about the fact and about the provenance of the original guilt. Nevertheless, because the 'differences in teaching concerning its [*peccatum originale*, GW] nature and its meaning were so great within their own ranks', they thought it better to avoid a definition.[19] There was also no agreement among the theological schools concerning its spread and effect, 'so that once again careful reserve recommended itself in the case of each definitive statement regarding this issue'.[20] Two topics of debate did, however, crystallise which demanded a clear decision: the question, on the one hand, of the decrease of original sin and, on the other hand, of its effect. To begin with, Canon 5 of the Decree on Justification made clear that concupiscence is not a sin in itself and that sin therefore is not predetermined. Thereby Trent clarified several insights which are remarkable in this form. *Firstly*, this Canon confirms that through the grace of baptism 'the culpability of original sin' is forgiven; it is therefore not simply 'scraped off' or not 'taken to account'.[21] According to Pröpper, in this first paragraph the Council succeeds in producing at last a clear terminological definition of 'the guilty character of the *peccatum orginale* [as] (*reatum*)', and can thus once more relate forgiveness to guilt.[22] Desire is no longer understood as 'true and essential sin'. It remains unclear, however, what significance it does have. *Secondly*, the Council argues in a twofold direction, as it is necessary to express critique of Luther's conception of sin *and* to address the idea of real forgiveness within the sin. The Council developed thus an argument in a series of steps. Although Paul names the remaining concupiscence 'sin', the Church has never included this in the concept of sin which is the basis of the Canon.[23] The desires which the baptised person experiences are therefore not 'true and essential sins'; rather they arise 'from sin' and give the person 'a tendency to sin' (DH 1515). The argument therefore concentrates—and not initially because of Luther's questions—upon the meaning of human freedom in the face of God's grace!

Hence it was necessary to come to agreement concerning the freedom of the will. In this debate the participants of the Council were able to draw upon previous discussions, especially as Luther had clearly positioned himself with respect to this question, not least in the course of the debate with Erasmus. The discussion took place in the Decree on Justification. In the first chapter postlapsarian humanity takes centre stage. 'After "all people had lost their innocence through Adam's transgression …", "become unclean" … and (as the Apostle says) "by nature children of wrath" (Eph 2: 30), they were—as described in the Decree on Original Sin—so much slaves to sin … and under the power of the devil and death, that not only could the heathens not be saved by the power of nature [Canon 1], but not even the Jews with the letter of the Law of Moses could be freed or raise themselves up. At the same time, however, the freedom of the will had not been taken away from them [Canon 5], although its powers had been weakened and bent.'[24] This instructive chapter has several intentions. It is meant to parry Luther's position, namely the loss of free will through Adam's sin. Thus, in contrast to Luther, it insists that in spite of original sin something remains that is worthy to be called free will. Within the Catholic Church, and this is almost more interesting, this instructional chapter presents a significant corrective to the Canons of the Second Council of Orange (529), in that it suspends the 'Augustinian tradition' and 'also (to put it mildly) [accents] the Canons of Orange in a new and downright corrective manner'.[25] Pröpper suggests that this position is confirmed by Canon 4 of the Decree on Justification, which emphasises the cooperation of the God-given free will. In this way both perspectives can be corrected: the Synod of Orange and Luther's conception of 'mere passivity'. Particularly significant is the clarity afforded the way grace works, since 'the absolute primacy of grace remains untouched, and only its sole efficacy is denied'.[26] This, the quintessence of the Decree on Justification—the originality of freedom that remains despite sin and that is opened up by the accommodating grace of God—is the starting point for the theory of penitence in the Decree on Penance.[27] It is only when the three Decrees, the Decree on Original Sin, the Decree on Justification and the Decree on Penance, are interpreted together that an understanding of Justification appropriate to the complexity of Trent's theological structure becomes possible. For penitence and justification are held together in the Decree on Penance.

In this Decree, however, two further basic hermeneutical tools of the Council become evident.[28] Firstly, no decision is to be made if such a decision would also condemn a Catholic position. Secondly, through this policy of non-decision, the Council also keeps traditions *open*. In the Decree on Penance the Council leaves a decisive theological issue open: namely, what kind of penitence is sufficient for the sacramental forgiveness of sins. The Decree on Penance decides for attrition, that is, fearful faithfulness as a God-given disposition for the reception of justifying grace in the sacrament (Chapter 4, DH 1678). Thereby the Council not only pits itself against Luther but also leaves open the issue of penitence transposed from the school of the Scholastics. Thus with Trent it remains conceivable that both forms of penitence—attrition, i.e. fearful faithfulness, and contrition, i.e. complete repentance—are sufficient for forgiveness in the sacrament. This open doctrinal situation develops during the post-Tridentine period into one of the great debates in the modern age.[29]

Because the question of justification becomes concrete when it comes to penitence and the active cooperation of human beings, a look at the Decrees is helpful. A close reading reveals that Trent breaks up the argument about penitence into minute pieces. This is done for good reason, as in the theologoumenon of penitence several theological frictions come to a head. At issue here are not only disputes concerning the principles of theological schools[30] but also Luther's allegation that the Christian faithful are made into hypocrites and sinners by a particular concept of penitence. The Decree on Penance adopts word for word the bull *Exsurge Domine*,[31] which had already spoken out against this allegation. The Decree on Justification distinguishes penitence in relation to two different stages of the Christian life. In Chapters 5 and 6 penitence plays a deciding role in the preparation for baptism,[32] and in Chapter 14 it plays a role in the condition of the person who falls into sin after baptism.[33] Chapter 5 is key because first of all it explains the relationship between grace and freedom. It stresses that, 'in the case of adults, justification must begin with the anticipatory grace of God through Jesus Christ' (DH 1525), so that, being prepared through this grace, the person may be justified 'by free consent and cooperation with this grace' [Canons 4 and 5] (DH 1525).[34] At the end of the chapter this line of thought is described as the coming together of grace and freedom.[35] 'When it says in the Scriptures: "Return to me and I will return to you" [*Zech 1,3*], we are reminded of our freedom; when we answer "Restore us to yourself, O Lord, that we may be restored" [*Lam 5, 21*], we confess that the grace of God anticipates us' (DH 1525).

The Decree on Justification thus reveals the centre of penitence. For repentance, as the awareness of one's own actions and the resulting change of life, is only possible on the basis of the '*liberum arbitrium*' (free will). In penitence cooperation with justifying grace takes place as a twofold movement, described by Trent as the opening act of grace and the free acceptance of it. Because free will was not completely destroyed by original sin, human beings can act in self-awareness of their own sinful history; they can acknowledge this and change their lives. Since this happens through the graced opening of freedom to oneself, neither the originality of freedom nor the efficacy of grace are changed.

Conclusion

On three occasions the Council made decisions that would change decisively the state of the discussion both prior to and following the Council. Firstly, original sin is accepted as Adam's guilt and the guilt of each human being, but also as personal action; secondly, attrition is determined to be a sufficient disposition for justifying grace in sacramental repentance, so that, starting from this disposition, a unique constellation for discussion is able to develop; thirdly, the amendment of the Second Council of Orange rehabilitates the freedom of the will, making a cooperation with justification—opened by grace—thinkable.

Thus, following the Council of Trent, three climactic controversies remain which require fundamental clarification. These controversies can be differentiated according to the above-named themes, and I will reconstruct two of these because of their relevance for the issue of free will. The decision to dogmatise both contrition and attrition results in a debate between the so-called Contritionists and Attritionists, concerning the significance and function of penitence with respect to justifying grace. Subsequent to the Council, a debate concerning justifying grace began, with the schools around Báñez on the one side and those of Molina and Suárez on the other. They disputed human freedom in the light of anticipatory and unearned grace.[36]

The starting points of the debate are Canon 5 of the Decree on Penitence and Canon 4 of the Decree on Justification. The third debate between probabilism and probabiliorism broke out over the question of the moral system for the evaluation of motives for actions.[37] At the heart of the debate is the postlapsarian state of humanity, with its actual sinfulness and its enduring, and variously valued, free abilities on the one side, and the effective, free and unearned grace of God on the other. As a Roman Catholic debate, the argument about penitence, in particular, is tied up with the sacramental efficacy of grace. Thereby Trent accepted the 'high-scholastic teaching, that the sacrament exercises an efficient causality upon the forgiveness of sins … the purely declaratory theory of absolution could no longer be held as the Catholic position'.[38]

Certainly, by means of a 'reframing' of available theologoumena, Trent made possible significant changes in western theology. Not only did the Council restore the significance of free will, it also changed the possibility of thinking about sin and guilt. While the dogmatising of attrition as sufficient disposition for the reception of the sacrament presents an open formulation that leads to controversies, nonetheless the Council retained the fundamental insight of the necessary personal act. In this insight the Council basically follows the fundamental theological approach of scholastic debates. At the same time, the metanarrative of Christendom, original sin, is much more carefully expressed and opens the insight that presents the question of sin as a question about guilt, which therefore can be related to free will. This tension between dogmatic statement and open theological issues provides the starting point for the ultimately speculative penetration of the theologoumena into the themes of sin, grace and freedom which characterises the post-Tridentine era. The fact that Enlightenment philosophy poses unrelenting questions to sensitive issues and deconstructs existing concepts can be better understood in the light of the theological and historical transformation of the theological theme of penitence despite the fact that truly satisfying solutions are missing from the theological concepts from the twelfth century onwards. The history of theology shows that the categories of freedom and autonomy which were opened up by the philosophy of the Enlightenment were able to take up those themes which had already been set out by Abelard and by the Council of Trent.

These theological questions must, however, resist two temptations. On the one hand, when the image of the court as the guiding category for the relationship between the sinner and God is retained, as is the case with Trent and in the documents of Vatican II and following, not only is the anticipatory merciful divine action undermined but also, above all, justification through penitence as internal conversion becomes unthinkable, since it focuses not upon sinful acts but rather upon motive. The consequence of this would be the end of the neo-scholastic, post-Tridentine theology of penance. On the other hand, the overemphasis on mercy brings with it the danger that the seriousness of the sinful act may not be appropriately taken into account, if mercy undercuts the accountability of the individual as acting subject. The danger here is the temptation to set aside the actual discrepancy between sin and justification. A further complication is a reference cited by the Second Vatican Council on the sacrament of penance with respect to the necessity of a compensation through penance for the insult done to God by the sin (compare *Lumen Gentium*, no. 11).[39] In the midst of this tension, mercy plays the role of mediator, since the concept of grace and pardon builds a soteriological bridge between the penitential and juridical aspects, connecting both facets of confession—the objective-forensic aspects, which are related to communion, and the subjective-individual aspects. These concepts must, however, be substantiated from the perspective of modern theory. How—from a practical perspective—is judgement to be understood? Does theological language make use here of a pre-modern or of a modern colouring of the idea of justice?

The self-modernisation of the Catholic Church and her theology would require an explicit clarification of whether the turn to individual morals really means individual conscience or rather a conscience created and judged in the collective understanding. Above all, however, mercy seems to have been assigned a role and it cannot be the task of a theological concept to fulfil it.

Notes

[1] Cf. Gunda Werner, 'Mercy and justice in the context of the sacrament of penance—a critical re-reading of contemporary semantics from the perspective of the hermeneutics of dogma', in Theodor Dieter, Andrea Grillo and James Puglisi (eds), *Signs of Forgiveness, Paths of Conversion, Practice of Penance. A Reform That Challenges All*

(Bern, 2017), 111–32.
2. Cf. G. Werner, '*Misericordiae vultus*. A systematic theologian's re-reading', in Judith Hahn and Gunda Werner (eds), *Pax cum Deo—Pax cum Ecclesia: Penitence and Punishment between Personal Insight and Objectivity* (forthcoming).
3. All references in relation to *Misericordiae vultus* are taken from https://w2.vatican.va/content/francesco/en/apost_letters/documents/papa-francesco_bolla_20150411_misericordiae-vultus.html, accessed 20 January 2018.
4. Pope Francis, Audience, 16 December 2015.
5. Among others Emil Fischer, *Die katholische Beichtpraxis bei Beginn der Reformation und Luthers Stellung dazu in den Anfängen seiner Wirksamkeit* (Zur Geschichte der evangelischen Beichte, 1) (Aalen, 1972). This position is shared by current research; see also Ernst Bezzel, *Freiheit zum Eingeständnis* (Stuttgart, 1982), and many others. Herbert Vorgrimler, 'Der Kampf des Christen mit der Sünde', in Magnus Löhrer and Johannes Feiner (eds), *Zwischenzeit und Vollendung der Heilsgeschichte*, vol. 5 (*Mysterium Salutis. Grundriss heilsgeschichtlicher Dogmatik*) (Zürich, 1976), 349–461, at 419. Vorgrimler stresses the necessary reform in the light of situations that had arisen in the practice of penance. Similarly H. Vorgrimler, *Buße und Krankensalbung* (Handbuch der Dogmengeschichte, vol. IV: Sakramente—Eschatologie, Faszikel 3) (3rd edn, Freiburg, 2014). H. Vorgrimler, *Sakramententheologie* (Leitfaden Theologie, 17) (Düsseldorf, 1987). Timotheus Rast, *Von der Beichte zum Sakrament der Buße, Eine katechetische Besinnung zur rechten Unterweisung über das Sakrament der Buße mit geschichtlicher und theologischer Begründung* (Düsseldorf, 1965).
6. James Dallen, *The Reconciling Community: The Rite of Penance* (Studies in the Reformed Rites of the Catholic Church, 3) (Collegeville, MN, 1986), 168f.
7. H. Schröer, 'Reue', IV, in *Theologische Realenzyklopädie* (hereafter *TRE*) 29 (1998), 105–7, at 105. All translations of secondary sources from German into English by Rowena Roppelt, translator of this article.
8. Dirk Ansorge, *Gerechtigkeit und Barmherzigkeit Gottes. Die Dramatik von Vergebung und Versöhnung in bibeltheologischer, theologiegeschichtlicher und philosophiegeschichtlicher Perspektive* (Freiburg, 2009).
9. Thomas Pröpper, *Theologische Anthropologie*, vol. II (Freiburg, 2011) 1061.
10. Falk Wagner, 'Bekehrung', II, in *TRE* 5 (1980), 459–69, at 459.
11. *Ibid*.
12. Martin Laube, *Freiheit* (Tübingen, 2014), 100.
13. Cf. church historian Günther Wassilowsky in his review of the theological-historical work of Andreas Holzem: http://www.sehepunkte.de/2016/04/26620.html, accessed 8 July 2016.
14. G. Werner, *Die Freiheit der Vergebung. Eine freiheitstheoretische Reflexion auf die Prärogative Gottes im sakramentalen Bußgeschehen* (Regensburg, 2016), 56.
15. Vorgrimler, 'Der Kampf des Christen mit der Sünde', 417. Vorgrimler differentiates the basic theories of penitence and describes the reformed position in which contrition is not free preparation for grace but rather understood purely as remorse.
16. Vorgrimler, *Handbuch*, 175.
17. Cf. Pröpper, *Theologische Anthropologie*, 1066.
18. Cf. *ibid*.
19. *Ibid*., 1068.

[20] *Ibid.*, 1086.
[21] Heinrich J.D. Denzinger, *Enchiridion Symbolorum* (43rd edn, Freiburg, 2010), 1515 (DH 1515).
[22] Pröpper, *Theologische Anthropologie*, 1073.
[23] Cf. *ibid.*
[24] DH 1521.
[25] Pröpper, *Theologische Anthropologie*, 1075.
[26] *Ibid.*, 1077.
[27] Cf. Vorgrimler, *Handbuch*, 175.
[28] Cf. Werner, *Die Freiheit der Vergebung*, 2016.
[29] Cf. Johann Joseph Ignaz von Döllinger and Fr Heinrich Reusch, *Geschichte der Moralstreitigkeiten in der römisch-katholischen Kirche seit dem 16. Jahrhundert mit Beiträgen zur Geschichte und Charakteristik des Jesuitenordens* (Nördlingen, 1889). Werner, *Die Freiheit der Vergebung*, 2016. G. Werner, 'Reuestreit [added 2017]', in Friedrich Jaeger (ed.), *Enzyklopädie der Neuzeit* (on-line edition: http://dx.doi.org/10.1163/2352-0248_edn_fulltextxml_a6019000; first published on-line 2017; first print edition 2017; accessed 13 February 2018).
[30] Cf. Werner, *Die Freiheit der Vergebung*. Werner, 'Reue [added 2017]', in *Enzyklopädie der Neuzeit* (on-line edition, 2017: http://dx.doi.org/10.1163/2352-0248_edn_fulltextxml_a6018000; accessed 13 February 2018).
[31] DH 1456.
[32] Cf. Piet Fransen, 'Dogmengeschichtliche Entfaltung der Gnadenlehre', in M. Löhrer and J. Feiner (eds), *Das Heilsgeschehen in der Gemeinde. Gottes Gnadenhandeln*, IV, 2, *Mysterium Salutis. Grundriss heilsgeschichtlicher Dogmatik*, IV, 2 (Einsiedeln, 1973), 631–765, at 718.
[33] DH 1525; 1526; 1527; 1542.
[34] The formulation sets itself against the 'mere passivity' of the Reformation.
[35] O.H. Pesch, 'Gottes Gnadenhandeln als Rechtfertigung des Menschen', in *Mysterium Salutis, op. cit.*, 852ff.
[36] Cf. the few references in Vorgrimler, *Handbuch*, 190f.; Döllinger and Reusch, *Geschichte der Moralstreitigkeiten*, 1885.
[37] *Ibid.* Döllinger deals mainly with this issue, 61ff.
[38] Vorgrimler, *Handbuch*, 187.
[39] http://www.vatican.va/archive/hist_councils/ii_vatican_council/documents/vat-ii_const_19641121_lumen-gentium_en.html, accessed 6 March 2018.

5
Luther in a Dublin library—reflections on the 500th anniversary of the Reformation

Graeme Murdock

In the spring of 2017 the Library of Trinity College Dublin marked the 500th anniversary of the Reformation with a small exhibition featuring some works from its collection of early printed books. This exhibition, 'Power and Belief: the Reformation at 500', presented a number of Bibles and other texts in a connected narrative about the origins and character of the Reformation. It attempted to provide pause for thought about the spiritual, cultural and political processes that informed the religious reform movements of the early sixteenth century, and highlighted how ideas about reform responded to the beliefs and rituals of late medieval religious life and how they engaged with Renaissance humanism and utilised the capacity of print technology. The exhibition focused on how reformers attempted to renew the practice of Christianity on the basis of biblical authority and to provide accurate vernacular translations of the Bible working from original languages. It also reflected on how reformers conceived of the history of the Church and on how reform movements across Europe were intimately connected, from the lands of the Bohemian crown to Saxony to England and to Ireland.[1]

Key texts that were displayed in this exhibition will be briefly considered here, with a particular focus on one intriguing little book published at Wittenberg in 1537.[2] The exhibition opened with a pamphlet about indulgences published in Leipzig in 1518 by Martin Luther (*Eyn Freyheyt dess Sermons bebstlichen [päpstlichen] Ablass und Gnad belangend* … [TCD Library catalogue number: DD.nn.50 no.12]). Tradition suggests that on 31 October 1517 Martin Luther attached a copy of a Latin text to the door of All Saints' Church in Wittenberg calling for a debate about the power and efficacy of indulgences. By 1518 Luther sought to reach a wider audience, well beyond the confines of Wittenberg, for his ideas. He published a short text in German on questions about the sale of indulgences. A second 1518 pamphlet, which was shown in the exhibition, responded to criticisms of his ideas. These 1518 texts were a publishing sensation, with multiple editions bringing Luther's challenge to existing church practices and ideas into homes across the German lands.[3]

Luther's use of print ensured that debate spread quickly about his emerging agenda of reform. He had to defend his ideas in person before the Holy Roman Emperor Charles V Habsburg at the 1521 imperial Diet in Worms. In January 1521 Luther had been excommunicated as a heretic by papal bull. The Saxon court argued that he should not be condemned without allowing for a hearing of his ideas in front of the emperor. Charles V was persuaded to allow Luther to appear before him. Pressed to recant, Luther instead defended his expressed concerns both about the practice of the sale of indulgences and about the authority of the pope. According to the official transcript of the diet, Luther declared: 'I am bound by the Scriptures I have quoted and my conscience is captive to the Word of God. I cannot and will not retract anything, since it is neither safe nor right to act against conscience.' Perhaps Luther may have added a final thought: 'I cannot do otherwise, here I stand, may God help me. Amen.' At first sight, Luther's reference to his conscience might seem to represent a rather modern-sounding struggle of the authentic inner self against a constructed set of external norms. Luther, however, was making a far more dangerous claim than merely asserting his own deeply held opinions. Rather he was suggesting that the supreme authority in Christian life was the Bible. It was by reading God's Word that Luther believed he had discovered the love and grace of God. It was the absolute truth of the Bible that inspired, or rendered captive, his conscience. He could not therefore deny the truth of conscience as a middle place between God and man, even if asked to do so by a Medici pope or a Habsburg emperor. His opponents knew exactly what he meant. The imperial orator responded by telling Luther that he should not be so arrogant as to claim to be the one and only man who had knowledge of the Bible.[4]

Following his dramatic appearance at Worms and subsequent retreat to the relative safety of the Wartburg, Luther proceeded with the work of translating the Bible that was at the heart of his movement of reform. The 2017 exhibition at Trinity College featured *Das Alte Testament*, published in Wittenberg in 1523 [D.dd.24]. Luther and his colleagues worked towards a complete German translation of the Bible in 1534. This 1523 volume included a translation of the first part of the Old Testament. The text featured striking woodcut illustrations, including one from the Book of Genesis showing Jacob's dream of a ladder connecting heaven and earth, with the depiction clearly set in a German landscape.

A third book in the exhibition drew attention both to Luther's innovative engagement with print and to his desire to influence German culture through song as well as printed words and images. This 1524 text presented hymns in an *Eyn Enchiridion oder Handbuchlein. Eynem ytzlichen Christen fast nutzlich bey sich zuhaben zur stetter vbung vnd trachtung geystlicher gesenge vnd Psalmen* [C.pp.37 no.6]. Luther intended his vernacular hymns to be sung in homes and in the streets as well as in churches. Two editions of this early collection of Lutheran hymns were published in 1524 by rival Erfurt printers, Johannes Loersfeld and Matthes Maler. The text held by Trinity Library is the only known surviving copy of the Maler edition of twenty-six hymn texts set to fifteen tunes.[5]

The book in the exhibition which we will consider in greatest depth draws attention to an evolving story about the history of the Reformation connecting Prague, Wittenberg, London and Dublin. In 1537 Luther added a preface to a text of letters and documents relating to Jan Hus which was printed at Wittenberg with the title of *Epistolae quaedam piissimae et eruditissimae Iohannis Hus, quae solae satis declarant Papistarum pietates, esse Satanae furias* ('Some very godly and erudite letters of Jan Hus, sufficient in themselves to show that the piety of the Papists is satanic madness') [A.1.34]. Luther's preface to this work explored his interpretation of the legacy of the early fifteenth-century Czech theologian. The book includes a collection of letters written by Hus from Constance. Hus had agreed in 1415 to attend a church council at Constance after receiving guarantees about his safety. Once there, however, he was arrested, tried and executed as a heretic. The 1537 text includes an account of his trial, as well as copies of letters written after Hus's death on his views and legacy.

Luther had a consistent interest in Hus throughout his career. In 1520 he wrote to Georg Spalatin that 'without knowing it, we are all Hussites'.[6] Luther and his followers turned to Hus, among others, not least to provide an answer to the question posed by Catholic polemicists—where was your church before Luther? Catholics asserted the historical continuity of Roman authority and asked Lutherans to explain why their church should not be dismissed as a novel heresy. The 1537 *Epistolae* pointed towards one answer to these charges by suggesting a medieval past of supporters of the true church who had been persecuted by Rome. It also attempted to undermine claims of Roman authority by attacking the papacy as a manifestation of Antichrist ('the pope has also made himself the lord of hell') and by attacking the authority of church councils. Luther co-opted Hus to suit his own purposes despite clear points of difference between their theological views. Luther's version of Hus was also one which contemporary Utraquists in the Bohemian lands could hardly accept. This usable version of the life and death of Hus as presented by Luther in the 1537 *Epistolae* focused on how Hus stood up for the authority of the Bible, for example on the question of lay access to Holy Communion in both kinds. Hus also provided a warning to Lutherans against accepting any suggestion that a church council should be called to arbitrate over Luther's criticisms of the papacy. Luther turned Hus into a prophet for his own movement, rehearsing the apocryphal prophecy that Hus had written from prison that 'they will roast a goose now [*hus* means goose in Czech] but in a hundred years they will hear a swan sing, and him they will have to endure'. Luther thought that he had fulfilled this prophecy, and the motif of the swan came to be commonly associated with him in depictions of the reformer and in different forms of decoration used in many Lutheran churches.[7]

A number of copies of the 1537 *Epistolae* have survived. The 'Universal Short Title Catalogue' suggests that copies are present in libraries in a number of German cities that almost evoke the reach of the Lutheran movement— Berlin, Dresden, Gotha, Göttingen, Halle, Jena, Lüneburg, Rostock, Wittenberg, Wolfenbüttel and Zwickau. Four other surviving copies of the *Epistolae* are listed in the 'Universal Short Title Catalogue' at Munich, in the national libraries of Austria and of Hungary and in the library of Harvard Divinity School. Copy in the Trinity College Library is not currently listed in this catalogue.[8] An inscription on the title-page of the copy of the 1537 *Epistolae* held in Dublin suggests that this book was once owned by the archbishop of Canterbury, Thomas Cranmer ('*Thomas Cantuariēn*'). David Selwyn's authoritative research on Cranmer's library confirms that this ownership inscription is the same as that which appears on all the surviving texts from Cranmer's library. These inscriptions are not in Cranmer's own hand but were likely written by one of his secretaries. This was perhaps done in 1553, before Cranmer's property was confiscated by the Catholic regime of Mary Tudor.[9]

How and why might this book have come into the possession of the archbishop of Canterbury? In 1532 Cranmer had been appointed as English ambassador to the court of the Holy Roman Emperor Charles V. In early 1532 Cranmer left England for Brussels and then followed the emperor as he travelled to attend the imperial diet at Regensburg in the summer of 1532. In July 1532 Charles V reached agreement with members of the alliance of Lutheran princes in the Schmalkaldic League to uphold the religious status quo in the empire pending a general church council. Cranmer was tasked with gaining the support of Lutheran princes in the empire for the cause of Henry's divorce from Catherine of Aragon, Charles V's aunt. He spent a good deal of time in Nuremberg, where church services and rituals had been reformed under the leadership of Johannes Brenz and Andreas Osiander. Osiander and his colleagues advanced ideas about salvation by faith alone and rejected the notion of transubstantiation in the Mass. They had also abandoned the rule of clerical celibacy. Cranmer's embrace of these ideas about reform was marked not least by his marriage at Nuremberg to the niece of Osiander's wife. He may have spoken with his young bride, Margarete, in Latin or perhaps through some German that he had learned. In the late summer of 1532 he followed the emperor to Vienna. His role as English ambassador was interrupted, however, when news arrived that the archbishop of Canterbury, William Warham, had died. Thanks to the influence of the Boleyn faction at court, Henry VIII decided to summon Cranmer back to England to succeed Warham.[10]

Cranmer was thereafter identified by leading Continental reformers as crucial to the success of their cause in England. In 1536 Martin Bucer at Strasbourg dedicated a commentary on Romans to Cranmer. In 1537 Andreas Osiander published his *Harmony of the Four Gospels* and dedicated the work to his old friend Thomas Cranmer ('*Cranamer*'). Osiander had been working on this project during Cranmer's stay in Nuremberg in 1532 and the preface fondly recalled the time that Cranmer had spent at his home, discussing theology and the need for church reform. Osiander also wrote of Cranmer's 'utmost loyalty towards his most serene highness the King, a contempt for earthly matters, a heavenly love for gospel truth, a passionate application to true religion and Christ's glory and finally a spirit equal to martyrdom'.[11] Osiander's dedication of this work to Cranmer was both well judged and well timed. In May 1538 Franciscus Burckhardt, vice-chancellor of Elector Johann Friedrich, led a Saxon delegation to England. The arrival in London of this delegation, which included Luther's close colleague Friedrich Myconius, raises the possibility that they may have brought a copy of Osiander's *Harmony* with them to give to Cranmer. While a copy of Osiander's *Harmony* owned by Cranmer has not survived, David Selwyn suggests that this text is likely to be among the many lost works from Cranmer's library and includes it in a list of books which the archbishop is known to have used and quoted in his own writings. Also, taking into account the personal dedication to Cranmer, it seems certain that this work once formed part of his library. We might consider that the 1538 Saxon delegation also brought other texts with them to give to Cranmer. If Cranmer had not already acquired his copy of the 1537 *Epistolae* by other means, then this visit by Myconius to England provides a plausible means for the little book now in Trinity's Library to have made its way from Wittenberg to London.[12]

Theological discussions took place at Lambeth Palace between the Saxon delegation and four English bishops, led by Cranmer, over the summer of 1538. These meetings had an immediate political context. Cranmer and Thomas Cromwell sought to encourage Henry to agree to reforms in the face of the king's traditionalism and opposition from a conservative faction at court. The presence of the Lutheran delegation was of potential use to English advocates of reform as the king sought to reach a political agreement with the Lutheran princes of the Schmalkaldic League. Henry was in great need of allies after the peace of Nice, agreed between the emperor and François I of France in June 1538. The Saxon and English churchmen agreed *Thirteen Articles* which were based on the 1530 Augsburg *Confession*, but optimism about this agreement was short-lived. Henry changed his position and supported a text of *Six Articles* that contradicted the articles agreed between Cranmer and Myconius. In October 1538 Myconius and the Saxon delegation left England disappointed with the lack of progress in persuading the king to accept crucial reforms, including clerical marriage and allowing the laity to receive Holy Communion in both kinds. With the risks to his wife and also to himself now heightened, Cranmer sent Margarete and their children to her family in Nuremberg, where they remained for four years. He was only able to publicly acknowledge his wife's existence after Edward VI's accession in 1547.[13]

Attempts by the English to revive contacts with Lutheran leaders and the Schmalkaldic League resumed in 1539. Cromwell negotiated the contract for Henry's marriage to Anne of Cleves but the annulment of this marriage and Cromwell's execution in July 1540 marked the end of this Lutheran period of influence over the direction of the Reformation in England. During Edward VI's reign Cranmer turned instead to south German and Swiss theologians in the emerging Reformed tradition. Nevertheless, the legacy of the late 1530s was of enduring significance not least in the production of English translations of the Bible. The 2017 exhibition in Trinity College featured early English Bibles published thanks to the efforts of Cromwell and Cranmer to follow the example that had been established in Saxony. The 1537 'Matthew' Bible [BB.b.11] was an officially sanctioned translation of the Bible, 'set forth with the Kinges most gracious lycence'. The name of the translator was given as 'Thomas Matthew' but the translator was in fact William Tyndale. Tyndale had left England to pursue his efforts to translate the Bible into English, but he was captured and burned as a heretic in the Netherlands in 1535 and the work of translation was completed by Miles Coverdale. The Trinity exhibition also included a 1540 edition of the 'Great' Bible [KK.b.20], first published in 1539 and placed by royal order in all England's parish churches to be read aloud to congregations during services.

Returning to the fate of Cranmer's copy of the 1537 *Epistolae*, in 1556 Cranmer was executed as a heretic during the reign of Mary. His library had been confiscated by the authorities and many texts which were not by prohibited authors came into the possession first of the earl of Arundel and then of his son-in-law, Lord Lumley. Many of Cranmer's books by Protestant authors seem to have been destroyed and only a small sample of his collection of works by reformers has survived. Works by prohibited authors such as Hus and Luther had possibly been separated out on the orders of the earl of Arundel or may have been given away at an earlier stage by Cranmer or others to sympathetic friends willing to take the risk of owning such books.[14] We have no information about who might have taken possession of the 1537 *Epistolae* either before Elizabeth's accession or during the early years of her reign. We have an indication of a later owner from a handwritten note in the middle of the front page, '*Liber Samuelis Burtoni Aedis Chri*'. Who might this graduate of Christ Church in Oxford be who was bold enough to add his own name alongside the martyred Archbishop Cranmer? The most likely candidate is a Samuel Burton, born in 1569, who attended Christ Church in the late 1580s. Burton then held a rectorship at Stratton on Fosse in Warwickshire from 1597 and was appointed archdeacon of Gloucester from 1607 until his death in 1634.[15]

Cranmer's copy of the 1537 *Epistolae* had come into the possession of a conformist cleric of the early seventeenth century. Samuel Burton was the cousin of another moderate figure in the church politics of the period, Joseph Hall, who was bishop of Exeter from 1627 and then of Norwich from 1641.[16] Arguments about Cranmer's legacy inevitably played a part in the sharp internal divisions within the English church during this period. While some Puritans complained that reforms under Cranmer had not gone far enough, some of the emerging Laudian party thought that Cranmer had gone too far. It seems fitting that Cranmer's book was in the safe keeping of a cleric like Burton who promoted loyalty to the monarch as supreme governor of the church and the religion of the 1559 *Book of Common Prayer* (which followed Cranmer's 1552 version without the added rubric concerning kneeling at Communion). Samuel Burton published his only known work in 1620, *A sermon preached at the generall assises in Warwicke*, in which he rehearsed anti-Catholic rhetoric and called for obedience to lawful authorities. He criticised Puritans who wasted their time worrying about maypoles and morris dances (his sermon followed the 1618 royal declaration of permitted sports and recreations). Taking Romans 13: 4 as his passage, he argued that 'the doctrine of Christ teacheth all due obedience' to the authority of magistrates. Noting that the pride of 'that Romish Antichrist' despised the need to obey lawful magistrates, Burton wished that preachers in England 'would press this point of obedience more closely to the consciences of the people'. He wondered, 'is it possible that in a reformed Church; a Church wherein the Romish pride and tyranny is so justly condemned, a Church wherein the Gospel is so plentifully preached; a Church which hath not locked up the Word of God; but laid it open, and put it into the hands of all her children there should be so little conscience made of yielding obedience to a most

Christian magistrate, commanding honest and lawful things?'[17]

Samuel Burton was the final known private owner of the 1537 *Epistolae*. We know nothing of the later fate of the book except for a comment made by Cranmer's first biographer, John Strype. In his 1694 biography Strype describes a book 'now in the possession of a reverend friend of mine near Canterbury: in which book the Archbishop's name is yet to be seen, written thus with his own hand, *Thomas Cantuariensis*, and a remarkable book it is, which we may conclude the Archbishop often perused, *viz. Epistolae et Historia Joannis Hus*. Printed at Wittenberg. 1537.'[18] David Selwyn suggested that this book recorded by Strype was likely to have been the text by Hus with a preface by Luther. Now that the copy of this book has been located, this suggestion has certainly been confirmed. While Cranmer may well have consulted and studied this text, there are no substantial marks or notes on the text in his hand.[19]

After this brief comment by Strype in the 1690s, Cranmer's copy of the 1537 *Epistolae* disappeared again from sight. As the Library of Trinity College does not have continuous accession records, we cannot be certain how and when this book travelled on the final leg of its journey from near Canterbury to Dublin. The book does not appear in a catalogue of the Library compiled in the 1710s but was certainly well known by 1872, when the catalogue entry presented a copy of 'Huss, Johannes, *Epistolae* ... Vitembergae (Joannes Lufft), 1537 ... [*Cum autographo Thomae Cranmeri, Cantuariensis archiepiscopi*]'. The book was regarded with obvious interest by librarians in Trinity College during the late nineteenth century. Records of the book's shelf-mark suggest that it was later placed on prominent display in the Library, presumably opened at the title-page to allow readers and visitors to view the inscription suggesting that the book had once belonged to Cranmer.[20]

In the context of Trinity College as an institution during the late nineteenth and early twentieth centuries, it is not surprising that the 1537 *Epistolae* was of interest largely because of the venerated place of Cranmer within the Anglican tradition. The story of Cranmer's martyrdom had featured prominently in John Foxe's *Acts and monuments* from 1563. Cranmer's death on 21 March 1556 continued to be marked in Anglican churches. His legacy as the 'godly father of the English Church' had been defined and promoted not least by his seventeenth-century biographer, John Strype. Strype described Cranmer as 'the first protestant archbishop of this kingdom, and the greatest instrument, under God, of the happy Reformation of this Church of England; in whose piety, learning, wisdom, conduct, and blood, the foundation of it was laid'.[21] Cranmer's language was ever-present in Anglican religious life, as his 1552 prayer-book remained almost unchanged at the heart of church services. We might note the conclusion of Diarmaid MacCulloch that Cranmer 'would not have known what Anglicanism meant, and he would probably not have approved if the meaning had been explained to him, but without his contribution the unending dialogue of Protestantism and Catholicism which forms Anglican identity would not have been possible'.[22] The high regard for Cranmer among Anglicans certainly provides the most plausible explanation of how his copy of the 1537 *Epistolae* passed from the hands of an early seventeenth-century archdeacon of Gloucester to a minister near Canterbury towards the end of the seventeenth century, and on into other clerical hands that at some point crossed the Irish Sea, to be donated or otherwise acquired by Trinity College before the middle decades of the nineteenth century. Once removed from display in the Library, and in changing times for Trinity College as an institution during the twentieth century, interest in and knowledge of this little book faded, so that it remained unknown to modern scholarship.

As we consider the impact of the Reformation on religious life and culture across Europe over the past 500 years we cannot wish away the violent contests over truth in word and deed of the early sixteenth century. The 1537 *Epistolae* in Trinity College Library brings this violent rhetoric and action into sharp focus. At the heart of the Reformation was a battle over legitimate authority in Christian religion. Reformers asserted the authority of the Bible as supreme and declared the authority of the bishop of Rome to be false. Jan Hus, Martin Luther, Thomas Cranmer and Samuel Burton all agreed that the papacy was a manifestation of Antichrist. On 6 July 1415 Jan Hus was burned as a heretic following the Council of Constance. In 1519 Martin Luther was burned in effigy in Rome. Luther's books were also burned in Rome after he was threatened with excommunication in a papal bull in the summer of 1520. When this bull arrived in Wittenberg, Luther had his revenge and staged a public burning of copies of the Roman text. He followed up by publishing a tract *Against the execrable bull of the Antichrist*. After the diet of Worms in 1521, Luther and his followers were declared heretics but the Catholic authorities had to content themselves with publicly burning Luther's books. Catholics later staged mock trials and burnings of effigies of Luther, but for Luther's supporters the hero of the Reformation proved himself to be incombustible both in person and in image.[23]

On 21 March 1556 Cranmer made a final declaration that the pope was Christ's enemy. Cranmer's Protestant books had been destroyed or dispersed before the archbishop was burned as a heretic. After Elizabeth's accession, owning a book that had once belonged to Cranmer became a matter of pride within the English church, and Samuel Burton added his name to the title-page of the book. While details of the passage of the 1537 *Epistolae* from Burton's hands to Dublin remain elusive, its evolving significance is clear as a token of the emotional and ideological importance of Cranmer within the emerging Anglican tradition in England and Ireland. Of less interest to later Anglican owners but of more significance for the history of the Reformation era, this book emphasises the influence of Luther and Lutherans within the early English Reformation. Finally, the 1537 *Epistolae* points backwards beyond the events in Wittenberg 500 years ago to the legacy of Jan Hus. By marking the 500th anniversary of the Reformation in 2017 we may perhaps have got our dates somewhat confused.

Notes

1. The Library of Trinity College Dublin held a much more substantial exhibition from its extraordinarily rich collection of early sixteenth-century German printed texts in 1980–1. A wonderful catalogue on this authoritative exhibition, which was curated by the late Prof. Helga Robinson-Hammerstein, appeared as *Reformation and Society in Germany, 1500–1530* (Dublin, 1981).
2. The exhibition was organised by Shane Mawe of TCD Library. Alongside early German printed texts the exhibition featured a number of early English and Irish Bibles, curated by Mark Sweetnam. Following the display of these texts in the Long Room, an on-line version of the exhibition was also prepared by Shane Mawe and appeared in conjunction with the Google Cultural Institute: https://artsandculture.google.com/exhibit/RALCdrBZ9S2VLA (accessed 30 June 2018).
3. Andrew Pettegree, *Brand Luther: 1517, Printing, and the Making of the Reformation* (New York, 2015).
4. Excellent biographies of Luther to appear for the 500th anniversary. See Scott H. Hendrix, *Martin Luther: Visionary Reformer* (New Haven, CT, 2016); Lyndal Roper, *Martin Luther: Renegade and Prophet* (London, 2016); and Heinz Schilling, *Martin Luther: Rebel in an Age of Upheaval* (trans. Rona Johnston) (Oxford, 2017).
5. On the 2013 attribution of this text see https://www.tcd.ie/library/epb/blog/tag/matthes-maler/ (accessed 30 June 2018).
6. See the excellent study by Phillip N. Haberkern, *Patron Saint and Prophet: Jan Hus in the Bohemian and German Reformations* (Oxford, 2016), 158, 207–10.
7. *Ibid.*, 189, 208.
8. For this text in the 'Universal Short Title Catalogue' see www.ustc.ac.uk (reference no. 651655). A digital copy of the 1537 *Epistolae* is available from the Bayerische Staatsbibliothek in Munich.
9. David Selwyn, *The Library of Thomas Cranmer* (Oxford, 1996), xxvi–lviii, and see p. 319 for an example of the inscription that also appears in the Dublin copy of the 1537 *Epistolae*.
10. Diarmaid MacCulloch, *Thomas Cranmer: A Life* (New Haven, CT, 1996); Susan Wabuda, *Thomas Cranmer* (New York, 2017).
11. Andreas Osiander, *Harmoniae evangelicae libri IIII Graece et Latine, in quibus evangelica*

historia ex quatuor evangelistis in unum est contexta, item annotationum liber unus elenchus harmoniae (Basel, 1537). Basil Hall, 'Cranmer's relations with Erasmianism and Lutheranism', in Paul Ayris and David Selwyn (eds), *Thomas Cranmer: churchman and scholar* (Woodbridge, 1993), 20–1.

[12] Selwyn, *The Library of Thomas Cranmer*, 243; David Selwyn, 'Cranmer's library: its potential for Reformation studies', in Ayris and Selwyn (eds), *Thomas Cranmer: churchman and scholar*, 39–74.

[13] Hall, 'Cranmer's relations with Erasmianism and Lutheranism', in Ayris and Selwyn (eds), *Thomas Cranmer: Churchman and Scholar*, 26–8.

[14] Selwyn, 'Cranmer's library: its potential for Reformation studies', 46–50.

[15] On Samuel Burton see the entry in the 'Clergy of the Church of England Database': http://db.theclergydatabase.org.uk/jsp/persons/CreatePersonFrames.jsp?PersonID=25113 (accessed 1 July 2018).

[16] Joseph Hall dedicated a 1609 devotional work, *Some few of David's Psalms metaphrased, for a taste of the rest*, to his 'loving and learned cousin' Samuel Burton. James Doelman, *King James I and the Religious Culture of England* (Woodbridge, 2000), 141.

[17] Samuel Burton, *A sermon preached at the generall assises in Warwicke, the third of March, being the first Friday in Lent* (London, 1620). Ann Hughes, *Politics, Society and Civil War in Warwickshire, 1620–1660* (Cambridge, 1987), 68–9.

[18] John Strype, *Memorials of the Most Reverend Father in God, Thomas Cranmer, Sometime Lord Archbishop of Canterbury* (London, 1694), book 3, 439.

[19] Selwyn, *The Library of Thomas Cranmer*, 43.

[20] Many thanks to Shane Mawe and David Selwyn for generously sharing their expert understanding of Trinity Library and Cranmer's library. Any mistakes in the interpretation presented here are my own.

[21] Hall, 'Cranmer's relations with Erasmianism and Lutheranism', 3; MacCulloch, *Thomas Cranmer*, 628.

[22] MacCulloch, *Thomas Cranmer*, 629.

[23] Robert Scribner, 'Incombustible Luther: the image of the reformer in early modern Germany', *Past and Present* **110** (1986), 38–68.

II.
LEGACIES OF THE REFORMATION

6
Luther's legacy for Pauline studies in modern debate

Martin Meiser

A contribution on Luther's legacy for Pauline studies today requires a sober comparison of Luther and of modern exegesis of Galatians and Romans. These two letters are both the centre of Luther's theology and the point of debate for the so-called 'New Perspective on Paul'.

Luther's commentary on Galatians, published in 1535, is one of the major works that he himself held in high esteem because of its doctrine.[1] Moreover, it is one of the works that was well received in his own time. Whereas his commentary on Romans 'was not published until 1908 ... , Luther's Galatians commentary of 1535, based on his 1531 lectures, circulated widely. Its English translation, first completed in 1575, went through numerous editions and versions and was widely influential.'[2]

It seems both historically odd and theologically prejudiced to examine the legacy of a theologian from five centuries ago concerning research that should be happening principally without specific denominational perspectives and addressing theological questions of our own times rather than those of long ago. On the other hand, the weight of biblical research is dependent on the weight of Christian history in general. Taken merely as a piece of ancient literature, the New Testament writings would not deserve such interest. In order to avoid ideological misunderstandings we have to speak of Luther's non-legacy as well as Luther's legacy. The latter is evident, in my view, in both exegetical observations and theological decisions.

The 'New Perspective on Paul'

Until the 1960s, Luther's interpretation of Paul was foremost in Protestant exegesis. In New Testament scholarship, the 1970s and 1980s were characterised not only by the so-called 'linguistic turn' but also by a geographic turn: German-speaking exegesis no longer took the lead but had to cede its position to North American exegetical scholarship. The influence of the so-called 'New Perspective on Paul' was both a part of and an effect of this shift.

The first scholar who was to undermine Luther's legacy concerning

Pauline studies after World War II was Krister Stendahl (1921–2008), Professor at Harvard University (1954–84) and later Lutheran bishop of Stockholm (1984–8). According to him,[3] the Pauline doctrine of salvation was not a fundamental theory on individual salvation and its anthropological presupposition but an ecclesiological theory aimed at establishing the rights of converted non-Jews. Because of Christ's death, Jews can be members of the church and heirs to the promises of the God of Israel despite any obligation to the Torah. Luther, Stendahl argued, misunderstood Paul in neglecting the ecclesiastical horizon and inferred problems of the Western tradition concerning the terrified conscience.[4] Romans 7 is a digression but subordinated the overwhelming intention to charge sin, not the Torah.

Similarly, early in the 1970s, Norman T. Wright read Rom 10:3 very differently from the traditional reading. He noted that 'Paul's critique of his fellow Jews was not that they were legalists trying to earn merit but that they were nationalists trying to keep God's blessing for themselves instead of being the conduit for that blessing to flow to the Gentiles'.[5]

The next proponent to be named here is Ed Parish Sanders, born in 1937 in Texas, Professor at McMaster University in Canada and later at Oxford and at Duke University, North Carolina. In his *Paul and Palestinian Judaism*[6] he proposed at least three points. (1) To characterise Judaism as a religion of work-righteousness is to construct a caricature of Jewish piety. The 'getting in' into the covenant with God is a result of the divine election of Israel; the 'staying in' within the covenant is a result of human obedience to the Torah, but there are possibilities for repentance and reconciliation. (2) The centre of Pauline thought is not the doctrine of justification but the doctrine of participation. 'I am crucified with Christ' (Gal 2:19b),[7] or 'it is no longer I who lives, but it is Christ who lives in me' (Gal 2:20a; see also Rom 6:3–4). These words are most important for Paul himself. (3) Paul's universalism in reflecting on sin is the effect not of theoretical reasoning on sin but of the Christ event. Sanders's formula 'From Solution to Plight'[8] includes the following thesis: because Paul emphasises Jesus Christ as redeemer of the whole of mankind, all human beings must have a problem from which they had to be redeemed, i.e. sin.

James D.G. Dunn, born in 1939, Professor Emeritus at Durham, focuses on Stendahl's theory on one important point: the function of the doctrine of justification is central not for salvation theology but for ecclesiology. Referring to ancient Jewish parallels, Dunn stresses the sociological function of the Torah, separating Jews from non-Jews. The Torah functions as 'identity marker' within Israel and as 'boundary' regarding the relation between Israel and non-Jews. In Gal 2:16 we read: 'No one will be justified by the works of the law'. In earlier contributions, James Dunn referred the formula 'works of the law' to rules marking the distinction between Jews and non-Jews: circumcision, the Sabbath, and laws concerning food and cleanliness.[9] Gal 2:16 does not deal with a general human inability to fulfil God's will but with a shift regarding the pre-conditions for belonging to the people of God. In this way, Gal 2:16 does not denigrate Christian ethics but denigrates prerogatives that could be misused by Jews in order to exclude non-Jews from the congregation. Owing to criticism,[10] Dunn admits in a later publication that it is a little too narrow to interpret Gal 2:16 in this way. He stresses, however, that Paul's rebuke of boasting with the Torah does not rebuke any claim to be able to avoid sin but the difference of status. 'The attitude of confidence expressed in "works of the law" is the assumption of the "Jew" that he will be acquitted at the final judgment, while others (Gentiles) will be condemned. It is *not* an assumption of sinlessness, of perfect keeping of the law; it *is* the assumption that his status within the covenant people, as attested by his "works of the law", will ensure his final acquittal.'[11] Romans 3:9–20 states that all human beings are under the power of sin and by this Paul 'clearly means to ensure that his fellow Jews recognise that they *specifically* are *not* exempt'[12] from the last judgement.

In some points, the so-called 'New Perspective on Paul' is not new. William Wrede and Albert Schweitzer postulated some of the central ideas.[13] Furthermore, we find the so-called 'New Perspective' anticipated also in ancient Christian exegesis. Romans 3:28 is interpreted as an apology for the salvation of Gentiles against Jewish rebukes[14] but it is also restricted to the 'getting in' according to Sanders, whereas Gal 5:6 and Jas 2:14–26 concern the 'staying in'.[15] The concentration on circumcision, Sabbath and dietary laws in the exegesis of Gal 2:16 occurs already in Theodoret of Cyrus's commentary on Galatians.[16]

Does the 'New Perspective on Paul' do justice to Luther?

Stendahl is correct when he considers Luther's theology of justification as a theology that refers to a problem in each human being as an individual.[17] Volker Stolle confirmed this view.[18] For Luther, however, human conscience was never a reliable indicator of the status of the human being before God.[19] Timothy George[20] quotes from Luther's 1535 commentary on Galatians: 'This is the reason why our theology is certain: it snatches us away from ourselves and places us outside ourselves, so that we do not depend on our own strength, conscience, experience, person, or works but depend on that which is outside ourselves, that is, on the promise and truth of God, which cannot deceive'.[21] Stendahl's description of Luther's way does not do justice to the motive of Luther's confession that he was not able to love God (cf. Deut 6:5; Mk 12:30)—he tried to fulfil the will of God owing to anxiousness with regard to God's punishment.[22]

In other cases, some insights from the New Perspective are present in passing mentions by Martin Luther himself, in Sanders's formula 'from Solution to Plight'[23] or in Dunn's thesis that Paul rejected the Jewish self-distinguishing from the Gentiles.[24] In addition, we can interpret Luther's distinction between absolute faith and incarnated faith[25] as the anticipation of Sanders's distinction between 'getting in' and 'staying in': absolute faith is the issue in our discussion of justification, while the incarnated faith is the issue in our discussion of works by the believer.

To be fair, in Luther's works these passages are passing mentions, not emphasised by Luther himself. Furthermore, Martin Luther cannot function as a single criterion to evaluate modern Pauline exegesis. We have to ask whether the so-called New Perspective did justice to Paul himself.

The New Perspective and Luther's (non-)legacy for Pauline studies

Luther's non-legacy
In an attempt at a historical embedding of Galatians and Romans, it is not useful to refer to Luther. He was active and intended to influence the theology and the church of his own days. He was not interested in independent historical research concerning Paul and his situation 1,500 years earlier. He does not deal with our questions concerning localisation of the addressees and dating of the letters. His one-sided contemporary reading is unique even in the history of exegesis before the Enlightenment.[26]

Luther's portrait of the Judaism or Jewish Christianity of Paul's days represents his perceptions of the Roman Catholicism of his own day. Furthermore, sometimes Luther describes the divine law as vexing the elected people.[27] The caricature of Judaism, already beginning even in the New Testament, has been a problem of Christian exegesis since the first days of Christianity.[28] In modern New Testament scholarship, we continually read texts of ancient Judaism in order to get a fair picture of the Jesus-preaching Paul within Judaism. Paul reclaimed his Jewish identity when he was active as a missionary of Jesus Christ. In his own biography he saw evidenced a witness of God's faithfulness to Israel (Rom 11:1). Luther's increasingly anti-Jewish attitude was fostered by a growing apocalyptic fear concerning his own work of reformation. The apocalyptic demonising of adversaries within Luther's works should make us cautious with regard to an uncritical revival.[29] His anti-Jewish stance, however, is present from the beginning, and it is not a phenomenon aside from his theological merits but is part of the centre of his own theology.[30]

Luther's formula *simul iustus et peccator*[31] describes, of course, not an ideal concept of Christian life but the real life of believers in Luther's view: 'If I look at myself, I can only confess that I am sinning; my righteousness is imputed righteousness'.[32] Luther was not the first to describe Christian life in this way. Augustine, centuries before him, stated that human beings are not able to escape sin within their earthly life.[33] The basis for Luther's thesis was his referring to Rom 7:7–25, to the life of the Christian and to Paul himself.[34] If we consider the context of Rom 6 and Rom 8, however, the thesis of Werner Georg Kümmel holds true: Rom 7 describes the non-Christian human being in the light of Christian insight.[35] The biblical ideal of Christian life is to be described by Paul's imperative in Rom 6:12: 'Therefore, do not let sin exercise dominion in your mortal bodies, to make you obey their passions'.

Luther's well-known identification of ancient Judaism as Paul's adversary and of Roman Catholicism and (in later times) the so-called Anabaptists and enthusiasts as his own adversaries[36] includes his self-identification with the apostle. Increasingly he would not maintain any distance between Paul and himself.[37] His comment on Gal 1:1 in 1535 is an example of his oscillating between historical explanations and justification of his stand against the pope and the Anabaptists. He begins with a reconstruction of the rebukes that the teachers in Galatia made against Paul:

> 'He was the last to turn to Christ. But we have seen Christ. We heard Him preach. Paul came later and is beneath us. Is it possible for us to be in error—we who have received the Holy Ghost? Paul stands alone. He has not seen Christ, nor has he had much contact with the other apostles. Indeed, he persecuted the Church of Christ for a long time … do you suppose that God would have left His Church floundering in error all these centuries?'[38]

In such a way, too, modern research could explain Paul's insistence on his apostolic ministry from just Gal 1:1 onwards. Following on, Luther identified his own position, criticised by the pope, with Paul's position challenged by the teachers in Galatia. Once more Luther reverts to history. He correctly observes that the first two chapters of Galatians are mostly dedicated to Paul's recommending his vocation, his ministry and his gospel. In this way, Luther concludes, every minister of the divine word can be certain concerning their own vocation, so that that they can boast before God and human beings of preaching the Gospel.[39] In the same way, he declares that he is right when—in his comment on Gal 6:14—he boasts about the cross of Jesus Christ with regard to the persecution by the pope of Rome.[40]

My only question here would be: from a theological point of view, are we allowed to emulate Paul fighting against others? I would be reluctant, remembering Christ's words: 'Do not judge in order not to be judged' (Mt 7:1).

Luther's legacy—exegetical observations
We should not only examine the great and, for the most part, prevailing lines in Luther's commentaries on Scripture but also his decisions concerning some detailed questions which continue to be debated in current exegesis. I want to list only a few examples, mostly drawn from Luther's commentary on Galatians from 1535.

In Gal 1 and 2, Paul does not retell mere history; we should observe the intention of his argument.[41] In Gal 1:13–14 Paul uses his own example in order to convince the Galatians to abstain from choosing a possibly wrong way.[42] Gal 1:17 proves that he had not learned the Gospel by human influence. He was not silently waiting for impulses from the other apostles but immediately began to preach the Gospel in Arabia.[43] In Gal 2:1, the 'fourteen years' are reckoned not from his call but from his visit in Jerusalem, mentioned in Gal 1:18–19.[44] Titus is a vivid witness for the efficacy of the Holy Spirit also among people who are not circumcised.[45] In Gal 2:15–16 the 'works of the law' are not only ceremonials but also concern the law in general,[46] including everything that is decisive for Jewish self-definition,[47] and there is no difference between the Decalogue and ceremonial law, against Jerome and others. That allows Luther to evaluate pagan examples of virtue in a positive way: they did works of the law but they are not justified by them, according to 1 Cor 4:4.[48] Gal 2:19 is interpreted as freedom from the law that is condemning me.[49] We die to the law not by imitation of Christ's crucifixion but by our faith that Christ's crucifixion is the sole basis of our salvation; the law does not have any claims against us.[50] Gal 3:2 is an argument from experience where any disagreement is impossible.[51] In the interpretation of Gal 3:5, both miracles and virtues are named as if Luther intended to write a modern commentary in which such questions are debated.[52] Gal 3:19 (the law is 'added because of transgressions') does not refer to increasing transgressions but to the so-called *usus elenchthicus legis*: the law reveals human sin and blindness, despised by God.[53] Gal 3:22 does not imply that God demands impossible things. What is impossible to fulfil by the law of works became possible by the law of faith.[54] How should we interpret Gal 3:24, '… the law was our disciplinarian until Christ came …'? The next parallel to Gal 3:24

is Rom 10:4: Christ is the end of the law in its accusing function.[55] Concerning Gal 5:18, Luther has in view the accusing function of law; passions vex Christians, but if they do not consent to these passions they are not 'under the law'.[56] Similarly, Gal 5:19–23 does not offer a portrait of sanctity comparable to Stoic doctrine intended to extirpate all passions. This is what Luther himself tried when he was a monk. Biblical saints are sinners too, like David and the apostle Peter. This is the consolation for our own conscience terrified by sin.[57]

Salvation history and anthropology within Paul
Stendahl is correct when he emphasises the totally different perspectives of Paul and Luther on their former lives. Whereas Luther was anxious regarding the Last Judgement and hated God and his Aristotelian 'justice', Paul was convinced of fulfilling God's will in being jealous for the Torah (Phil 3:6!). Stendahl, however, downplays the role that Romans 7 had for Paul.[58] The one-sidedness of emphasising salvation history and the shortening of the anthropological dimension in Pauline thought have been issues of critique.[59] Functionalising the doctrine of justification as mere ecclesiastical strategy completely fails to recognise the universal claim of Paul's theology of salvation.[60] Paul's theology is relevant not only to issues of mission but also to issues of anthropology.[61] To be sure, Bultmann was wrong in stating that the fulfilment of the Torah also provokes the curse:[62] the Torah curses everyone who does *not* fulfil it (Deut 27:26 in Gal 3:10). We should not construct false contrasts where no contrasts are evident. Maybe Paul got this concept on the basis of salvation history. We should not overlook the fact, however, that Paul is truly convinced of the sinfulness of all human beings. Rom 7 is by no means simply a mere excursus but unfolds anthropological concerns already evident in Gal 3:10. Luther was correct in observing in his *disputatio de homine* that Paul did use the term in Rom 3:28 in a universal fashion[63] and he sees the justification of the human being as the anthropological definition of the human being.[64]

Concerning Paul, it has to be said, moreover, that isolated references including forms of the root δικ- (righteous) show that motifs of the theology of justification are not only a mere late product of Pauline theology.[65]

Participationism and justification
Sanders is principally correct in emphasising the relevance of participationist terminology in Paul. The aim of this terminology and theology is to underline the obligations imposed on the believers in being bound to Jesus Christ. This aspect is well known from ancient Christian exegesis.[66] I suggest, however, that terms like 'relevant' or 'irrelevant' are not sufficiently precise. In order to recon-

struct the concepts of Pauline thought we have to ask for coherence in terms of logic.[67] Concerning that point we can simply state that justification is the basis of participation and participation is the effect of justification.[68]

In a distinct way, Sanders's claim for participationist elements in Pauline theology is an important element in Luther's theology too. Against Sanders's charge of Luther's alleged neglect of participationist elements in Paul's theology, Klaus Haacker quotes Luther's exegesis of Gal 2:20, which in fact reveals the presence of participationist motifs in Luther. 'By faith, you will be unified with Jesus Christ in a way, that from you and from him quasi one person comes into being which cannot be separated but continuously adheres to him who says "I am like Christ," and Christ says, "I am like this sinner, who adheres to me, and I to him".'[69] We could add another passage from Luther's comments on Gal 2:20: Paul explains what constitutes true Christian righteousness. This righteousness is the righteousness of Christ Who lives in us. We must look away from our own person. Christ and my conscience must become one, so that I can see nothing else but Christ crucified and raised from the dead for me. If I only look at myself, I am gone.[70]

'From Solution to Plight'—and Israel's Scripture
Even if Paul's knowledge is described correctly by the formula 'from Solution to Plight' (Sanders), it is important for the apostle that his idea of the Torah as condemning the whole of humankind is to be found within the Torah itself. While we could doubt whether Gal 2:16 really includes an allusion to Psalm 143:2 at the end,[71] at least in Gal 3:23–25 two things are clear: the horizon of the text is salvation history, but the basis of salvation history is the state of all human beings identified as sinners by the Torah.[72] For Martin Luther, our human conscience is no real source of knowledge about our state before God (see above). The *extra nos* of the biblical Word was decisive for him.[73]

Remembering the Reformation today

Repentance as thoroughgoing self-criticism
Reformation from the outset was a plea for repentance. The first of the famous *Ninety-Five Theses*[74] is a warning against mere external acts of repentance, following Johannes Tauler and Johann von Staupitz.[75] On the other hand, the third thesis, following monastic tradition,[76] makes it clear that repentance does not solely mean inner repentance. Such repentance is worthless unless it produces various outward signs of mortification of the flesh. Theses 43 and 44 emphasise helping the poor. Thus repentance does not mean wallowing in self-pity but

implies sober eagerness for thoroughgoing self-criticism based on the biblical Word. For non-religious people, too, it could be an impulse for thoroughgoing questioning: are our actions adequate?

Freedom

Luther did not focus on political freedom or promote a vulgar freedom apart from the divine Word. Rather he was concerned with the freedom of our conscience, whereby we are free from reproaches by the law, from sin and from fear of death.[77] Salvation is not (at least this was Luther's thesis since 1517)[78] dependent on the quality of the repentance that asks for God's mercy. Luther repeatedly emphasises, against Aristotle, that good works will follow from righteousness but do not constitute righteousness.[79] In this way we are able to act responsibly and at the same time we can stop being continually anxious about whether we have done enough in helping others. Good works will flow from our being justified by God's grace;[80] indeed, Luther was not so silly as to deny the necessity of good works.

Luther repeatedly emphasised the distinction between Law and Gospel,[81] commenting that Paul did not deal with political, economic etc. righteousness but with spiritual righteousness.[82] One thing one might ask is whether these distinctions are correct when applied to Paul. Another thing is to realise that only clarity of mind can help us to avoid mistakes and abuses. A result of seeking such clarification might be another impact of freedom—the distinction between God's Word and human thinking.

Notes

[1] Julius Köstlin, *Martin Luther. Sein Leben und seine Schriften* (5th edn, ed. Gustav Kawerau), vol. II (Berlin, 1903), 594.

[2] John Riches, *Galatians through the Centuries*, Blackwell Bible Commentaries (Malden, 2008), 33.

[3] Krister Stendhal, 'Paul and the introspective conscience of the West', *Harvard Theological Review* **56** (1963), 199–215; reprinted in *Paul among Jews and Gentiles* (London, 1977), 78–96.

[4] This theory was later taken up by Ed Parish Sanders. Cf. E.P. Sanders, *Paul, the Law, and the Jewish People* (Minneapolis, 1983), 18: 'The subject of Galatians is not whether or not humans, abstractly conceived, can by good deeds earn enough merit to be declared righteous at the judgment; it is the condition on which Gentiles enter the people of God'.

[5] Norman T. Wright, 'Justification: yesterday, today, and forever', *Journal of the Evangelical Theological Society* **54** (2011), 49–63, at 53.

[6] E.P. Sanders, *Paul and Palestinian Judaism: A Comparison for Patterns of Religion* (London, 1977).

7 English translations from the New Revised Standard Version (1989).
8 E.P. Sanders, *Paul and Palestinian Judaism*, 443.
9 James D.G. Dunn, 'New Perspective on Paul', in J.D.G. Dunn, *The New Perspective on Paul: collected essays*, Wissenschaftliche Untersuchungen zum Neuen Testament 185 (Tübingen, 2005), 89–110, at 95–101, with references on p. 100 to 1 Macc 1:62–63; Dan 1:8–16; Tob 1:10–13; Judith 10:5; 12:1–20. J.D.G. Dunn, *The theology of Paul the Apostle*, New Testament Theology (Grand Rapids, 1993), 354–66.
10 Charles E.B. Cranfield, '"The Works of the Law" in the Epistle to the Romans', *Journal for the Study of the New Testament* 43 (1991), 89–101, at 91–4.
11 J.D.G. Dunn, 'Yet once more, "The Works of the Law": a response', *Journal for the Study of the New Testament* 46 (1992), 99–117, at 109 (italics by J.D.G. Dunn).
12 *Ibid.*, 106.
13 According to William Wrede, *Paulus*, RV I 5–6 (Halle, 1904), reprinted in Karl Heinrich Rengstorf (ed.), *Das Paulusbild in der neueren deutschen Forschung*, Wege der Forschung 24 (Darmstadt, 1982), 1–97, at 67, 71–2, Paul's theology was a theology of mission; the theory of justification was a theory of fighting against Judaism. Albert Schweitzer, *Die Mystik des Apostels Paulus* (Tübingen, 1930) (UTB 1091), ed. Werner Georg Kümmel (Tübingen, 1981), 220. Schweitzer described the doctrine of justification as 'Nebenkrater der paulinischen Mystik' ('secondary crater of Pauline mysticism').
14 John Chrysostom, *in Romans* (PG 60, 446); Theodoret of Cyrus, *in Romans* (PG 82, 85 B); Augustine, *div. qu.* 76,2 (CCL 44 A, 220); the Venerable Bede, *in Iacobum* 2,20 (CC.SL 121, 199).
15 Origen, *in Romans* 3,9 (FC 2,2, 136): *indulgentia namque non futurorum, sed praeteritorum criminum datur*.
16 Theodoret, *in Galatas* (PG 82, 473 A).
17 Concerning this paragraph cf. Klaus Haacker, 'Verdienste und Grenzen der "neuen Perspektive" der Paulus-Auslegung', in Michael Bachmann (ed.), *Lutherische und Neue Paulus-Perspektive, Beiträge zu einem Schlüsselproblem der gegenwärtigen exegetischen Diskussion* (WUNT 182) (Tübingen, 2005), 1–15, at 9–11; Mark A. Seifrid, 'Paul's use of righteousness language against its Hellenistic background', in D.A. Carson, P.T. O'Brien and M.A. Seifrid (eds), *Justification and Variegated Nomism* (WUNT II 181) (Tübingen/Grand Rapids, 2004), 39–74, at 67–74. Seifrid offers a very nuanced portrayal of intra-Reformation divergences.
18 Volker Stolle, *Luther und Paulus. Die exegetischen und hermeneutischen Grundlagen der lutherischen Rechtfertigungslehre im Paulinismus Luthers*, ABG 10 (Leipzig, 2002), 223–7.
19 *Ibid.*, 44.
20 Timothy George, 'Modernizing Luther, domesticating Paul: another perspective', in Carson *et al.* (eds), *Justification and Variegated Nomism*, vol. I (WUNT II 181) (Tübingen, 2004), 437–63, at 445.
21 WA 40/I, 589, 25–28. Cf. also WA 40/II, 282, 23: 'If I only look at myself, I am gone' (*Si vero in me tantum intueor Christo excluso, actum est de me*). Stendahl and other adherents to the New Perspective are neglecting Luther's *extra nos* (George, 'Modernizing Luther', 446).
22 Wilfried Härle, 'Paulus und Luther. Ein kritischer Blick auf die "New Perspective"', *Zeitschrift für Theologie und Kirche* 103 (2006), 362–93, at 380–2.
23 WA 40/I, 304, 30–2: 'Together with Paul, we constantly confess: either Christ died in

vain, or the Law does not justify. Christ, however, did not die in vain. Therefore the Law does not justify' (*Nos vero cum Paulo constanter affirmamus ... aut Christum gratis mortuum esse, aut legem non iustificare. Sed Christus non est gratis mortuus, Ergo lex non iustificat*).

[24] WA 40/I, 334, 34–7: the following passing mention, based on Acts 10:11 and actualised for the Galatian conflict, reveals that Luther was aware even of a possible protest of Jewish-born believers against grace for the Gentiles: 'We who are God's people, vexed (i.e. by the law) all the day. Those, however, who are not God's people, who did not have the law nor did any time something good, are put on a par with us' (*Nos enim qui sumus populus Dei, vexati sumus tota die, Illi vero qui non sunt populus Dei, qui legem non habent neque unquam boni quidquam fecerunt, redduntur nobis pares*).

[25] WA 40/I, 415, 12–20.

[26] Cf. M. Meiser, *Galater*, Novum Testamentum Patristicum 9 (Göttingen, 2007), 41–3, concerning Galatians.

[27] WA 40/I, 334, 34–7.

[28] Cf. Heinz Schreckenberg, *Die christlichen Adversus-Judaeos-Texte und ihr literarisches und historisches Umfeld (1.–11. Jh.)*, EHS 23/172 (4th edn, Frankfurt/Bern, 1999).

[29] Cf. Stolle, *Luther und Paulus*, 289.

[30] Heiko A. Obermann, *Wurzeln des Antisemitismus: Christenangst und Judenplage im Zeitalter von Humanismus und Reformation* (Berlin, 1981), 125.

[31] Cf. WA 56, 272, 17; 347, 2–4, 9–11.

[32] Cf. WA 40/I, 19–21: *Papa iubet respicere non deum promittentem, non Christum Pontificem, sed nostra opera et merita. Ibi necessario sequitur dubitatio et desperatio, Illic vero certitudo et gaudium Spiritus, Quia in Deo haeret, qui mentiri non potest*.

[33] Augustinus, *ench.* 23, 91 (CCL 46, 98); *div. qu.* 70 (CSEL 44 A, 197); *civ.* 19,4 (CSEL 40/2, 375); *serm.* 30,6 (CCL 41, 386).

[34] WA 40/II, 89, 16–18.

[35] Werner G. Kümmel, 'Römer 7 und die Bekehrung des Paulus', reprinted in Kümmel, *Römer 7 und das Bild des Menschen im Neuen Testament*, TB 53 (München, 1974), IX–160.

[36] WA 40/I, 309, 23–8.

[37] Cf. Stolle, *Luther und Paulus*, 236–7.

[38] WA 40/I, 55, 8–15. Theodore Graebner, *A Commentary on the Epistle of St Paul to the Galatians by Martin Luther. A New Abridged Translation* (Grand Rapids, MI, 1937), 6.

[39] WA 40/I, 56, 16–24. Similarly cf. WA 40/I 353, 26–30: *Idem et nos hodie possumus dicere ad eos qui iactant se Evangelicos et ex Tyrannide papae liberatos esse: Num vicistis Tyrannidem Papae et libertatem in Christo adepti estis per Phanaticos spiritus aut per nos qui praedicavimus fidem in Christumn? Hic si veritatem fateri volunt: coguntur dicere: Certe per praedicationem fidei*.

[40] WA 40/II, 170, 27–31.

[41] WA 40/I, 126, 20–24.

[42] WA 40/I, 134, 15–20.

[43] WA 40/I, 143, 30–144, 29.

[44] WA 40/I, 152, 13. Luther did not identify the contents of the texts of Acts 15 and Gal 2. Acts 15 is a record of an event which took place much earlier (WA 40/I, 151, 31–152, 13).

[45] WA 40/I, 153, 31–154, 17.

[46] Also, according to some voices in modern scholarship, the restriction of the syntagma

'Works of the Law' to boundary-markers in the line of James Dunn is impossible when we remember Gal 3:10, Gal 5:3 and Rom 3:20. The vigorously debated parallel 4QMMT C 27 does not imply a holistic dimension of this formula. It differs herein from Gal 2:16; cf. C. Landmesser, 'Umstrittener Paulus. Die gegenwärtige Diskussion um die paulinische Theologie', *Zeitschrift für Theologie und Kirche* **105** (2008), 387–410, at 404–5. Cf., however, also J.D.G. Dunn, '4QMMT and Galatians', *New Testament Studies* **43** (1997), 147–53, at 150: we should take seriously the difference of situation. In 4QMMT, an inner-Jewish debate is encompassed, while in Gal 2:16 we find a general debate between adherents of a position, which in general is denigrating the role of the Law, and their opponents.

[47] WA 40/I, 216, 18–217, 16.
[48] WA 40/I, 218, 12–219, 33.
[49] WA 40/I, 275, 29–30. Paul here does not speak of crucifying the flesh but of that higher crucifying wherein sin, devil and death are crucified in Christ and in him. By his faith in Christ, he is crucified with Christ. Hence these evils are crucified and dead unto him.
[50] WA 40/I, 280, 14–281, 20.
[51] WA 40/I, 329, 13–16.
[52] WA 40/I, 351, 29–30.
[53] WA 40/I, 481, 13–16.
[54] WA 6, 24, 12–15 (= Theses 9–11).
[55] WA 40/I, 533, 31–534, 12.
[56] WA 40/II, 98, 20–30.
[57] WA 40/II, 102, 17–103, 28. With regard to his staying in a monastery cf. also WA 40/III, 91, 32–92, 31, referring also to Johann von Staupitz consoling him (WA 40/II, 92, 24–29).
[58] The apostle deals with the problem of why a life of bearing fruit for God should not be possible by obeying the Torah. His answer: as soon as a human being learns the commandment, s/he is inclined to contradict, and the human being before Christ and remote from Christ is not able to overcome the forces of sin her/himself. Sanders correctly emphasises that Paul charges sin, not the Torah, but it is not correct to neglect the fundamental anthropological dimension.
[59] Cf. Hans Hübner, 'Pauli Theologiae proprium', *New Testament Studies* **26** (1980), 445–73, at 463; Eduard Lohse, 'Theologie der Rechtfertigung im kritischen Disput—zu einigen neuen Perspektiven in der Interpretation der Theologie des Apostels Paulus', *Göttingische Gelehrte Anzeigen* **249** (1997), 66–81, at 70; Seifrid, 'Paul's use of righteousness language against its Hellenistic background', 64; Friedrich W. Horn, 'Juden und Heiden. Aspekte der Verhältnisbestimmung in den paulinischen Briefen. Ein Gespräch mit Krister Stendahl', in Michael Bachmann (ed.), *Lutherische und Neue Paulus-Perspektive, Beiträge zu einem Schlüsselproblem der gegenwärtigen exegetischen Diskussion*, WUNT 182 (Tübingen, 2005), 17–39, at 31; Douglas J. Moo, *Galatians*, BECNT (Grand Rapids, 2013), 159; Jens Schröter, 'Der Mensch zwischen Wollen und Tun. Erwägungen zu Römer 7 im Licht der "New Perspective on Paul"', in Paul-Gerhard Klumbies and David S. du Toit (eds), *Paulus—Werk und Wirkung. FS Lindemann* (Tübingen, 2013), 195–223, at 220.
[60] Landmesser, 'Umstrittener Paulus', 404–5.
[61] Christine Gerber, 'Blicke auf Paulus. Die New Perspective on Paul in der jüngeren

Diskussion', *Verkündigung und Forschung* **55** (2010), 45–60, at 59.

[62] Rudolf Bultmann, *Theologie des Neuen Testaments* (9th edn, ed. Otto Merk) (Tübingen, 1984), 188–9. Cf., however, Luther, WA 40/I, 396, 34–397, 13: *Sunt ergo omnino duae pugnantes sententiae Pauli et Mosi; Pauli: Quicunque fecerint opera Legis, maledicti sund; Mosi: Quincunque non fecerint opera legis, maledicti sunt.* Afterwards this antagonism is resolved; however, no one is able to fulfil the law, cf. Rom 7; Psalm 143:2 (WA 40/I, 408, 22–29).

[63] WA 39/I, 177, 1 (= Thesis 34).

[64] WA 39/I, 176, 33–35 (= Thesis 32).

[65] Dieter Sänger, 'Die Adresse des Galaterbriefs. Neue (?) Überlegungen zu einem alten Problem', in D. Sänger, *Schrift—Tradition—Evangelium. Studien zum frühen Judentum und zur paulinischen Theologie* (Neukirchen-Vluyn, 2016), 229–74, at 274.

[66] Cf. Meiser, *Galater*, 111 (re. Gal 2:19); 114–16 (re. Gal 2:20); 168–70 (re. Gal 3:27).

[67] Cf. also Morna D. Hooker, 'Paul and covenantal nomism', in M.D. Hooker and S.G. Wilson (eds), *Paul and Paulinism* (London, 1982), 47–56, at 55. 'What Sanders fails to bring out is the inner logic which leads Paul to argue that the death and resurrection of Christ mean the end of the reign of the Law.'

[68] Landmesser, 'Umstrittener Paulus', 400.

[69] WA 40/I, 285, 24–27; Haacker, 'Verdienste und Grenzen der "neuen Perspektive"', 11.

[70] WA 40/I, 282, 16–23.

[71] In his early lessons on Galatians, Luther notices the allusion to Psalm 143:2 (WA 2, 493, 15–18). In his great commentary from 1535 (WA 40/I, 239, 12–246, 28) he does not!

[72] D. Sänger, '"Das Gesetz ist unser παιδαγωγός geworden bis zu Christus" (Gal 3,24). Zum Verständnis des Gesetzes im Galaterbrief', in D. Sänger, *Von der Bestimmtheit des Anfangs. Studien zu Jesus, Paulus und zum frühchristlichen Schriftverständnis* (Neukirchen, 2007), 158–84, at 183–4.

[73] Cf. Stolle, *Luther und Paulus*, 473: Luther's *extra nos* is an important corrective in order to avoid the confusion between Christian faith and pious mental state.

[74] 'When our Lord and Master Jesus Christ said, "Repent" (Mt 4:17), he willed the entire life of believers to be one of repentance' (WA I, 233, 10–11).

[75] Volker Leppin, *Die fremde Reformation. Luthers mystische Wurzeln* (München, 2016), 56–7.

[76] Berndt Hamm, *Der frühe Luther* (Tübingen, 2010), 98.

[77] WA 40/II, 2, 28–4, 29.

[78] Hamm, *Der frühe Luther*, 108.

[79] WA 2, 492 20f.; WA 39/I, 83, 32–3 (= Thesis 31).

[80] Cf. Luther on Gal 5:6: *Opera fieri dicit ex fide per Charitatem, non iustificari hominem per Charitatem* (WA 40/II, 35, 24–25) … *Charitatem vero facit* (e.g. Paulus) *fidei velut instrumentum, per quod operetur* (WA 40/II 36, 13–14). Cf. also the dilution of an objection based on Luke 7:47, 'her sins, which were many, have been forgiven; hence she has shown great love': *Christus loquitur de dilectione, quae manat ex fide* (WA 39/I, 91, 17–19).

[81] WA 40/I, 207, 17–18: *Qui igitur bene novit discernere Evangelium a lege, is gratias agat Deo et sciat se esse Theologum.* Cf. further WA 40/I, 336, 32–5.

[82] WA 40/I, 40, 16–22; WA 40/I, 292, 22–293, 17; WA 40/I, 393, 21–9; WA 40/I 409, 30–410, 15.

7
Challenging memories—the Reformation in France and the Huguenots in Ireland

Ruth Whelan

The quotation from the Epistle to the Galatians, 'For freedom Christ has set us free', chosen as the theme for the Reformation Quincentenary event in Dublin is a wonderful theological statement and it recalls Luther's treatise *On the Freedom of a Christian* (1520). Nevertheless, in these two thumbnail sketches of the Reformation in France and the Huguenots in Ireland it would be misleading to evoke the theme of freedom without contextualising it and even calling it into question. For the past is not always as straightforward as we like to make it, and when we remember it, as Miroslav Volf points out, 'it breaks into the present and gains a new lease on life'.[1]

Not that French Protestants are shy about presenting the Reformation in France as one of the early stages in the great French and European struggle for freedom. At the beginning of the year of commemoration, François Clavairoly, the president of the Fédération protestante de France, made the following remark in an article entitled 'Je crois que Jésus était un peu un protestant d'origine':

> 'Certes, la Réforme emporte avec elle toute cette dynamique civilisationnelle, construisant de nouveaux horizons de pensée, et modelant l'Europe dans un esprit de délibération et de liberté démocratique'.[2]

The French are not alone in taking this view. In November 2016, when the Reformation bus began its tour in Geneva (where I happened to be visiting professor at the Institut d'histoire de la Réformation), journalists, politicians and even academics all sang from the same hymn-sheet, unambiguously attributing the origin of modernity to the Reformation. In January 2017 Patsy McGarry picked up the same tune in the *Irish Times*, when he observed that the Reformation led to 'the ascendancy of the individual, the existence of democracy as we now know it, and the evolution, geopolitically, of "the West"'.[3]

These generalisations contain some elements of truth, of course, but they also fall short of it. The question framed in another context by the theologian

Lytta Basset may be applied to this one-sided way of remembering the Reformation:

> 'Comment pouvons-nous discerner que nous n'avons pas pris en compte toute la réalité humaine? Précisément quand nous fuyons dans les idéaux—une histoire dorée, mythique, une société idéale, une éducation modèle, qui n'ont jamais existé.'[4]

The unquestioned association of the Protestant Reformation with liberty, democracy and modernity is an epic narrative, a mythical history that sweeps away the shadow side of the Reformation, which is not just a success story, as Bishop Heinrich Bedford-Strohm, the presiding bishop of the Evangelische Kirche in Germany, observed at the start of the commemorations.[5] Nor is it a story of linear progress towards the values of our modernity, as my two thumbnail sketches will demonstrate, however briefly.

Why is it important to challenge the epic narrative of the Reformation, which was so often repeated during the Luther 500 commemorations? Commemoration is a collective act of memory and as such it requires of us that we 'remember *rightly*', to borrow another phrase from Miroslav Volf.[6] That is to say, there is an ethical dimension to remembering and commemoration which involves a commitment to being truthful about the whole past, including its shadow side. I will return to the theme of the ethics of memory very briefly in conclusion.

From Reformation to Revocation: Protestantism in France in the sixteenth and seventeenth centuries

The history of French Protestantism in this period may be organised into four sequences, beginning with the emergence of a Protestant minority around 1525 and ending with its willed exclusion from the kingdom 160 years later,[7] for it was the Revocation of the Edict of Nantes in 1685, and the escalating persecution which preceded it, that brought the Huguenots to Ireland.

An emerging, clandestine minority: c. 1525–60

Although Luther's books were censured by the University of Paris in April 1521, and then forbidden, they were known to be in circulation in the mid-1520s among small groups of educated people. Their impact was limited, however; the impetus for reform came more from a group referred to as the *Évangéliques* who were protected by Marguerite de Navarre, herself an author and sister to François I, king of France. Among them were the humanists Jacques Lefèvre d'Étaples and Guillaume Briçonnet, bishop of Meaux, men influenced by Erasmus and the movement known as *devotio moderna*, who promoted or carried out the translation of the Bible into French and were imbued with a Christocentric spirituality. Their objective (like Luther's) was to reform the church from within by recruiting humanists who, having acquired a deep knowledge of Scripture, would be equipped to preach the Gospel in the vernacular to the people. It was this biblical humanism that brought Jean Calvin into contact with the *Évangéliques* between 1527 and 1532. Clément Marot, the first translator of the Psalms, soon to be sung in Reformed worship, was also part of the network connected to Marguerite de Navarre.

The imprisonment of François I by Charles V in 1525, after the French defeat at the battle of Pavia during the Italian War (1521–6), and Marguerite de Navarre's departure for Spain to negotiate his release left the biblical humanists without political protection. Voices calling for repression of the 'damnable Lutheran heresy' won the day; some of the biblical humanists in the Meaux circle were arrested or fled for safety. In February 1526 the *parlement* of Paris issued an order forbidding any Lutheran or other teaching that questioned Catholic dogma and outlawing the sale or possession of the Old or New Testaments in French. The first suspected 'Lutheran', an Augustinian monk named Jean Vallière, was burned at the stake in Paris in 1523; other executions followed. And the repression continued to escalate, particularly after the *affaire des placards* (17 October 1534), when posters virulently critical of Catholic dogma appeared overnight in Paris (including on the door to the king's bedchamber), Amboise, Orléans and Tours. Calvin left France for Basel and later Geneva, where he came under the influence of Guillaume Farel, and from there to Strasbourg, finally returning in 1541 to Geneva, where he remained until his death.

Despite the severe repression in France, conventicles continued to meet clandestinely in Paris and other towns. Their members were drawn mostly from the educated élite but also from the clergy. In the 1540s they were increasingly influenced by the separatist model of reform (as opposed to the humanist model of reform from within) that was being elaborated in Switzerland, and also by treatises written by Calvin urging them to come out into the open, to 'flee from Egypt' and break definitively with 'papist' practices. In the 1550s the 'Calvinisation' of the reform movement in France proceeded apace. By September 1555 the first church reformed on the Calvinist model had been founded in Paris. Others followed over the next five years in towns throughout the country, at first in their tens and ultimately in their hundreds. In 1559 the first clandestine synod was called in Paris to draw up a constitution on the Genevan

Pl. 1—Lucas Cranach the Elder, *Martin Luther* (1520).

Pl. 2—St Finian's Lutheran Church, Dublin.

Pl. 3—The opening of the Conference: (l–r) Dr Gesa Thiessen, Pr Martin Sauter, Prof. Jürgen Barkhoff, CoI Archbishop of Dublin Michael Jackson, Pr Stephan Arras, Provost Patrick Prendergast, Revd Dr Donald Watts, Prof. Ruth Whelan, RC Bishop of Limerick Brendan Leahy, Nuncio Charles Browne, Peter Adams, Prof. Kajsa Ahlstrand and Prof. Maureen Junker-Kenny.

Pl. 4—The Reformation 2017 Travelling Exhibition, Trinity College, Dublin.

Pl. 5—The Reformation 2017 Travelling Exhibition, truck interior.

Pl. 6—(l–r) Kajsa Ahlstrand, Volker Leppin, Maureen Junker-Kenny and Graeme Murdock.

Pl. 7—The Reformation 2017 Travelling Exhibition, Trinity College, Dublin.

Pl. 8—(l–r) John McCafferty, Kajsa Ahlstrand, Ruth Whelan, Martin Meiser and Maureen Junker-Kenny.

Pl. 9—Gesa Thiessen.

Pl. 10—Interior of the Reformation 2017 Travelling Exhibition, Trinity College, Dublin.

Pl. 11— Interior of the Reformation 2017 Travelling Exhibition, Trinity College, Dublin.

Pl. 12—The Symposium reception, Trinity College, Dublin.

Pl. 13—'Power and Belief: The Reformation at 500' exhibition in the Long Room, Trinity College Library, 2017.

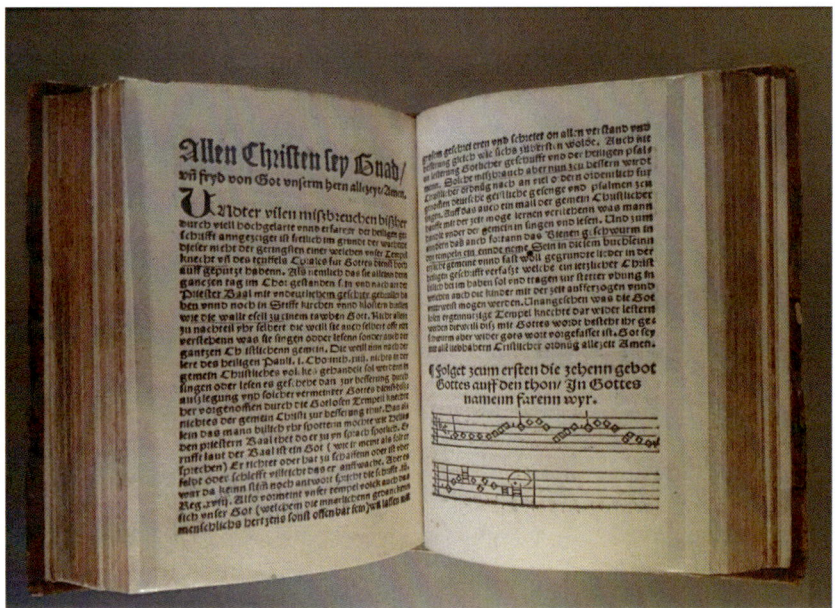

Pl. 14—'Power and Belief: The Reformation at 500' exhibition in the Long Room, Trinity College Library, 2017.

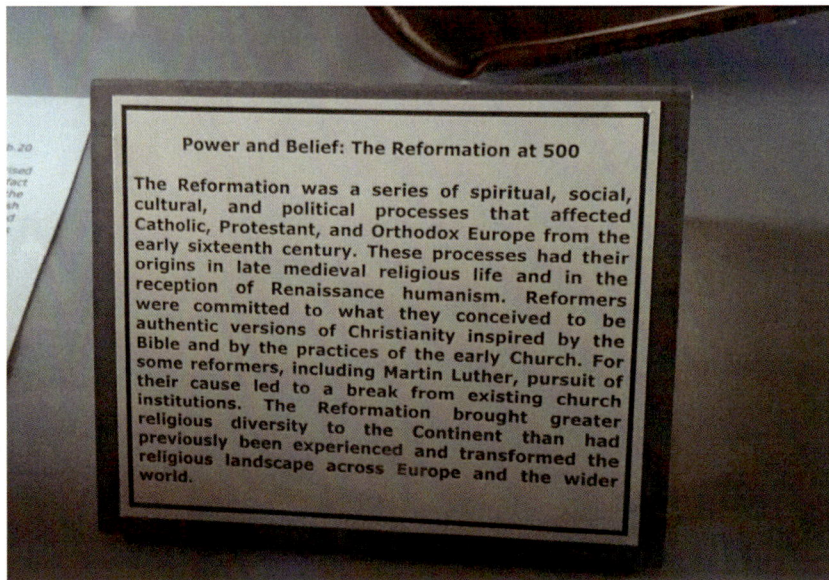

Pl. 15—'Power and Belief: The Reformation at 500' exhibition in the Long Room, Trinity College Library, 2017.

Pl. 16—Reformation 1517–2017 Commemoration Service at St Finian's Lutheran Church, Dublin: (l–r) Prädikant Frithjof Berndsen, Pr Martin Sauter, Revd Damian McNeice, RC Archbishop of Dublin Diarmuid Martin and Pr Stephan Arras.

Pl. 17—Pr Stephan Arras and Dr Stephanie Springer (EKD).

Pl. 18—Dr Stephanie Springer (EKD) and Dr Hans Ulrich Anke (EKD).

Pl. 19—Dr Markus Grimmeisen, Prof. Wolfgang Marx and Prof. Werner Blau.

Pl. 20—Volunteers from Germany accompanying the Travelling Exhibition at the Commemoration Service, St Finian's Church.

Pl. 21—Reception in Lutherhaus after the Commemoration Service at St Finian's Church.

Pl. 22—Dr Helga Robinson-Hammerstein, 7 May 1938–26 February 2018.

model of church *Discipline*. It was deemed important to create a common structure for these conventicles emerging from clandestinity.

The structure created was federal, designed to hold together the emerging churches in a network but to grant priority to none, in an explicit rejection of the hierarchical structure of the Roman communion. In practice, however, the Reformed church in Paris came to have priority: it was, after all, in the capital city and enjoyed proximity to the court. All ministers were considered equal, although the most gifted preachers, those who published extensively or were based in Paris, came to exercise greater moral authority. Church governance was exercised collectively by means of a pyramidal presbytero-synodal structure. At the local level, the consistory was a committee made up of the ordained minister(s) and elders elected by the heads of household from among themselves for a limited period. At the regional level, the colloquy was a regularly convened meeting of ministers from churches in the region, accompanied by at least one elder, to discuss matters pertaining to church discipline or the moral oversight of the congregations concerned. At the provincial and national levels were the synods, where those in attendance, whether ministers or elders (exclusively male), each had a vote. In theory, any layman could become an elder and exercise leadership in these churches. In practice, although the levels of literacy were higher among Protestants (the word entered the French language in 1546) than Catholics in early modern France, the majority of lay elders were notables drawn from the educated élite, the landed aristocracy or the minor nobility.

The only extant image of the interior of a Reformed church from this period is the picture painted in 1569–70 by Jean Perrissin of the *Temple de Paradis* in Lyons, which was constructed in 1564 (Fig. 1). Its architecture offers an immediate insight into the religious culture of the newly founded 'Calvinist' churches in France. The building expresses the Reformed doctrine of *Sola Scriptura*, the Bible as the central authority in faith and practice, whose meaning is explicated by the pastor in the vernacular to the people through the regular meetings of the church (twice on Sundays and at least once mid-week, although this image is of a wedding). At the centre of the edifice, which was constructed as a rotunda, is the pulpit, which is surrounded on the ground floor and in the gallery by plain wooden benches (galleries were a constant feature in all Reformed temples of the period, although many were built as basilicas).[8] There are no obstacles between the faithful and the preacher. Visitors often commented on the absence of central pillars in temples (as they were called), which were obviously constructed to facilitate hearing by a maximum number of people, who also had a clear view of the pastor from everywhere in the building.

Fig. 1—The interior of the *Temple de Paradis* in Lyons by Jean Perrissin, currently on display in the Musée international de la Réforme, Geneva.

The emerging Reformed churches taught (and still do) that there are two sacraments, baptism and the Lord's Supper, both instituted by Jesus Christ, but neither baptismal font nor communion table are in evidence here. They were set up in the temple as required (four times a year for Communion) and placed underneath the raised pulpit, thereby signifying the Reformed teaching that sacraments are not independent of the Word but rather outward and visible signs that confirm and seal the Word to the covenant community of the church. Note the absence of religious art, ritual objects or decoration (considered idolatrous), with two exceptions: on the first gallery behind the pulpit hangs an escutcheon with the royal and municipal coat of arms, signs of the loyalty and submission of French Protestants to their king. Affixed on either side are two tablets of the Law, on which the Decalogue is engraved—another visible sign of the centrality and authority of the Word. The responses of the congregation (not heard or seen here) took the form of unaccompanied singing of psalms, 'en langue commune et connue du peuple', as psalm-singing in Calvin's view

Fig. 2–Geographical distribution of reformed churches in France in the sixteenth century.[9]

had 'grande force et vigueur pour émouvoir et enflammer le cœur des hommes pour invoquer et louer Dieu d'un zèle plus véhément et ardent'.[10] Finally, the seated dog and the hats still on the men's heads indicate that the architectural space of the temple is not in itself sacred (the one man at the back with his hat off may be fanning himself in the heat). When they prayed, early French Protestant men removed their hats, signifying in that simple yet theological gesture the sacredness only of that interaction between humans and the invisible yet present God of the covenant, whose tables of the Law hung prominently above their heads.

Initially, the protection of the royal family and the desire to reform the church from within had nourished the hope that the Reformation would become a national phenomenon. The repression and persecution that ensued meant, however, that over the course of the sixteenth century Protestants in France became definitively a minority: in 1562 they made up approximately 10% of a total population of some eighteen to twenty million; by the end of the century that proportion had shrunk to 7–8%. The geographical distribution of Protestants in the kingdom was strikingly uneven, with almost two-thirds residing in what is known as the 'Huguenot crescent' in the south-west, south and south-east of the country (Fig. 2).

This geographical distribution also had a cultural dimension. Protestantism in France was mostly, although not entirely, an urban phenomenon, with those living in the northern half of the kingdom being clearly in the minority (with the exception of parts of Normandy) in the towns where they lived, while those in the 'Huguenot crescent' were often in the majority, especially in the large urban centres of La Rochelle, Montauban and Nîmes. Consequently, during the wars of religion in the sixteenth century, and the later resistance to enforced conversion after 1685, the most vehement opposition to the anti-Protestant policies of successive monarchies was to come from the south of the kingdom.

A politicised minority (1560–1629) and a history of violence[11]
The emergence from clandestinity of the Reformed churches met with a renewed determination on the part of the monarchy to detect and punish any and all apprehended in prohibited 'secret conventicles'. As a result, from 1560 French Protestants formed a specifically militant party with political objectives. They were widely designated Huguenots from this time, possibly as a derivative from the German *Eidgenossen* (pronounced 'Eignots') or confederates, a term that had subversive connotations in a monarchy.[12] The growing power of the Huguenot party, which was led by princes of the blood, caused the queen-regent, Catherine de Médicis, to opt for a politics of conciliation and limited civil toleration of the Protestant minority, but those policies were opposed by the Catholic majority, and particularly by the powerful Guise family, who in the 1570s headed the Catholic (or Holy) League with its crusading anti-Protestantism.

The first of eight civil and religious wars was triggered by the massacre of several dozen Protestants whom some of the duke of Guise's associates discovered worshipping according to Reformed rites in a barn in Wassy (1 March 1562) and by the political aftermath of that massacre. Over 36 years (1562–98) the Huguenot party engaged in armed conflict with the monarchy and the Guise family, a conflict that left France in a state of war for decades, mobilised thousands of men on each side and affected the whole population of the kingdom. Each of the wars concluded with a peace treaty and general amnesty, together with guarantees granted to the Protestant minority of civil toleration and freedom of conscience and worship (to a greater or lesser degree in the different treaties). The terms of the peace treaties were difficult to implement, however, and the periods of toleration were short-lived until the Edict of Nantes (1598), promulgated under Henri IV (formerly Henri de Navarre), brought the wars of religion to an end.

During the long years of war, apart from the expected military acts of violence, there was verbal and physical violence, on both sides of the conflict, which left its mark on contemporaries because of its unprecedented atrocity. There was a difference in kind, however, between the violent acts of Protestants and those carried out by Catholics. With the exception of the massacre of priests, monks and notables in Nîmes on Michaelmas night, 29 September 1567 ('la Michelade'), Protestants tended to engage in iconoclasm or acts of derision, designed to publicise their mockery of Catholic ritual and sacred objects. They beheaded statues and covered them in dung, stamped on relics and flung them into heaps of manure, or tied a priest to an ass backwards and paraded him through the town of Montauban on Christmas Day 1561. In the symbolic world of early modern society, they were demonstrating the association which they believed existed between idolatry and filth, or turning the priest into a reverse, parodic image of the Saviour Who rode on a donkey.

Catholic violence tended to be carried out by crowds who engaged in large-scale killing of men, women and children and disposed of the bodies in rivers or left them to rot without burial. Such acts, often accompanied by mutilation of corpses, were motivated by the conviction that heresy was a pollutant, even a contagion, which had to be eliminated from the body politic, and the mutilation was intended to make visible on the body physical the diabolical impulse of the heretic.[13] However, it was the mass murder in Paris on St Bartholomew's Day, 24 August 1572—and in the following weeks and, indeed, months in the provinces—that sent shock waves through the Protestant community in France. It signalled the failure of the Reformation in France to establish a comprehensive national church that would embrace all the people of the kingdom. As a result, it was the direct cause of the first 'Refuge', as it is called—that is, the voluntary exile of thousands of Protestants, who fled to England, Holland and Switzerland. Its atrocity marked the individual and communal memories not just of French but also of European Protestants, including those in Ireland. For them it became a symbol of Catholic treachery and fanaticism.

A minority recognised by the Edict of Nantes (1598–1685)
The Edict of Nantes is often referred to as Henri IV's 'great achievement', as it caused the warring parties in the kingdom to lay down arms and accept, however reluctantly, a negotiated peace settlement. Under its terms Protestants were granted freedom of conscience and worship, were provided with a strictly limited number of churches and civil liberties and, given the violence exercised against them during the wars, were also permitted to maintain military strongholds or *places de sûreté* for their protection for a period of eight years. The Edict was contested—the *parlement* in Rouen (one of eight charged with administering royal decrees) refused to register it for over a decade—but it provided the terms for a relatively peaceful, if increasingly hostile, coexistence between the Catholic majority and the Protestant minority in France. It did not, however, end armed conflict. A final period of war, known as the 'wars of Rohan' (their leader was Henri II, duc de Rohan), between 1621 and 1629, famously remembered for the siege of La Rochelle, was only brought to an end by the Peace of Alès (28 June 1629). This last treaty reiterated the guarantees of civil toleration, freedom of conscience and worship granted by the Edict of Nantes but prohibited French Protestants from holding political assemblies and deprived them of their political strongholds. The treaty of Alès thereby put an end to the 'Huguenot party' as a political force. Consequently, French Protestants became entirely dependent on the will of the monarch.

Each of the wars of religion had ended with a negotiated peace settlement which anticipated in some respects the terms of the Edict of Nantes, but Henri IV's 'great achievement' had matured in the sobering experience of peacemaking during the civil wars.[14] The Edict inaugurated the legalised coexistence of two confessions in one kingdom, which was a significant departure from the traditional model of religious coexistence, namely the principle of *cujus regio ejus religio*—the religion of the ruler determines the religion of the ruled. It did not, however, grant equality to the two confessions.[15] While it no longer referred to Protestants as heretics but rather as members of a religious denomination, the terminology it imposed signalled the inferior status of the Protestant minority *vis-à-vis* the religion of king and kingdom. Thus the Reformed churches of France, although legally permitted, were henceforth referred to as the *religion prétendue réformée*, or 'the pretended or so-called Reformed religion'. Furthermore, the concept of toleration at work in the Edict was the negative one of its time: it meant putting up with what could not be prevented.

Tolerating French Protestants was the lesser of two evils (the other being civil war), but the religious unity of the kingdom remained the ideal to be pursued. Consequently, although the Edict was declared 'perpetual and irrevocable', certain expressions in the preamble to it revealed that confessional coexistence was envisioned as a provisional measure on the way to religious reunification.[16] In a word, although the pacification of Nantes was exceptional because of its duration (over 80 years), it locked French Protestants and their churches into an *intolerant* coexistence.

Towards the elimination of the Protestant minority
After 1629 and the dismantling of the military force of the 'Huguenot party', French Protestants tended to stress their absolute loyalty to their king, whom they viewed as their sole protection against a hostile Catholic clergy who never ceased regarding them as heretics to be brought back into the fold. During the reign of Louis XIII and the minority reign of his successor, some anti-Protestant measures were taken to undermine the religious and civil liberties of the Huguenots, notably by abolishing their churches and schools, where possible, and by prohibiting them from holding national synods after 1659. But it was from 1661, with the personal reign of Louis XIV, that the drive began to restrict or eliminate the provisions granted by the Edict of Nantes by interpreting and applying it *à la rigueur* (strictly, narrowly or stringently).

Between 1661 and 1668, 250 of the existing 860 Reformed churches were closed or razed to the ground. Psalm-singing outside temples (e.g. while working or travelling) was prohibited. Burials were only permitted at dawn or dusk, and priests were authorised to attend Protestants on their deathbeds in order to urge them to convert. From 1669 to 1679 this legal harassment went hand in hand with missions held by Catholic clergy with the aim of persuading Protestants to abjure their heresy. A fund was created to indemnify those who abjured against loss of income or family support. In response, the Protestant minority went on the defensive. They appealed judicial decisions that went against them, and communicated their objections to the king through their representative at court. Their pastors engaged tirelessly in religious controversy and published their efforts, sometimes in Paris or Rouen but more often in Holland or Switzerland. Exile began to seem the best option; some Protestants left and others began to plan for a future abroad, but in 1669 the first of a series of ordinances (reiterated in 1682, 1685 and 1686) prohibiting French subjects from emigrating without royal permission made exile problematic. Although addressed to all subjects of the Crown, the principal target of these ordinances was the Protestant population.

From 1679, with the conclusion of the Dutch wars, Louis XIV was able

CALLED TO FREEDOM

Fig. 3—A nineteenth-century copy of a 1686 political cartoon of coerced abjuration.

to give his full attention to the reduction of Protestantism within the kingdom. In the years that followed, a plethora of royal *arrêts* banned Protestants from most of the professions (including that of midwife), forbade Catholics from embracing Protestantism and authorised severe penalties for relapsed Protestants (i.e. those who had embraced Catholicism but then abandoned it); any Reformed temple where the 'relapsed' had attended religious services was razed to the ground. The *arrêts* exempted those who abjured from repaying their debts for three years, a measure designed to impoverish their undoubtedly Protestant creditors. Most notoriously of all, the *arrêts* permitted Protestant children aged seven and upwards to abjure. Despite the royal prohibition against emigration, Protestants began sending their children abroad. Many left and others began planning their departure, but the greatest exodus of Protestants from France began in 1681, when soldiers were billeted in their homes with instructions to make as much of a nuisance of themselves as possible.

The *dragonnades*, as they are known (after the word *dragon*, 'soldier'), began in Poitou-Saintonge on the west coast in March 1681, and the results were spectacular. Some 38,000 Protestants abjured in a few months; others fled abroad, bringing tales of the abuse to the countries where they sought refuge and adding the word 'refugee' to the English language. In the few years that followed, 'booted missionaries' were also billeted on Protestants in the towns and villages of the 'Huguenot crescent', with similarly dramatic results. Often referred to as 'the great *dragonnade* of the South', it ravaged the Béarn (22,000 abjurations), Dauphiné and Vivarais (50,000 abjurations); in Montpellier 6,000 Protestants abjured in three days at the end of September 1685. By that autumn, officials had reported some 300,000–400,000 abjurations to the court, making it opportune to revoke the Edict of Nantes. The escalating persecution over the previous decades had eroded the numbers of adherents of the 'so-called Reformed religion' to approximately 4% of the population, and reports from the provinces indicated that the majority of them had embraced the king's religion. There was therefore no further need for the provisions made at Nantes for the Protestant minority, or so it was claimed.

The impact of the Edict of Revocation, signed at Fontainebleau on 17 October 1685 (and registered by the *parlement* of Paris five days later), on the Protestant communities of France was immediate. Pastors were given fourteen days to leave the country and forced to leave their children over the age of seven behind, in the mistaken belief that if the heads were cut off, the body of believers would perish. Approximately 20% of ordained ministers chose abjuration over exile, but the majority left France for Holland (over 50%), England or Switzerland. Over the same period of time, French Reformed temples were razed to the ground, and some of the buildings of their academies and schools were transferred into Catholic ownership. Assembling for worship in any place whatsoever was prohibited, even in private homes and certainly on the sites of the razed temples, where some had initially tried to congregate. The prohibition on emigration was reiterated, but the punishment for those apprehended was changed from imprisonment to a life sentence on the galleys (for men) and prison (for women). Parents were required to have their children baptised in Catholic churches and to send their children to Catholic schools. Similar discriminatory measures were implemented against religious minorities in other European countries, e.g. Catholics in the kingdoms of England and Scotland, and in Ireland, where Catholics were a subjugated majority. But the Edict of Fontainebleau was unique in prohibiting emigration (the *jus emigrandi*) and in denying French Protestants the right to worship in the privacy of their homes, although the text of the Edict had seemed to hold out the possibility of some sort of *devotio privata*. These policies of subjugation, intimidation and even terror had the desired effect initially, but within a year the failure of the Edict of Fontainebleau to bring about its desired outcome was obvious. Not only were the 'New Catholics' not attending Mass or baptising their children but thousands of them had also managed to emigrate to other European—and, for the most part, Protestant—countries.

The Huguenot diaspora

Refugees on the move
Despite the risks involved in emigration and the severe penalties imposed on those who were caught, an estimated 180,000 French Protestants—men, women and children—escaped from France between 1685 and 1715, with two major waves occurring in the years immediately following the Revocation (1685–8) and the Peace of Ryswick (1697). It was the greatest mass movement of population in early modern Europe. The major push factor was, of course, the persecution, with the losses and terror it generated, but there were also pull factors. French churches and communities had been in existence in Holland and England from the time of the first 'Refuge' (after the St Bartholomew's Day massacre), and French was spoken in the neighbouring Swiss cantons. Ironically, the *dragonnades* in 1681 had paved the way for this latest flood of refugees, as funds had been collected and structures put in place to assist French Protestants fleeing at that time. In 1685 and afterwards, some of those countries, e.g. England, Holland and Brandenbourg, even offered incentives (such as tax exemptions, free guild membership or naturalisation) to attract refugees who were skilled workers to settle there.

The routes that the Huguenots took into exile and the countries where they settled were often determined by their own place of origin, financial or social standing, trade or skills and contacts abroad. On the whole, the refugees came from the northern provinces (Normandy, Picardy, Paris and the surrounding area, Champagne or Berry), from provinces on the eastern borders (e.g. Dauphiné) and those on the west coast. In other words, the majority of refugees came from areas in France along coasts or borders, which offered better possibilities for escape, however risky that proved to be. Those leaving from the west coast embarked at Bordeaux, La Rochelle or Nantes for Holland or England. Those escaping from the north or east went overland in carriages, on horseback or on foot, frequently by night and always in disguise, to Holland or Switzerland. They were mostly urban people of some financial means, at least in the beginning. The journey was costly: passage on ships or guides for those fleeing overland had to be paid (often exhorbitantly, given the risks) and the costs of travel met. Of the 100,000 who managed to escape between 1685 and 1687, at least half of them were young men travelling alone or in small groups but planning to send for fiancées, wives,

The Reformation in France and the Huguenots in Ireland

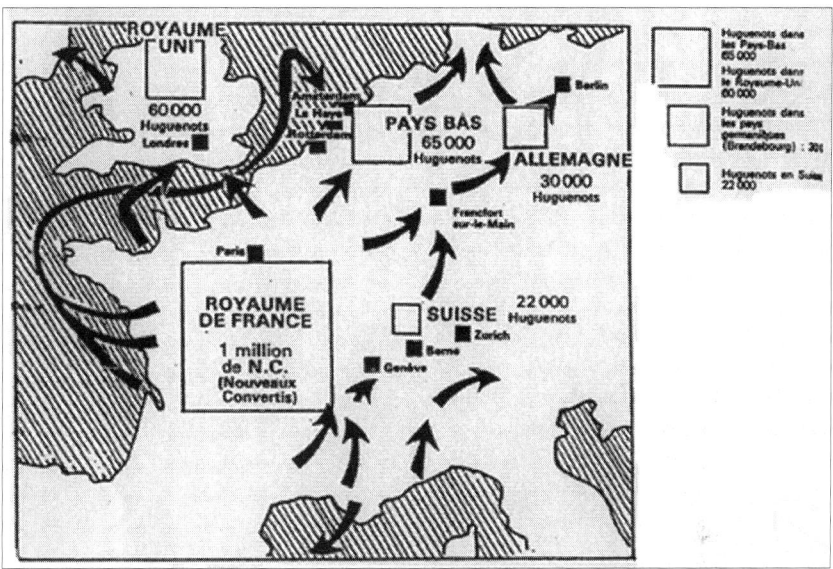

Fig. 4—Principal countries of the second 'Refuge'.[17]

children or parents when they had settled and found ways to make a living.

The map (Fig. 4) shows the movement of Huguenot refugees out of France, although the latest estimates of their numbers and where they settled are slightly different.[18]

As is readily visible, there were four major destinations: England, 50,000–55,000; the United Provinces (Holland), 35,000–50,000; Germany, 38,000–44,000; and Geneva and Switzerland, 20,000 out of a total of 60,000 who passed through the Swiss cantons to other destinations. Their first choice of destination were the cities and ports closest to France—London, Rotterdam or Geneva. Those travelling on to Germany usually went via Frankfurt/Main, which acted as a reception and clearing centre for the refugees. By the end of 1687 reception centres were saturated, in particular Geneva, where on a few days in August 1687 some 350 refugees arrived each day and, over the space of that same year, 12,000 people (the equivalent of 40% of the population of that city state). Often couples with children were given financial assistance before being moved on to other destinations in Switzerland. So from 1689 plans were being put in place to relieve the pressure by redistributing the refugees throughout Protestant Europe, plans that had to be put on hold because of the Nine Years War. In the meantime, the more adventurous refugees, perhaps the more desperate, travelled on to secondary destinations in countries further away from home: to Denmark and Sweden, 3,000; to the Dutch Cape, 178 families; and to British North America, 3,000. Ireland was one such secondary destination.

The Huguenots in Ireland
Estimates vary as to how many Huguenots settled in Ireland: between 5,000 and 8,000 over the whole course of the immigration (from the 1660s to the 1750s), according to current research. Ireland was not an obvious destination for Huguenots, whether they were coming as economic migrants in the 1660s or as refugees from 1681 onwards. Protestants were in the minority and they governed a hostile Catholic and Gaelic-speaking majority, whom they deeply distrusted—as did the refugees, according to the Geneva-born Michel David, pastor of the French community in Kilkenny, according to a comment he made in a letter written in April 1701.

> 'Nous serions bien peu en sûreté (il serait à souhaiter que nous le fussions du moins un peu plus) si les naturels du pays n'étaient pas tenus fort bas … Ils sont tous fort animés de l'esprit du papisme, de sorte qu'ils sont toujours disposés à nous égorger, quelques civils qu'ils nous soient, s'ils avaient ouverture et pouvoir pour cela.'[19]

Consequently, although there is some evidence of spontaneous immigration in 1681 and 1682, not many made their way independently to Ireland. For the Huguenots, the island had the added disadvantage of being 'un endroit si éloigné du reste du monde', as Élie Bouhéreau remarked when moving here in 1697, that he feared he could be of no further use to his contacts on the Continent (he was appointed first Keeper of Archbishop Marsh's Library in 1701!).[20] In reality, then, the Huguenots came to Ireland because the authorities actively recruited them.

There were four successive settlements, each one independent of the others, in the 1660s, 1680s, 1690s and 1750s (the first three are considered here). James Butler, first duke of Ormond, who was appointed lord lieutenant in 1661, instigated the first two settlements. In 1662 he sent agents to France to attract Huguenots to Ireland to assist in the foundation of new industries, particularly for the woollen and linen trades. The Irish parliament passed an 'Act for encouraging protestant-strangers and others, to inhabit and plant in the kingdom of Ireland', whose terms were valid for a period of seven years. The act enabled those who took advantage of it to become naturalised subjects and freemen of the towns and guilds, provided that they took the oaths of Allegiance and Supremacy. Two dozen houses were constructed in Chapelizod, Dublin, to ac-

Fig. 5—Map by Grace Lawless Lee (1936).[21]

commodate them. Woollen manufactures were established in Clonmel and Carrick-on-Suir, but the planned settlement met with only limited success, despite the advantages on offer. Although some 200 families had immigrated by 1668, their numbers had declined sharply ten years later.

In 1681, in the wake of the *dragonnades*, Ormond once again put measures in place to attract skilled Protestant workers to Ireland. He urged the Irish privy council to vote funds for the relief of the refugees, and authorised the mayor of Dublin to make a door-to-door collection for the fund. He also commissioned promotional literature to 'advertise' the advantages of the island and present it as a safe haven for French Protestants, and his recruitment agents were active in London and Holland, alongside those recruiting for other destinations whose distance from France made them unattractive, e.g. some of the German states and the American colonies.[22] By 1685 an estimated 600 refugees had arrived and some 140 men had become freemen of the city of Dublin, where the majority of the refugees settled. Attempts were also made in 1684 to establish a Huguenot colony in Wexford, which was short-lived. However, the political crisis following the appointment of the Catholic Richard Talbot, earl of Tyrconnell, as viceroy to Ireland, the Glorious Revolution (1688) and the military conflict when the island became a theatre of war between the armies of James II and William III decimated the Huguenot communities. Among those Protestants fleeing the island at the time were some 280 Huguenots who left Dublin, never to return.[23]

The major settlement of French Protestants in Ireland occurred in the 1690s under the leadership of the Huguenot Henri de Massue, 2nd marquis de Ruvigny, made earl of Galway in 1697 and appointed lord lieutenant of Ireland that same year. There were three main motivations behind this latest plan to create Huguenot colonies in Ireland: the island had been ravaged by the war; its agriculture, industries and infrastructures needed rebuilding; and the decline in its Protestant population needed to be reversed. On the Continent, the refugee crisis had not abated. In fact, failed harvests in 1691 and 1693 in the Swiss cantons exacerbated it, and Zurich was determined to move the refugees on in large numbers to other destinations. Ruvigny had been granted the forfeited estates of the Jacobite Patrick Trant in the Irish midlands in recognition of his military leadership during William III's Irish campaign. In conjunction with other Huguenot leaders in Switzerland, he instigated a project on a vast scale, the 'Projet pour l'établissement des réfugiés en Irlande'.[24] The aim was to transport up to 40,000 French refugees to Ireland (600 families in the first year of the project, 1693, and the rest to follow) and establish them in specially constructed colonies throughout the island. The Irish parliament in 1692 passed a new 'Act for the encouragement of Protestant strangers to settle in the kingdom of Ireland', and in 1693 Dublin Civic Council renewed the by-law that permitted skilled refugees swift access to civic franchise and the guilds.[25] From then to the end of the century some 2,000–3,000 refugees were transported to Ireland via Holland and England. They settled in some major centres, e.g. Dublin, Cork and Portarlington, and many minor ones (see Fig. 5). One of the major ones was the newly created settlement of Portarlington on the forfeited estates granted to Ruvigny, which was largely made up of Huguenot soldiers who had fought in the Williamite wars and were thereafter pensioned on the Irish establishment. This ambitious project, like the previous ones, met with only limited success, however.

The planned immigration schemes that sought to bring French Protestants to Ireland failed for a number of reasons. Economic factors were an important impediment to their success. An economic downturn in the 1680s, poor harvests and widespread poverty in Dublin meant that work was scarce and food expensive and in short supply. In the 1690s, the large sums of money required for transporting and accommodating thousands of refugees, promised by government sources in Holland and England, did not materialise. In addition, as Ruvigny explained in a letter written from Dublin Castle in 1698 by his secretary Élie Bouhéreau, Ireland was a poor country, devastated by war, and was already contributing proportionately more than England to provide pensions for the refugees: £8,000 per annum, as compared to £15,000 from the English treasury.[26] Nevertheless, economic factors alone cannot account for the Huguenots' reluctance to make Ireland their home.

The planned immigration schemes targeted Huguenots in the belief that their industry and skills would make a significant contribution to the economy of Ireland, but the instigators of those schemes also firmly expected the French migrants and refugees to bolster the Protestant interest in Ireland. From the outset, that meant requiring them to conform to the Church of England and preventing them from making common cause with Presbyterian dissenters, whose Reformed ecclesiology was similar to that of the French and whose nonconformity was seen as a threat to the security of the kingdom.[27] To that end, the Lady Chapel in St Patrick's Cathedral was adapted for the use of the immigrants, and solemnly inaugurated in April 1666 as a venue for them to worship according to Anglican rites, using a French translation of the Book of Common Prayer. The compromise was not acceptable to many Huguenots, who viewed the rites of the Church of England as perilously similar to those of Roman Catholics and were uneasy about its episcopal structures. Some of their pastors vehemently refused to take Anglican orders, which the bishops required of them if they were to serve in the established church and, most importantly, if they were to be remunerated by it. They rightly believed that such a requirement implied that there was something lacking in their Reformed ordination, and that to accede to it would call into question the legitimacy of the Reformed church, which they served at such personal cost.

Although the 1692 act provided for freedom of worship, and French Reformed churches were founded in Dublin, Portarlington and Cork, the Anglican hierarchy remained hostile. In fact, they repeatedly sought ways to make the refugees conform and brought pressure to bear on them, their leaders and their ministers in the years that followed. For the refugees who refused to conform, the difference between Catholic and Anglican oppression was largely one of degree rather than kind; conflict and serious rifts occurred between the refugees over the issue of conformity in the late 1690s and early 1700s. Furthermore, the limitations that the ruling Anglican minority sought to impose on the religious freedom of the refugees were widely known and reported on the Continent. That unacceptable turn of events, together with the refugees' own fear of 'popery', made Ireland an ambivalent refuge for people fleeing from persecution.

Despite these disadvantages, some French Protestants, especially those who conformed, managed to establish themselves as members of the middle class and become prominent in banking and finance, the wine trade, paper-making, property development or government administration. In the past, some historians claimed that, because they were victims of persecution in France and outsiders subject to constraints in Ireland, those who settled here were unlikely to support the penal legislation against Irish Catholics.[28] The evidence, however, points to the contrary—namely that their commitment to the Protestant interest and their self-identification with the Irish Protestant élite were unquestionable. Five Huguenot regiments participated in William III's Irish campaign. They, and others who later settled here, were not slow to celebrate the reduction of Ireland, the victory at the Boyne (1690) and the treaty of Limerick (1691) alongside the triumphantly victorious Protestants.[29] The French immigrants may not have been the agents of the dispossession of Irish Catholics in the aftermath of the war of the two kings but they were willing beneficiaries of it.

Inevitably, given both their experience in France and their dependence on government and civic bodies for their transfer to Ireland, the Huguenots shared the confessional ideology of the Protestant élite, with its expected polarities between Protestantism and popery, settler and native. Indeed, Jacques Fontaine, pastor of the French church in Cork between 1694 and 1698, and later appointed a Justice of the Peace in 1702, prided himself on the 'strict justice' that he administered to the native Irish, claiming that he sent eight or ten of them to prison at every assizes for collusion with French privateer activity off the south-west coast.[30] Gaspard Caillard, pastor of the French Reformed Church in Peter Street, Dublin, preached two sermons in the 1720s that argued in favour of imposing civil restrictions on Catholics. Significantly, Catholic persecution, treachery and violence figure prominently among his justifications for penal legislation. In summing up, he urged his listeners to keep alive the memory of both the St Bartholomew's Day massacres (1572) and the Gunpowder Plot (1605) as active reminders of the dangers of Roman Catholicism.[31] The association of these two key dates from the recent history of French and English Protestants speaks to an acceptance of the politics of exclusion as a guarantee of the continuing existence of the Irish Protestant élite, with whom the Huguenots had fully identified.

Conclusion

Clearly, the history of the Reformation in France and the Huguenots in Ireland is nothing if not ambiguous. Far from the one-sided tale of its 'shaping Europe in a spirit of democratic deliberation and freedom', it is rather a more complex story of the pursuit of religious freedom that did not shy away from violence or the promotion of oppression when such actions or policies served the interests of those concerned. There is therefore no *necessary* connection between the Reformation and freedom, nor does the prior experience of persecution *necessarily* result in a commitment to toleration in the positive sense of the word. Recalling that more complex reality truthfully is essential to remembering *rightly*. Why is this important?

Let us switch perspectives for a moment and turn to a remark made by a Catholic (and fictional) garda (policeman) in Julie Parsons's most recent novel. Musing on the conflict between Republicans and Unionists in twentieth-century Ireland, he observes, 'How we were taught our history, we couldn't help but admire the hard men, the tough guys'.[32] The comment, with its underlying and persistent sense of victimhood, is an example of what Tzvetan Todorov has designated a 'literal' memory—that is, an interpretation of the past that turns a recalled event into 'un fait intransitif, ne conduisant pas au-delà de lui-même', which establishes a continuity between the past and the present and extends the consequences of past wrongs to each aspect of the present.[33] For Todorov this constitutes an abuse of memory—and, we might add, the history of conflict in twentieth-century Ireland amply illustrates that kind of abuse, perpetrated by Catholics and Protestants alike. That is not, however, the only way of remembering.

Recalling the shadow side to the history of the French Reformation and the Huguenots in Ireland disturbs the partisan bias (whether religious or political) evident in the unchallenged association of that history with the rise of modern freedoms. In doing so it opens up that history to interrogation, analogy and generalisation, as Todorov argues, so that lessons may be extracted from it in new situations—which is what he calls exemplary memory. Yet, as the Huguenots' own use of the St Bartholomew's Day massacres illustrates, and as Miroslav Volf points out, 'exemplary memory' is morally ambiguous; the lessons it delivers are not necessarily 'the right' ones.[34] This is a complex issue that cannot be resolved here. So let us instead end by noting one of the lessons that French Protestants have actually drawn from their history, transforming it into an unambiguous ethical imperative for the present. Rather than retrospectively admiring 'the hard men, the tough guys', with their dreams of national Reformation and political dominance, French Protestants have turned the minority status that history imposed on them into an 'elective affinity' with the persecuted and excluded other.[35] In that way, recalling the whole past, with its rights and its wrongs, can become an inspiration for the pursuit of justice, if we choose to make it so.

Notes

[1] Miroslav Volf, *The End of Memory: Remembering Rightly in a Violent World* (Grand Rapids, 2006), 21.

[2] François Clavairoly, 'I think Jesus was a bit of a protestant', *Réforme* **3688** (12 January 2017), 14: 'Of course, the Reformation carries along with it that whole civilising dynamic, constructing new horizons of thought, and shaping Europe in a spirit of democratic deliberation and freedom'.

[3] Patsy McGarry, 'The Reformation continues to shape our world 500 years on from Luther's "Theses"', *Irish Times*, 7 January 2017.

[4] Lytta Basset, *Oser la bienveillance* (Paris, 2014), 167: 'How can we discern that we have not taken the total human reality into account? Precisely when we take flight into ideals—a gilded, mythical history, an ideal society, a model education, which never existed.'

[5] In an interview on German radio in early October 2016, as reported by Déborah Berlioz, 'Guérir les mémoires', *Réforme* **3680** (10 November 2016), 7.

[6] Volf, *End of memory*, 10.

[7] These sequences are borrowed from Jean Baubérot and Marianne Carbonnier-Burkard, *Histoire des Protestants: Une Minorité en France (XVIe–XXIe siècle)* (Paris, 2016), 13–255.

[8] Hélène Guicharnaud, 'An introduction to the architecture of Protestant temples constructed in France before the Revocation of the Edict of Nantes', in Paul Corby Finney (ed.),
seeing Beyond the Word: Visual Arts and the Calvinist Tradition (Grand Rapids, MI, 1999), 133–55.

[9] From Baubérot et Carbonnier-Burkard: *Histoire des Protestants*, with kind permission of the authors.

[10] Jean Calvin, 'Préface à la première édition du psautier 1543': 'in a language commonly known to the people'; 'singing has great force and vigour to move and inflame people's hearts to invoke and praise God with a more vehement and ardent zeal'; text in modernised French available at http://www.eglise-baptiste-albi.org/articles/calvin_preface_psautier.php; and in English translation at http://spindleworks.com/library/calvin/calvinpsalterpreface.html.

[11] Patrick Cabanel, *Histoire des Protestants en France: XVIe–XXIe siècle*, (Paris, 2012) 204–304.

[12] Raymond A. Mentzer and Bertrand Van Ruymbeke (eds), *A Companion to the Huguenots* (Leiden, 2016), 2.

[13] Denis Crouzet, 'Identity and violence: French Protestants and the early wars of religion', in Ruth Whelan and Carol Baxter (eds), *Toleration and Religious Identity: the Edict of Nantes and Its Implications in France, Britain and Ireland* (Dublin, 2003), 73–91.

[14] Mark Greengrass, 'An Edict and its antecedents: the pacification of Nantes and political culture in later sixteenth-century France', in Whelan and Baxter (eds), *Toleration and*

Religious Identity, 146.
15. Baubérot and Carbonnier-Burkard, *Histoire des Protestants*, 89.
16. See http://huguenotsweb.free.fr/histoire/edit_nantes.htm: 'et s'il ne lui [Dieu] a plu permettre que ce soit *pour encore* en une même forme et religion': 'as it has *not yet* pleased God to permit a single form of worship and religion' (emphasis added).
17. Downloaded from https://www.museeprotestant.org/de/notice/le-refuge-huguenot/.
18. Yves Krumenacker, 'La circulation des huguenots sur les routes du Refuge', *Revue d'Histoire de l'Église de France* **98** (2012), 311–27.
19. Michel David to Louis Tronchin, 2 April 1701: 'We would not be very safe (and it would be desirable for us to be a bit more so), if the natives were not kept right down. … They are all very driven by the spirit of popery, with the result that, no matter how civilly they behave towards us, they are always ready to cut our throats if they had the opportunity and the power to do so.'
20. Élie Bouhéreau to Louis Tronchin, 21/31 May 1697: 'a place so far away from the rest of the world'.
21. Grace Lawless Lee, *The Huguenot Settlements in Ireland* (Dublin, Green and Co., 1936).
22. Ruth Whelan, 'The Huguenots and the imaginative geography of Ireland: a planned immigration scheme in the 1680s', *Irish Historical Studies* **35** (140) (2007), 481–2.
23. Raymond Hylton, *Ireland's Huguenots and their Refuge, 1662–1745: an unlikely haven* (Brighton, 2005), 34–5, 52.
24. 'Project for establishing refugees in Ireland', see Michelle Magdelaine, 'L'Irlande huguenote: utopie ou réalité?', in Michelle Magdelaine, Maria-Cristina Pitassi, Ruth Whelan and Antony McKenna (eds), *De l'Humanisme aux Lumières, Bayle et le Protestantisme* (Paris and Oxford, 1996), 273–87.
25. Edward Whelan, 'Poverty, war, intolerance and vested interests: challenges to the Dublin Refuge, 1680–1702', *Proceedings of the Huguenot Society* **29** (2010), 397–8.
26. From Henri de Ruvigny, Dublin Castle, 25 January 1698, Bibliothèque de Genève, MS Court 11, ff 188v–189r.
27. Richard L. Greaves, *God's other Children: Protestant Nonconformists and the Emergence of Denominational Churches in Ireland, 1660–1700* (Stanford, 1997), 81–7.
28. See the Conclusion to C.E.J. Caldicott, H. Gough and J.-P. Pittion (eds), *The Huguenots and Ireland: Anatomy of an Emigration* (Dublin, 1987), 424.
29. R. Whelan, 'Marsh's Library and the French Calvinist tradition: the manuscript diary of Élie Bouhéreau (1643–1719)', in Muriel McCarthy and Ann Simmons (eds), *The Making of Marsh's Library: Learning, Politics and Religion in Ireland, 1650–1750* (Dublin, 2004), 224–5.
30. Jacques Fontaine, *Persécutés pour Leur Foi. Mémoires d'une Famille Huguenote* (ed. Bernard Cottret) (Paris, 2003), 182; Thomas Doyle, 'Jacobitism, Catholicism and the Irish Protestant elite, 1700–1710', *Eighteenth-Century Ireland* **12** (1997), 45–6.
31. R. Whelan, 'Repressive toleration: the Huguenots in early eighteenth-century Dublin', in Whelan and Baxter (eds), *Toleration and Religious Identity*, 179–95.
32. Julie Parsons, *The Therapy House* (Dublin, 2017), 122.
33. Tzvetan Todorov, *Les abus de la mémoire* (Paris, 1998), 30: 'an intransitive fact leading nowhere beyond itself'; and pp 31–3 for the notion of 'exemplary memory'.
34. Volf, *End of Memory*, 91.
35. *Ibid.*, 204; Baubérot and Carbonnier-Burkard, *Histoire des Protestants*, 3–7.

8
'They also appointed bishops for themselves'—religious change in sixteenth- and seventeenth-century Ireland

John McCafferty

Writing about 100 years after the events that he was describing, the Franciscan Observant friar Mícheál Ó Cléirigh recorded this about 1537, the year John Frederick I presented Luther's 'Schmalkaldic' articles to the League: 'a heresy and new error sprang up in England through pride, vain-glory, avarice and lust … so that the men of England went into opposition to the Pope and Rome and they also appointed bishops for themselves'.[1]

This description of the schismatic effect of the legislation of Henry VIII's Dublin parliament in the years 1536–7 makes reformation a conjoined twin of moral turpitude and English isolationism. Writing only a few years later, the Old English Capuchin friar Nicholas Archbold had this to say about the trajectories of the English reformation: 'nothing being so hatefull to heretics as Religious men: especially to Calvinistical heretics: such as now Ingland wholly began to be fil'd with: Henrician Protestancie, turning daily into Calvinistical Puritanitie'.[2]

Henry VIII hated Martin Luther, not least because of the latter's determination that the king's marriage to Catherine of Aragon was both licit and valid. By the time Henry died, eleven months after Luther, English Protestant sights were fixed on Geneva rather than on Wittenberg, as Friar Nicholas clearly saw. Yet Archbold and Ó Cléirigh were very clear on two things: Henry VIII's reformation was *sui generis* and it was an English thing. This mattered to them and it mattered to Ireland, because religious change in the 1530s was brought about by a simple statutory ratification of existing English legislation in a Dublin parliament. Ireland, quite simply, got a minimally glossed English reformation. From the outset, and through all the ensuing vagaries of Tudor religious policy, the Crown's reflexive inclination was to export English solutions to Irish shores. The story of Ireland's experience of Martin Luther's reformation and all that radiated out from it is not one of a call to interior freedom. It is a story of statecraft.

Ireland's break with Rome was a second-hand affair, achieved using borrowed clothes. The Irish 'reformation' parliament of 1536–7 enacted Acts of Supremacy, Appeals, Slander, First Fruits, Against the Authority of the Bishop of Rome—all woven from the same words as those passed at Westminster just a few years previously. Alterations were close to invisible, consisting only of the necessary replacements of the word 'England' with 'Ireland' in draft bills and some small adjustment in official titles, such as 'Armagh' for 'Canterbury'.[3] But Ireland was not England and the Crown government from Dublin was not in the same position as Crown government from Westminster. During the sixteenth century, English law and authority would expand out from the 'Pale' (four eastern seaboard counties) and a number of other cities and semi-autonomous territories to effectively encompass the whole island by 1607. This expansion was not achieved without violence, displacement of local élites and much confiscation of land. As a result, religious change became braided up with warfare, destruction and the trauma of military campaigns. Even in the very early days, in those gap years between Westminster's statutory break with Rome and that of Dublin, bloodshed was present. In July of 1534, Archbishop of Dublin John Alen, a Norfolk-born client of Henry VIII's reform-inclined minister Thomas Cromwell, attempted to get out of the city by boat. His vessel was grounded on a sandbank in Dublin Bay and he was compelled to overnight in the nearby village of Raheny. He was murdered there by associates of Silken Thomas Fitzgerald, Lord Offaly, son of the earl of Kildare, former viceroy of Ireland, who was at that very moment imprisoned in the Tower of London.[4] The revolt of the Fitzgeralds of Kildare, an Old English lineage with extensive connections to Gaelic Ireland, absorbed Crown government on the island of Ireland for almost two years. It was this violent seigneurial revolt that delayed the legislative process. But it did more. The Kildare rebels sought Continental allies for their local conflict on the grounds of Henry VIII's supposed heresy and his actual schism.[5] Religious choice in Ireland was repeatedly presented by the State in early modern Ireland as being between a 'foreign' and therefore treasonous Catholic counter-reformation or a 'domestic' and therefore loyal Protestant reformation. That State was itself contested, however; its boundaries were fluid and frequently violent, and its means were often prerogative and coercive. Protestant evangelisation found itself swept along by the tide of the State's exigencies and regularly ducked under the waters of the many political events attendant on decades of conflict, both major and minor, and on the impact of the domestic and foreign policy considerations of the Crown of England.

    Catholic and Protestant writing about the Tudor reformations in Ireland, whether produced later in the sixteenth century or in any of the following centuries right up to the middle of the twentieth, liked to depict the religious trajectory of the island as a kind of titanic aetiology which pitted Romans against heretics or papists against Protestants.[6] Such enduringly confessionalised history was perhaps inevitable in a scenario in which virtually all of the adherents of the major Protestant groupings were settlers and arrivals entering the country from the middle of the sixteenth century to the end of the seventeenth. The numbers of natively born Protestants in the first generations of the established church in Ireland were vanishingly small. There are problems with providing detailed explanations for this development. Since the slow-moving dissolution of Irish religious houses under the Tudor monarchs through to the extremely destructive wars of the seventeenth century, conflagrations and dispersals of historical materials have been common. Even the vast holocaust that was the destruction of the Public Record Office of Ireland in 1922 (containing many Church of Ireland records) was presaged by a disastrous fire in the Bermingham Tower of Dublin Castle in the eighteenth century. So if the Irish reformation process is a derivative of the English one, it is nowhere near it in terms of evidential base. Very little is known of what went on in the naves of churches and in the spiritual lives of churchgoers in Ireland from 1536/7 to the accession of Elizabeth I in 1558. From the 1570s onwards it is increasingly clear that those in communion with Rome were no longer attending Church of Ireland services, or were doing so under duress or with intent to disrupt.

Martin Luther made the vernacular crucial to his reform movement. His prose shaped the early modern German language itself. If asked to find an equivalent author with equivalent impact on the Irish language, many scholars would turn to *Foras feasa ar Éirinn* ('Compendium of wisdom about Ireland') by the Hibernophone French-educated Old English priest Seathrún Céitinn. *Foras feasa ar Éirinn* is a history of the island that rejects and refutes English allegations of Irish barbarity. It posits the existence of a *naturaliter* Catholic kingdom peopled by a *naisiún* (his borrowing of the recent Spanish neologism *naçion*) or nation whose primary identity resides not in their ethnicity but rather in their natality on the island of Ireland and their allegiance to the Holy See.[7] Put simply, this enduring driver of Irish self-identity, endlessly copied in manuscript form right into the nineteenth century, is no Protestant work. It points back, indirectly, over its shoulder to a specifically Irish piece of legislation passed by the Dublin parliament in 1536–7. This was the Act for the English Order, Habit and Language. Just as the legal basis for the king's headship of the church was no novelty, this statute was very far from an innovation. Parliaments of the *Anglo-Hibernici* or 'English of Ireland', as they called themselves, had on numerous occasions, such as 1297 and 1366, mandated the speaking of English and insisted on English-style haircuts, clothes and pastimes. The roots of this legislation lay deep in ethnic politics yet now they were being grafted onto a process intended to break the island's church from Rome. All benefices were now to be given to an English-speaker unless—after a very minutely delineated process—all efforts to find one had failed. All priests were to take an oath on their ordination day to learn the 'English tongue … to the uttermost of his power, wit and cunning'. They were also to make Anglophones of their congregations, especially the children, and to preach in that language and make the bidding prayers in it.[8] There was absolutely no pastoral provision for the language spoken by between 80% and 90% of Ireland's population. Complex English events would make a Protestant reformation of Henry VIII's schism and so see its early Lutheran influences shoved aside in favour of Calvinist churchmanship. That Protestantism would be an English-speaking one, wrapped up with widespread confiscation and redistribution of land as the sixteenth century went on. Contrary to the vernacularising principles of the Continental Reformation, evangelisation was now yoked to Anglicisation. What the English had to say about their own language in the 1571 Thirty-Nine Articles—'it is a thing plainly repugnant to the Word of God, and the custom of the Primitive church, to have public Prayer in the church, or to minister the Sacraments in a language not understanded of the people'—was only ever intermittently applied to the Irish language in Ireland.[9] Despite Elizabeth I's provision of £66 13s 4d for a Gaelic font, the sole Protestant text in Irish until the arrival of a Common Prayer Book in 1608 was Seán Ó Cearnaigh's short primer, the *Aibidil Caiticiosma* of 1571, which was produced in a tiny edition of 200 copies. Its appearance, incidentally, had less to do with an impulse to preach in Irish and more to do with a defensive reaction to the apparent Presbyterianism of John Carswell's Gaelic translation—*Foirm na n-Urrnuidheadh*—of the Scots Book of Common Order. So the first book in Irish came about, too, as a result of something that had happened on the other side of the Irish Sea. The New Testament, *Tiomna Nuadh ar Dtigherna*, was published in Dublin in 1602 but there was no Old Testament until 1685. A full Irish version of the Bible finally appeared five years later.[10] Wales, the nearby non-Anglophone comparator, had a printed Welsh New Testament by 1567. Nine years after Martin Luther's *Ninety-Five Theses* there was a full German Mass, and by 1534 the complete German Bible had been published. These trajectories speak for themselves. Use of Irish in the established church during this period was rare, the enthusiasm of a minute minority, and almost endlessly postponed even as Ireland became the scene of escalating confessionalisation from the 1560s onwards.

England's emergence as a Protestant confessional state with a Catholic minority is marked with a variety of key dates: the Supremacy Act in 1534,

Elizabeth I's Act of Uniformity in 1559, the moment of her distinctive church settlement, the Thirty-Nine Articles in 1571 and the seminal moment of the Authorised Version (King James) of the Bible in 1611. These were English solutions, speaking English, for English conditions. Insofar as they were evangelical, they were evangelical for England only. The matching Irish dates are instructive: 1536 for Supremacy, after a violent rising; 1560 for an Act of Uniformity which actually prioritised Latin over Irish in non-Anglophone areas; 1634 for a belated reception of the 1571 Thirty-Nine Articles—itself a belated English reaction to the double predestination Calvinism and the formal identification of the pope as Antichrist by the Church of Ireland in 1615. While the Authorised Version of the Bible was available to English-speakers in Ireland from 1611, Irish-speakers would have to wait until 1685–90 to see a full Bible in their own language. Protestant evangelisation in Ireland was much muted by Dublin Castle's insistence on Anglicisation. On Elizabeth I's 1558 accession day, 48 of the 62 decrees of the Council of Trent had already been passed. The Tridentine church as it operated in Ireland was comfortably trilingual in Irish, English and Latin. That church also retained conventual life. Most numerous were the Franciscan Observants, who were a highly mobile and highly resilient group, deeply embedded in local communities across the whole island. Painfully aware of the grief visited on their outspoken English confrères by Henry VIII for supporting Catherine of Aragon, the Irish friars are likely to have acted as a kind of mesh keeping explicit commitment to the Roman obedience intact during the 1530s.[11] The friars drew membership from hereditary Gaelic élites whose custody of traditional learning and manuscripts assisted in cultivating arguments that Catholicity was the natural state for the island, that Protestantism was at once foreign and heretical and that to relinquish Rome was a betrayal of blood and of ancestors. Reports from all of the religious orders and from the growing number of Catholic bishops on the island from the 1560s all indicate a pastoral emphasis on the country's two vernaculars. Priests, active not only in towns but also in country districts (often commandeering ruined churches or using inn yards for services), made translations of basic prayers and the *Credo*. There was versification and singing of catechetical material. Orders such as the Jesuits and Capuchins brought emotive preaching and public performances of weeping, all tending to create emotional communities bonded on Catholic identity. So, ironically, while the Roman church would not budge from Latin liturgy it capitalised on the Irish language. In terms of the written word, manuscript transmission remained a dominant mode in Irish up to the nineteenth century. Nonetheless, Catholics did make a quick riposte to tardy Protestant efforts at the provision of printed material in Irish. The first

Continental printing in Irish was done by Jacobus Messius at Antwerp in 1611, but thereafter this work was carried out in-house by the Irish Franciscans at St Anthony's, Louvain. The press there, initially financed under the terms of the will of a former secular priest of the Armagh diocese, required constant transfusions of cash, as Irish was printed with bespoke fonts based on a version of insular hands rather than on romans. It is clear from extant archiducal and episcopal permissions for Flanders that such activity was explicitly intended to rebut the very minimal Irish-language output of the Protestant side. The friar Bonabhentura Ó hEodhasa's *An Teagasg Críosdaidhe* (Antwerp, 1611; Louvain, 1614) was a catechism by a trained professional poet who summarised his book's prose contents in verse—a rhyming strategy in keeping with Franciscan evangelisation in the vernaculars of both Europe and the New World.[12] Tuning global Catholicism in for Irish-speaking audiences was a method employed in a series of Franciscan publications produced in Louvain and Rome right up to 1676.[13] The extent to which Irish Catholicism was not just the product of oppositional sectarianism but was also influenced by the paths chosen by what had become a worldwide church is easily discernible in these vernacular texts.

These texts were produced in or near a network of expatriate Irish colleges. That college system was a model borrowed from the English Catholic exiles. By Elizabeth I's death in 1603 there were already five seminary-college venues on offer—Paris (1578), Lisbon (1590), Salamanca (1592), Douai (1594) and Antwerp (1600). By the time Charles I came to the throne in 1625 there were a further ten—Compostela (1605), Louvain (1607), Lille (1610), Rouen (1612), Tournai (1616), Charleville (1620) and Prague (1620), along with a second college (1623) and a third (1624) in the important university city of Louvain, and one in Rome (1625). By this stage most of these institutions were run by the Jesuits for the formation of secular clergy, but they were complemented by three Franciscan Observant colleges, one Capuchin and one Dominican. These latter reflected the durability of the regulars in Ireland, their prestige and consequent privileges, which they deployed not only in the pastoral service of Irish Catholicism but in settling its direction. The regulars, along with the Jesuits, had agendas which were both specifically Irish and highly transnational. The effect was to provide an exemplary context for congregations across the island when their priests were interested in and preaching about, for example, the fate of Christians in contemporary Japan.[14]

Those clerics and theologians who gave the Irish State church its first formulary in 1615 were overwhelmingly English-speaking immigrants or the children of such immigrants. This had profound consequences. From the outset, the bishops and higher clergy of the Church of Ireland were imported. There were two main reasons for this. During the medieval period, the English Crown tended to give the more lucrative sees to Englishmen, not just as a reward to individual clients but also as a reflection of its distrust both of local Anglophone élites and of Gaelic Irish clergy. This segued nicely into the new conditions—reform would be entrusted to newcomers to the Irish scene. The second reason was that the Tudor monarchs (including the Catholic Mary I) came to believe that placement or 'plantation' of English populations was the best means by which Ireland could be 'civilised' or properly colonised. Protestantism became tightly woven into plantation. Over the much longer term, Ireland's Anglican and Presbyterian populations were massively composed of English and Scottish settlers respectively. Protestants of Irish birth—whether Old English or Gaelic Irish—were vanishingly rare.

In 1552 John Bale, ex-Carmelite friar, playwright, historian and Protestant polemicist, was appointed to the midland diocese of Ossory. He had no experience of local conditions. Rome, on the other hand, would come predominantly to favour locals for its episcopal appointees. Bale's *Vocaycon*, an account of his time in Kilkenny (written with exile hindsight from Germany), has been harvested by many historians to provide examples of ignorance of local conditions, Anglicising belligerence and—perhaps—as a sign of a small Protestant nucleus.[15] Bale claimed to have had success with some of the younger people in his episcopal city. His vivid prose choler is, however, both arresting and unsubstantiated. Nevertheless, it is one of the first sustained literary attempts to create binaries of, respectively, English, Protestant and civilised versus Irish, papist and barbarian. The closing scenes of his autobiographical tract, in which the reader is offered sketches of Mary I's proclamation, a reversal of iconoclasm and his own flight in fear of his life, do seem to suggest that whatever conformities had been secured from the Old English population under Henry VIII and his son Edward VI were outward, bounded and only very rarely Protestant.[16] Late medieval Catholicism in Tudor Ireland was minimally disrupted or rather only disrupted in institutional form. Any proselytising was minimal.

There are some native Protestant voices. James Ussher (1581–1656) was from an Old English Dublin Protestant family.[17] One of the first students of Trinity College Dublin, he rose to become archbishop of Armagh and an internationally famous scholar whose work on the medieval Irish church and on patristic material has had enduring value. Various aspects of Ussher's career are revealing of the contours of reformation in Ireland. He entered Trinity College in 1594. A university in Dublin had been a goal of the city's patricians for several centuries. After its foundation, many of those same wealthy families, including Ussher's own numerous Catholic relatives, had turned their backs on the place. They preferred to send their sons abroad or to the Inns of Court in London, where there was no religious test. This sectarianisation of public spaces extended even to the dead, who now began to be buried apart or who were occasionally exhumed in spasms of ritual 'cleansing'.[18] The city's medieval churches became the demesne of predominantly immigrant congregations, while Catholics celebrated their rites in 'mass-houses' which were often opulent affairs and well known to the authorities. Ussher's theological and antiquarian intellectual interests led him to a dual engagement with England. He travelled and stayed there for long periods, studying and collecting manuscripts. He died in England in 1656, a refugee from an Ireland which during the 1640s had been the locus for a resurgent and flamboyantly Tridentine Roman church. More inwardly, Ussher's scholarly preoccupations were those of his English contemporaries. The nineteenth-century edition of the archbishop's collected works dedicates 522 pages to his refutations of the Jesuit Cardinal Robert Bellarmine, a *bête noire* of the English church and especially of its first Stuart supreme governor, James VI & I. Ussher's commanding work on the early Irish church was both in approach and inspiration firmly within the tradition of English defences of the deep antiquity of a Church of England 'independent' of Rome.[19] Even Irish-born Protestants were entirely attuned to English cadences and rhythms. Early modern Ireland never enjoyed the capacity to generate a distinct reformed tradition.

The even smaller numbers of Irish-speaking Protestants did deploy the language of liberty but did so in a very particular context. William Daniel or Uilliam Ó Domhnuill was born in 1570 and was of a generation who did not recall anything before Elizabeth I's reign. His 1602 *Tiomna Nvadh ar Dtigherna* or New Testament has an English preface, added to the *c.* 500 copies printed at the very outset of the new reign of James VI & I. The Scottish king's accession marked for Ireland the cessation of the Nine Years War, perpetrated, as Ó Domhnuill puts it, by 'unnaturall barbarous rebell and proud bloudie Spaniard'. The absolute precondition for peace in Ireland, he believes, is the 'utter extirpation of ydolatrie and superstitition'. Satan was an upholder of an anti-kingdom of 'darkenesse with … rotten pillars of falsehood and ignorance'. The antidote to all of this is, of course, the Gospel's saving light transmitted in the vulgar tongue 'as all the Churches of God doe confesse'. Ó Domhnuill's contrast of a Protestant international here with Antichrist's activities is also a neat bow in the direction of James VI & I's well-known aspiration to be a latter-day Constantine for western Christianity.[20] It also positioned Ireland in time and space as part of a reformed international engaged in an epoch-long struggle.[21]

Yet in the midst of his universal view, Ó Domhnuill stitched Gospel and governance in Ireland together by insisting on the anti-Gospel, anti-government nature of the Ulster earls and their allies in the recent war, who 'proclaimed themselves absolute Lords of the land: having cast lots for the lives, lands and goods of those few who that professed either religion or subjection unto God and his anointed'. Elizabeth I's rule—'under her wings', as he puts it—guaranteed estates, liberties and the Gospel light because she saw to it that 'good laws' and good people were sent over from England.[22]

Returning to the same theme in 1609 as a preface to his Gaelic *Leabhar na nurnaightheadh gcomhchoidchiond* or Book of Common Prayer, he makes this stark summary: 'the land having partly swallowed up in displeasure the disturbers of our peace and partly spewed them out into strange countries, craving better inhabitants to enjoy her blessings, and discovering her rich bosom for their kind entertainment'. He transmutes war deaths, forced exile, aggressive centralisation of power, large-scale confiscation of land and plantation of new populations as actions of providence in support of the Gospel. This then left him free to extol Arthur Chichester, the viceroy and chief proponent of plantation, as a security solution, for having 'often played the part of a religious bishop'.[23] Gospel liberty, in Ó Domhnuill's printed voice, can only be realised in the extirpation of Irish barbarity and the extension of English rule.[24] This internalisation of colonising politico-religious discourses is indicative of the remarkable degree to which the whole matter of religious change in early modern Ireland melted into its wars and politics.

In 1541 the Irish parliament declared Henry VIII king of Ireland. This rejection of the style of 'lord of Ireland', used by English monarchs since the twelfth century, was an outworking of the break with Rome and a signal of intent. Contemporaries believed that *Laudabiliter*, a papal bull dated to 1155, used the alleged 'Donation' of Constantine to grant dominion over the island for the purposes of church reform to Henry II. Henry VIII's claim to the realm could no longer be dependent on the Holy See,[25] yet shifting to kingly dominion by creating a paper kingdom utterly dependent on the English Crown had many effects. This declarative statute, celebrated with solemn Mass at Christ Church Cathedral, Dublin, volleys of shots and free wine, magicked all of the inhabitants of the island kingdom into subjects of Henry VIII and his heirs and successors. The Irish Crown also maintained that supreme headship of the church and later, under Elizabeth and after her, supreme governorship was vested in itself. Full participation in the commonwealth had become dependent on conformity to the established church. Full loyalty to the Crown became, as the sixteenth century progressed, increasingly understood as subsisting in such conformity. Penal legislation against Catholics and those exercising papal jurisdiction was never as harsh in Ireland as it was in England. Those fines for failure to attend Church of Ireland services, set as 12d per Sunday under Elizabeth I, were intermittently applied, as the state had neither the resources nor the inclination to cause mass unrest. The continuing loyalty of large numbers of civic officials and lawyers to the papacy meant that mechanisms of enforcement could not function properly and there were, usually for English foreign policy purposes, sustained periods of *de facto* toleration for recusancy. The full story of anti-Catholic legislation is both knotty and lengthy. In many ways, though, the creation of a body such as the ecclesiastical High Commission of 1564 charged to investigate and punish popery only served to further a discourse that maintained that Protestantism was simply an aspect of statecraft.[26]

In 1542, a year after the Act for Kingly Title, the Jesuit emissaries Alphonse Salmeron and Paschase Broet grimly concluded after meeting with the Gaelic leaders of Ulster that Ireland would stay in schism with Henry VIII.[27] By the 1570s, however, the Old English population, traditional loyalists, were beginning to articulate a political loyalty to the Protestant monarch but a spiritual loyalty to the pope in Rome. These same Old English, many of whom had benefited from the dissolution of monasteries, were now applying some of those revenues to the support of Catholic clergy on their lands. Those clergy, in turn, sharpened by training in the controversial schools of Continental colleges, educated their children and policed confessional boundaries by insisting more and more that it was not spiritually safe to attend Church of Ireland services even for the sole purpose of staying on the right side of the law. Those clergy were also the sons, nephews and grandchildren of families within the host population. They had a ready network of supporters, protectors and hosts.[28]

Most Protestant clergy found themselves inheriting the capacious structures of the medieval Irish church, consisting of over 4,000 parishes and 30 dioceses. The inherent claim presented by the title *Ecclesia Hibernica* or Church of Ireland meant that there was little appetite for a rational restructuring which might put the Protestant church on a missionary footing. To do so would have impinged on an array of claims that the English Crown was making about Ireland as a whole. These clergy of the established church from the 1570s onwards, educated in Oxford, Cambridge, Edinburgh, Glasgow, Aberdeen, St Andrews or Trinity College Dublin, were well trained but they were overwhelmingly newcomers who often spoke a language different from that of their flock. Their finances, and those of their bishops, were disastrous. Need for revenue pushed them into permanent pluralism. Need for revenue made litigants and tithe-collectors of pastors whose legally defined parishioners were decidedly not of their flock. The many armed conflicts of sixteenth-century Ireland were not the only reason why the physical infrastructure of the later medieval church—its chapels, churches and cathedrals—collapsed or were collapsing by the 1590s. Only in the royal capital of Dublin and areas of significant planter settlement, such as the larger towns of Ulster counties, was a relatively normal and functional Protestant parochial system possible.[29]

On 27 September 1992, Pope John Paul II beatified sixteen Irish men and one Irish woman at a ceremony in St Peter's Square. Their cause was based on martyrdom. Three were bishops. In 1579 Patrick O'Hely of Mayo went to his death, as did Archbishop Dermot O'Hurley of Cashel in 1584 after extensive torture, and then, after various long spells of imprisonment in the 1590s, Cornelius O'Devaney of Down & Connor went to the gallows in Dublin at Candlemas 1612.[30] In 1561 David Wolfe, a Jesuit and a native of Limerick, landed at Cork to begin his work as papal commissary to Paul IV. Wolfe's mission was to stabilise the Irish Catholic Church, acting in person and on the ground as a source of delegated papal authority. He was also told to talent-spot. Those he sought were candidates for bishoprics. For the first three decades after the break with Rome bishops across Ireland variously exercised their powers as Crown appointees, as papal ones or even as both. Many dioceses, even archbishoprics, were left vacant by both Crown and Holy See for long stretches of time. With increasing tempo from 1576 onwards, Rome and then the Crown began to fill up the empty benches, so that by the accession of Charles I in 1625 both sides boasted a full set of bishops. These men claimed the same jurisdiction, the same titles, the same lands. The executions of O'Hely, O'Hurley and O'Devaney spelled out those claims in blood. Dublin Castle insisted that such actions were judicial consequences of treason and not of their Catholic orders. Exercise of foreign authority within the realm was treasonous and therefore punishable by death. On 18 November 1581 the Nugent or 'Baltinglass' rebels, seigneurial insurgents, walked to their place of execution reciting the *Ave Maria*. When offered the spiritual services of Thomas Jones, Church of Ireland minister and future bishop of Meath, they called out '*Vade satana, vade satana, vade post me satana*'.[31] At O'Devaney's 1612 execution in the Dublin suburb of Oxmantown, thousands of the Old English inhabitants turned out to watch this Gaelic Irish prelate wend his way to the gallows. After his death officials were overwhelmed by the rush for relics. Slightly less than 100 years previously, in 1518, a Dublin provincial synod had barred clergy from Ulster, O'Devaney's home province, from holding benefices in their dioceses. The scaffold became a place to display opposition to the government's religious policies and to create scenes of Catholic solidarity. The scaffold was also a place where the slow collapse of medieval ethnic antagonisms would begin to reveal the outlines of a new Irish identity based on creed and birth on the island of Ireland.[32]

The use of religious rhetoric for political purposes and the use of political rhetoric for religious purposes meant that the air of early modern Ireland was filled with sounds that have echoed, often very deafeningly and corrosively, around the heads and hearts of the inhabitants of the island for many centuries since that time. This has had the effect of making it very difficult to hear anything at all of the interior religious thoughts and emotions of those who lived in early modern Ireland. Protestant reformation in early modern Ireland was pushed into the service of an expanding and colonising state. Catholic reformation in early modern Ireland was deemed subversive of that state but also aimed itself to hold onto the denizens of the island as a prelude to a re-Catholicisation of England. Both of the churches, then, were working off scripts dictated by Anglo-Irish relations. 'Vos enim in libertatem vocati estis' (Gal 5: 13) was not, perhaps, the most frequently deployed scriptural text in an island whose experience of religious change was worked out in an atmosphere of contested authority, frequent violence and fracturing identities.

Notes

1. Royal Irish Academy, Dublin, MS 23 P7, fols 54v–55r. Translation taken from John O'Donovan (ed.), *Annála ríoghachta Éireann: Annals of the Kingdom of Ireland*, vol. V (Dublin, 1854), 1445.
2. Nicholas Archbold, 'Historie of the Irish Capuchins', Troyes Bibliothèque MS 1103, 54.
3. For a recent overview see Henry A. Jefferies, *The Irish Church and the Tudor Reformations* (Dublin, 2010).
4. Richard Hawkins, 'Alen (Allen), John', in James McGuire and James Quinn (eds), *Dictionary of Irish Biography* (Cambridge, 2009) (http://dib.cambridge.org/viewReadPage.do?articleId=a0091).
5. Mícheál Ó Siochrú, 'Foreign involvement in the revolt of Silken Thomas, 1534–5', *Proceedings of the Royal Irish Academy* 96C (1996), 49–66.
6. Mark Empey, Alan Ford and Miriam Moffitt (eds), *The Church of Ireland and Its Past: History, Interpretation and Identity* (Dublin, 2017). See also Alan Ford, *The Protestant Reformation in Ireland, 1590–1641* (Dublin, 1997), and Karl Bottigheimer and Ute Lotz-Heumann, 'The Irish Reformation in European perspective', *Archiv für Reformationsgeschichte* 89 (1998), 268–309.
7. Bernadette Cunningham, *The World of Geoffrey Keating* (Dublin, 2000). See also Mícheál Mac Craith, 'From the Elizabethan settlement to the Battle of the Boyne: literature in Irish 1560–1690', in Margaret Kelleher and Philip O'Leary (eds), *The*

Cambridge History of Irish Literature (Cambridge, 2006), vol. I, 191–231.

[8] John McCafferty, *The Reconstruction of the Church of Ireland: Bishop Bramhall and the Laudian Reforms* (Cambridge, 2007), Chapter 1.

[9] J. McCafferty, 'Voices in Prefaces: speaking Irish in an English Reformation', *Studies: An Irish Quarterly Review* 106 (2017/18), 484–92.

[10] Marc Caball, 'Language, print and literature in Irish, 1550–1630', in Jane Ohlmeyer (ed.), *The Cambridge History of Ireland, Volume II: 1550–1730* (Cambridge, 2018), 411–33. Nicholas Williams, *I bPrionta I Leabhar: Na Protastúin agus prós na Gaeilge, 1567–1724* (Dublin, 1986).

[11] J. McCafferty, 'A mundo valde alieni: Irish Franciscan responses to the Dissolution of the Monasteries, 1540–1640', *Reformation and Renaissance Review* 19 (2017), 50–63; Brendan Scott, 'The religious houses of Tudor Dublin: their communities and resistance to the Dissolution 1537–41', in Seán Duffy (ed.), *Medieval Dublin VII* (Dublin, 2006), 214–32.

[12] Fearghal MacRaghnaill (ed.), *An teagasg Críosdiadhe* (Dublin, 1976); Salvador Ryan, 'Bonaventura Ó hEoghusa's "An Teagasg Críosdaidhe" 1611–1614: a reassessment of its audience and use', *Archivium Hibernicum* 58 (2004), 259–67.

[13] For a recent overview of exile literature see Raymond Gillespie and Ruairí Ó hUiginn, *Irish Europe, 1600–1650: writing and learning* (Dublin, 2013).

[14] The literature on the Irish Continental colleges, individually and collectively and by religious order, is enormous. Overviews which provide access to this area include Liam Chambers and Thomas O'Connor (eds), *College Communities Abroad: Education, Migration and Catholicism in Early Modern Europe* (Manchester, 2017); Liam Chambers and Thomas O'Connor (eds), *Forming Catholic Communities: Irish, Scots and English College Networks in Europe, 1568–1918* (Leiden, 2018); Mary Ann Lyons and Thomas O'Connor (eds), *Strangers to Citizens: the Irish in Europe, 1600–1800* (Dublin, 2008); John J. Silke, 'The Irish abroad, 1534–1691', in T.W. Moody, F.X. Martin and F.J. Byrne (eds), *A New History of Ireland, Volume III: Early Modern Ireland 1534–1691* (Oxford, 1976; repr. 1989), 615–33.

[15] John Bale, *The vocacyon of Ioha[n] Bale to the bishiprick of Ossorie in Irela[n]de his persecucio[n]s in ye same, & finall delyueraunce …* ('Rome' [false imprint], 1553); Steven Ellis, 'John Bale, bishop of Ossory, 1552–3', *Journal of the Butler Society* 2 (1984), 283–93; Elizabethanne Boran, 'Persecution and deliverance in sixteenth-century Kilkenny: the *Vocacyon* of Johan Bale (1553)', *Old Kilkenny Review* 69 (2017), 71–92; Andrew Hadfield, 'Translating the Reformation: John Bale's Irish *Vocacyon*', in Brendan Bradshaw, Andrew Hadfield and Willy Maley (eds), *Representing Ireland: Literature and the Origins of Conflict, 1534–1660* (Cambridge, 1993), 43–59.

[16] Bale, *Vocacyon*, fols 29v–33v.

[17] A. Ford, *James Ussher: Theology, History and Politics in Early-Modern Ireland and England* (Oxford, 2007).

[18] Clodagh Tait, *Death, Burial and Commemoration in Ireland, 1550–1650* (Basingstoke, 2002), especially Chapter 5.

[19] U. Lotz-Heumann, 'The Protestant interpretation of the history of Ireland: the case of James Ussher's *Discourse*', in Bruce Gordon (ed.), *Protestant History and Identity in Sixteenth-Century Europe, ii: the Later Reformation* (Aldershot, 1996), 107–20; J. McCafferty, 'St Patrick for the Church of Ireland: James Ussher's *Discourse*', *Bullán* 3

(1997–8), 87–101.
20 *Tiomna Nvadh ar Dtigherna* (Dublin, 1602), fols 1r–2v.
21 Daniel would go on to participate in the Church of Ireland convocation of 1615 which identified (Article 80) the pope as that Antichrist.
22 *Tiomna Nvadh ar Dtigherna*, fols 2r–2v.
23 *Leabhar na nurnaightheadh gcomhchoidchiond* (Dublin, 1609), 'The Epistle Dedicatorie'.
24 *Ibid*.
25 Brendan Bradshaw, *The Irish Constitutional Revolution of the Sixteenth Century* (Cambridge, 1979); James Murray, *Enforcing the English Reformation in Ireland* (Cambridge, 2009).
26 Jefferies, *The Irish Church and the Tudor Reformations*; A. Ford, '"Force and fear of punishment": Protestants and religious coercion in Ireland, 1603–33', in Elizabethanne Boran and Crawford Gribben (eds), *Enforcing Reformation in Ireland and Scotland, 1550–1700* (Aldershot, 2006), 91–130.
27 Alphonse Salmeron and Paschase Broet to Cardinal Cervini (Santa Crucis), Edinburgh, 9 April 1542, in *Epistolae PP. Paschasii Broëti, Claudi Jaji, Joannis Codurii et Simonis Rodericii Societatis Jesu ex autographis vel originalibus exemplis potissimum depromptae, Monumenta Historica Societas Iesu 24* (Madrid, 1903), 23–31.
28 Patrick J. Corish, *The Catholic Community in the Seventeenth and Eighteenth Centuries* (Dublin, 1981), 18–42.
29 Jefferies, *The Irish Church and the Tudor Reformations*, 241–84; Ford, *Protestant Reformation, passim*; J. McCafferty, *Reconstruction*, Chapter 1.
30 Benignus Millett, 'Patrick O'Healy OFM and Conn O'Rourke OFM'; J.J. Meagher, 'Dermot O'Hurley'; and Kieran Devlin, 'Conor O'Devaney, OFM and Patrick O'Loughran', in Patrick J. Corish (ed.), *The Irish Martyrs* (Dublin, 2005), 32–65, 66–80 and 107–37.
31 J. McCafferty, 'Protestant prelates or godly pastors? The dilemma of the early Stuart episcopate', in A. Ford and J. McCafferty, *The Origins of Sectarianism in Early Modern Ireland* (Cambridge, 2005), 54–72; Tadhg Ó hAnnracháin, '"In imitation of that holy patron of prelates the blessed St Charles": episcopal activity in Ireland and the formation of a confessional identity, 1618–1653', in Ford and McCafferty, *The Origins of Sectarianism*, 73–94.
32 C. Tait, 'Adored for saints: Catholic martyrdom in Ireland *c*. 1560–1655', *Journal of Early Modern History* 5 (2001), 128–59; A. Ford, 'Martyrdom, history and memory in early modern Ireland', in Ian McBride (ed.), *History and Memory in Modern Ireland* (Cambridge, 2001), 43–66.

9
The Lutheran rectory in German culture and literature

Jürgen Barkhoff

The Lutheran rectory occupies a prominent place in the German cultural imagination and is a central *lieu de mémoire* of German cultural memory. It is credited with having had a dominant formative influence on the intellectual and cultural life of the educated middle classes in Germany, their lifestyle, mentality, habitus and values, and forms a cornerstone of the identity narratives of the German *Bildungsbürgertum* well beyond the religious sphere. The term *Kulturprotestantismus*, which is hard to translate but describes the immense cultural influence of Protestantism, captures this importance of the Protestant vicarage for German intellectual life and culture, education and art. As is the norm for identity narratives, this prominence presents itself as an intriguing mix of fact and fiction. It is at the same time a historical reality that can be underpinned with historical and sociological data and a carefully crafted cultural myth, created and maintained by a variety of strategies and media and not least by a rich body of literature about life in the Protestant rectory.

This literature, both fictional and (auto-)biographical, has its origins in the rectory, written often by Protestant clergy themselves but even more often by their sons and, more rarely and more recently, their daughters.[1] The most influential of these texts were written during the seminal period around 1800, the Enlightenment and German Romanticism, during which the intertwined identity narratives of *Kulturprotestantismus* and *Bildungsbürgertum* took shape. Later peaks in these emerging identity narratives can be observed during crisis moments in the identity of Protestant clergy, such as the mid-nineteenth century, when its dominance among the university-educated middle classes waned, or in the late nineteenth century, when in the wake of the *Kulturkampf* official administrative functions were taken away from the clergy. Another peak occurred in the early twentieth century, when secularisation gained momentum especially among the working classes, from which the Protestant clergy were very much separated by social class, political outlook and cultural habitus. In these situations, a flood of ego-documents, often nostalgic, idealising or defensive in tone, attempted to reinforce and stabilise a threatened identity narrative.

What do these accounts of life in the rectory have to offer? Commencing in the Enlightenment, they portray the central position of the Lutheran pastor in the life and education of his parish and his multiple and interlocking roles as preacher, spiritual guide, educator, adviser, reformer and chronicler. They give detailed insights into family life in the rectory and the position and situation of the pastor's wife, highly visible and highly active in the parish while at the same time very much defined by her husband's role and in his shadow. They thematise the exposure of the whole household to the scrutiny of the parishioners, as its members were expected to be a model family and to lead by example.[2] Some of those accounts describe the sociological basis of the Protestant vicarage, which, especially in the early centuries after the Reformation and in the countryside, was often characterised by poverty and real want. They sketch the often-difficult relationships with the classes above and below them, i.e. the nobility and the farmers and craftsmen. They tell us about the pride and class-consciousness of the pastors as a well-educated part of the local élite, of their ambitions and projects, but equally about their self-doubts, frustrations, crises and despairs. They portray the Protestant rectory as a place of exemplary virtue and principled values, of great hospitality and lively debate, of intellectual and artistic stimulation, but also as a place of strict paternal authority, stifling conformism and overbearing moral burden to lead an exemplary life—a situation which put immense pressure especially on the offspring. They do so often in an idealised way that constructs the cultural myth and shows it at work, but equally in a critical or satirical way that unmasks pious pretensions, shows the men of God in their all-too-human weaknesses and reflects on the darker aspects of family life under a dominant father in whom are fused the aspects of paternal command, the authority of the local preacher, educator, shepherd and the ultimate power of a patriarchal Father-God.

This chapter will in its first part briefly sketch the theological, cultural, historical and sociological background to which the enormous influence of the Protestant rectory on the cultural and intellectual life in Germany can be attributed. Particular attention will be given to the period of the Reformation and its aftermath, when Luther established the Protestant pastorate by ending celibacy, and to the eighteenth century, in which bourgeois identity was forged from the ideals of the Enlightenment. In the second part we will briefly examine a small selection of literary portrayals of the Lutheran rectory, taken mainly from the seminal period during the late eighteenth and early nineteenth centuries. The authors under consideration are Johann Wolfgang von Goethe, Johann Heinrich Voß, Eduard Mörike, Jakob Michael Reinhold Lenz, Jean Paul and Friedrich Nietzsche.[3]

Before the First World War, in a much-quoted analysis of 1,600 relevant entries in the *Allgemeine Deutsche Biographie*, the Professor of Canon Law Johann von Schulte, a member of the Old Catholic Church, came to the conclusion that since the Reformation 54% of German writers and scholars came from Protestant rectories. This staggering figure seemed to offer a statistical basis for the Protestant supremacy in German cultural life and became a myth in itself. Recently, however, Oliver Janz has pointed to significant methodological flaws in von Schulte's study, relating mainly to the way in which the entries included for assessment were selected.[4] Nevertheless, even a highly selective list like the following of only the most important canonical household names of writers, thinkers and learned men who came from Protestant parsonages in Germany (and Switzerland) is exceptionally impressive and offers compelling evidence for the centrality of Protestant influence on German literature and culture: Andreas Gryphius (1616–64), the towering figure of the literary Baroque; the literary critics Johann Christoph Gottsched (1700–66) and Johann Jakob Bodmer (1698–1783), whose aesthetic disputes paved the way for a more innovative and individualistic Enlightenment poetics; Christian Fürchtegott Gellert (1715–69), the writer and moralist whose popular idylls, fables and hymns greatly influenced bourgeois literary taste; the rebellious 'Storm and Stress' (*Sturm und Drang*) author Jakob Michael Reinhold Lenz (1751–92), who served as a model for Georg Büchner's ingenious depiction of mental illness in his novella *Lenz*; the three most important authors of German Enlightenment writing, who all combine sharp analysis and satirical wit with a deep humanity—Gotthold Ephraim Lessing (1729–81), whose plea for religious tolerance in *Nathan der Weise* remains immensely topical, Christoph Martin Wieland (1733–1813), prolific author in many genres and fellow Weimarian of Goethe and Schiller, and the physicist and satirist Georg Christoph Lichtenberg (1742–99); Leonhard Euler (1707–83), the Swiss mathematician and astronomer; the Romantic philosopher brothers August Wilhelm (1767–1845) and Friedrich Schlegel (1772–1829); the Romantic writer Matthias Claudius (1740–1815), whose *Der Mond ist aufgegangen* is one of the few Romantic expressions of folk piety that have survived until today in broad German cultural memory; Jean Paul (1763–1825), author of the equally brilliant and terrifying *Rede des toten Christus vom Weltgebäude herab, daß kein Gott sei*, which in many ways prefigures *fin de siècle* nihilism; the Romantic philosophers Friedrich Schleiermacher (1768–1834), the 'father' of hermeneutics and modern theology, and Friedrich Wilhelm Joseph Schelling (1775–1854), the main proponent of a pantheistic Romantic philosophy of nature which conceptualised human subjectivity as in intimate correspondence with the *Welt seele*; the Romantic and chief architect of German classicism Karl Friedrich Schinkel (1781–1841); Heinrich Schliemann (1822–90), the pioneering archaeologist and discoverer of historical Troy; the classicists and historians who developed and dominated nineteenth-century historiography, Johann Gustav Droysen (1808–84), Christian Matthias Theodor Mommsen (1817–1903) and Jacob Burckhardt (1818–97); the philosopher Wilhelm Dilthey (1833–1911), who developed hermeneutics into the principle methodology of *Geisteswissenschaften*; the zoologist and author Alfred Brehm (1829–84), who established *Brehm's Tierleben*, a compendium to be found in most middle-class households; the enduringly popular novelist of adolescence Hermann Hesse (1877–1962), influenced by Jungian psychology and Indian mysticism; and the two great proponents of late nineteenth- and early twentieth-century scepticism and nihilism, Friedrich Nietzsche (1844–1900) and Gottfried Benn (1886–1956). It was only much later, in the second half of the twentieth century, that all these pastors' sons were joined by pastors' daughters, who, like Gabriele Wohmann (1932–2015) and Ruth Rehmann (1922–2016), in their literary works advocate, in a Lutheran tradition, a strong connection between the private and the public and reflect both nostalgically and critically on their upbringing in a Protestant pastorate from a female perspective, most intensely and radically in Rehmann's *Der Mann auf der Kanzel. Fragen an einen Vater* (1979). This autobiographical novel questions, in the wake of the 1968 cultural revolution, the authoritarian oppressiveness of her home and the silence and acquiescence of her father towards the Nazi regime, supported by Luther's *Zwei-Reiche Lehre*, the traditional closeness of throne and altar in Prussian state religion and a long history of obedience towards the state authorities.

Three aspects immediately stand out when perusing this astonishing list. The first relates to the time-line; the density of talent and achievement really unfolds from the mid-eighteenth century onwards, is at its peak during the late Enlightenment and Romanticism, and lasts right through the nineteenth century. The second relates to the range of interests and disciplines: the intellectual pursuits of the Lutheran offspring centre around but are by no means limited to *Geisteswissenschaften*, with a particular emphasis on philosophy, literature and history. The seminal period around 1800 was one in which the concepts and ideals of the Enlightenment, such as critical inquiry, the methodical and scientific pursuit of knowledge, and an interest in history, coupled with the belief in progress, self-reflection, moral autonomy and civic responsibility, became dominant paradigms that informed the self-definition and value systems of the educated middle classes and, in turn, of society as a whole. This made the Lutheran parsonage—in its unique mixture of spirituality and rationality, belief and questioning, sense of tradition and innovative spirit—a particularly stimulating and fruitful environment. The third aspect relates to the relationship with religion: the above overview already makes us appreciate that many of the literary or philosophical themes and preoccupations of these pastors' sons and daughters are inspired by, or engage with, religious impulses and reinterpret and develop them further in more secular contexts.

Which specific elements in its history, religious outlook, self-definition and daily practice made the Lutheran vicarage a place of such disproportionate richness and intensity of education, intellectual endeavour, the arts and cultural productivity? Two fundamentals of the Lutheran Reformation are of critical importance here: the abolition of celibacy and the introduction of mandatory academic training for Protestant clergy. The first established the household and the family of the Lutheran pastor as the centre of parish life and thus overcame the strict separation of the spheres of the sacred and the everyday. As Martin Greiffenhagen has observed, a dialectical process of concurrent and intertwined 'Verweltlichung und Vergeistigung' (secularisation and spiritualisation) occurred around the Lutheran vicarage.[5] As a husband, father and member of the community, the pastor was much more involved in the everyday life of his parishioners than the Catholic priest had ever been or could ever be. His duties were not at all restricted to the preaching of God's Word, the distribution of the sacraments, spiritual guidance and support for his parishioners, and care of the poor and the sick. The pastor was also an educator, an administrator, a general figure of authority and, especially in rural parishes, until the end of the nineteenth century often a gardener, beekeeper, farmer or even breeder of cattle. This led to a daily and very practical involvement of the pastor and his family with every aspect of the life of his parishioners, and eliminated—at least to a degree—the aura of remoteness and spiritual otherworldliness which had often characterised priests before. At the same time, the pastor was the spiritual and moral authority and often the most educated man in his parish, and he and his family were expected to lead an exemplary life in every respect. In the pastor's home, education and cultural pursuits, family life and hospitality could not be separated from the preaching of the Gospel and prayer. As a result, all everyday pursuits were imbued with a certain spirit of piety and godliness, a kind of sanctification of the everyday. Physicotheology, a theological movement influenced by Enlightenment rationalism and its interest in natural sciences, which sought evidence of God's infinite love and wisdom in the beauty, orderliness and usefulness of the natural world, supported this fusion by lending theological authority to the view that God could also be found and praised by studying nature, looking after bees and cattle, or improving agricultural methods.

Over time, education and culture in particular profited from this fusion of the sacred and the secular. The enlightened belief in the centrality of education, culture and the arts for self-development and societal progress alike was reinforced by the semi-religious aura which these pursuits acquired in the German Protestant rectory. They were seen and practised as closely related and structurally similar experiences and pursuits. In subsequent German cultural history this made itself felt in many ways, for example in the Romantic project of *Kunstreligion*, in the metaphysical dimension of German music aesthetics, the rituals of *Hausmusik* in bourgeois households, and arguably even the general high respect and value attributed to art and culture in German public life throughout the nineteenth and twentieth centuries.

This was, of course, a gradual development over a very long period. In the aftermath of the Reformation, the first married priests and their families—especially after Luther married Katharina von Bora in 1525 and established his community in the old monastery in Wittenberg—had to fight for their legitimacy against the polemics of their Catholic adversaries. Many of the parsonages, especially in the countryside in the first centuries after the Reformation, also had to fight against poverty, material want and low social prestige, conditions which often left little room for cultural pursuits. The development of the Protestant pastorate into the epitome of cultured and educated middle-class values and lifestyle is a phenomenon of the Enlightenment and develops from the mid-eighteenth century onwards, mainly in the cities. The idealised image of Luther's family as the paradigm of the Protestant family, omnipresent and emulated in Lutheran circles, is an invention of the nineteenth century, developed and propagated not least to fight decline and self-doubt in periods of increasing modernisation and secularisation which threatened the pivotal role of the Protestant clergy.

Equally important is the second, closely related, element in the redefinition of the status of clergymen through the Reformation: the mandatory university training. As in Protestantism the proclamation of the Word of God and the interpretation of the Bible are decisive means of grace, the responsibility of the Lutheran clergyman as a convincing and effective preacher who is able to guide his flock to salvation is at the heart of his professional identity. Consequently the self-definition of the preacher becomes closely connected to that of the scholar. The black gown, which only in the nineteenth century became the official livery of Lutheran clergy in Germany, was that of a professor of theology, as in Luther's Wittenberg. It is not a priest's cassock, accentuating privileged access to a sacramental space or a mystical realm, but a sign of academic standing and intellectual dignity. Luther's understanding of Protestant ministry was equally directed against Catholic obscurantism and subjective religious enthusiasm (*Schwärmertum*) among his own followers and in Protestant sects which privileged mystical inspiration and emotional closeness over knowledge and understanding of the Word of God. Against this the authority of the well-trained Protestant clergy rested on their learnedness and their ability to convey their understanding of the Bible publicly and with clarity. This necessitated solid academic training, historical knowledge and a knowledge of Hebrew, Greek and Latin as the languages of the Bible and the church. The most important skills for the work of salvation, however, were the proper interpretation of the written word and the art of rhetoric for preaching. A highly conscious and reflexive attitude towards language, both as written text and spoken word, was not only a professional requirement in the Protestant rectory but also a seminal ingredient of a vocation fulfilled and a Christian life well lived. It is not surprising that the young men and—later and, for a long time, to a lesser degree—young women who grew up and were educated in such an intellectual and spiritual climate were drawn to reading, writing and a literary culture, especially as they experienced their father not only as preacher but also as their teacher. It is equally unsurprising that the two 'fathers' of hermeneutics, Schleiermacher and Dilthey, came from this very background. While the Bible was the principal text of instruction in the rectory, the pastor's library contained many other and increasingly more non-religious books, dictionaries, historical and scientific works, travelogues, the literature of classical antiquity and also more recent and contemporary works of fiction. Heinz Schlaffer in his history of German literature argues that the emergence of a distinct German literary culture in the second half of the eighteenth century would not have been possible without this fertile intellectual climate, and contests that in this environment secular literature participated in the aura of authority and holiness of the Bible.[6] The philosopher Walter Schulz goes even further, arguing in a similar vein that Protestantism had a considerable influence on modern philosophy in general and German idealistic philosophy in particular, as its thought systems echo a Protestant inclination toward structure and system.[7]

A third result of the Reformation of relevance for the strong link between the Protestant vicarage and middle-class culture was that as a profession it aimed to be, and increasingly was, exclusively *bürgerlich*. After the Reformation, joining the Protestant clergy was not an option for sons of the nobility, as it had been and continued to be with the Catholic priesthood. As a result, the Protestant pastor was a distinct and exclusively middle-class phenomenon that found itself between the nobility and the peasantry, had contact with both and often served as a mediator between them. Socially and economically well below the nobility and excluded from political roles, and in rural areas often in uncomfortably close social proximity to the farmers and craftsmen around them, Protestant clergy developed their social distinction and cultural capital out of their learnedness, their culture, their superior morality and—supported by the doctrine of the Two Kingdoms—their authority in the spiritual realm. From early on, sons of Protestant clergy stepped into their father's footsteps and established veritable dynasties of Lutheran clergy, often uninterrupted for centuries. In these dynasties, professional identity, a sense of family and class-consciousness merged and developed into a strong sense of pride and distinction, which at least partially compensated for the lack of economic and political power. With genealogical trees, family chronicles and the careful nurturing of rituals and traditions, these pastor's lineages developed a specific memory culture of their own. In this process of social distinction university training and learnedness was a crucial element of demarcation both towards the nobility and later, from the second half of the nineteenth century, increasingly also towards the growing entrepreneurial and administrative middle classes, especially when the Protestant clergy lost their dominant position among the university-educated. It is worth noting in this context that in the 1820s almost one third of all graduates from German universities were Protestant pastors, but that this figure had dwindled to less than one tenth by 1875.[8]

Other, more general, aspects of mentality can be identified in the documents and narratives emanating from the vicarages and also have to be taken into account. First and foremost is the Protestant work ethic with its sense of duty, the pressure to fulfil the expectations of a demanding father and figure of authority, the ambition to emulate or surpass his achievements or excel in another field—or to rebel. In the 1930s and '40s, when the discourse about the cultural hegemony of the Protestant rectory in the spirit of the times took on a distinctly biologistic dimension, the psychiatrist and pastor's son Ernst Kretzschmer spoke of a veritable 'Geniezüchtung' in the 'kastenartig scharf geprägte Schicht' of the 'alten Gelehrten- und Pastorenfamilien' in which the 'einseitige Examensauslese und die vorwiegend ständische Heirat' resulted in a 'einheitlich scharfe Prägung des exquisit Sprachlich-Logischen'.[9] While such language and argument sound alien and suspect today, the general relevance of such observations comes into focus when compared with the situation on the Catholic side. Here the academically and rhetorically talented sons who entered the priesthood had no opportunity to create offspring, pass on their culture and shape them according to their ideals and values. Celibacy meant that their talent was lost in each generation and for all subsequent ones, while in Protestantism it was cultivated and passed on from generation to generation.

Overall, the interrelated factors described above, although necessarily given in broad strokes and without detailed historical differentiation, can explain the predominance of the Protestant élites in German culture and also the identification of Protestant mentality with German middle-class culture in general. They also help to illuminate the unique artistic, cultural and scientific productivity of the Protestant rectory.

Turning now to literary portrayals of life in the Protestant pastorate, it is noteworthy that one of the earliest, best known and most quoted does not take lived reality as its point of departure but rather fiction. Johann Wolfgang von Goethe, in the second book of his autobiography *Dichtung und Wahrheit* (1811), paints against the increasing fragmentation of modern life an idyllic and idealised image of the Protestant rectory as a model of a holistic life that allows for a harmonious unity under one roof of the private and the public, of family life, work and piety, and of an everyday life imbued with spirituality:

> 'Ein protestantischer Landgeistlicher ist vielleicht der schönste Gegenstand einer modernen Idylle; er erscheint, wie Melchiesedek, als Priester und König in einer Person. An den unschuldigsten Zustand, der sich auf Erden denken lässt, an den des Ackermanns, ist er meistens durch gleiche Beschäftigung, sowie durch gleiche Familienverhältnisse geknüpft; er ist Vater, Hausherr, Landmann und so vollkommen ein Glied der Gemeine. Auf diesem reinen, schönen, irdischen Grunde ruht sein höherer Beruf; ihm ist übergeben, die Menschen ins Leben zu führen, für ihre geistige Erziehung zu sorgen, sie bei allen Hauptepochen ihres Daseins zu segnen, sie zu belehren, zu kräftigen, zu trösten …'[10]

As its title highlights, *Dichtung und Wahrheit* is at all times a sophisticated reflection of the complicated relationship between fiction and fact, and this certainly also applies to Goethe's handling of this topic. Already in its first sentence, the poet flags that he is presenting 'eine moderne Idylle', a literary genre and not a realistic portrayal. Moreover, he concludes his subsequent praise of the intellectual, moral and pastoral qualities of the ideal Protestant pastor with an explicit reference to the immensely influential literary model for his own and many other portrayals of a Protestant vicarage, *The Vicar of Wakefield* (1766) by the Irishman (and Trinity College graduate) Oliver Goldsmith. Goethe had become familiar with this eighteenth-century bestseller—which so effectively mixes the (in many ways) conflicting genres of idyll and satire— through Herder, and he makes it very clear that his own idealised view of the

Protestant parsonage and the pastor at its centre is owed to this literary model and not to real-life experience:

> '… man verleihe ihm Gutmütigkeit, Versöhnlichkeit, Standhaftigkeit und was sonst noch aus einem entschiedenen Charakter Löbliches hervorspringt, und über dies alles eine heitere Nachgiebigkeit und lächelnde Duldung eigner und fremder Fehler; so hat man das Bild unseres trefflichen Wakefield so ziemlich beisammen'.[11]

Moreover, Goethe goes one decisive step further: immediately following the report about Herder's reading of Goldsmith's novel to their common group of friends, Goethe positions in the text the passage about his first visit to the Protestant vicarage in Sesenheim and his later love interest, Frederike Brion, one of the pastor's daughters. The enthusiastic description of his first visit to the vicarage culminates in the observation that 'Meine Verwunderung war über allen Ausdruck, mich so ganz leibhaftig in der Wakefieldschen Familie zu finden'.[12] Goethe in his autobiography thus perceives and interprets his experience of a real-life vicarage through the model and prism of Goldsmith's text. What he points to here is that literature pre-structures and guides our experience and hence co-creates reality—not vice versa, as is generally assumed. Early on in the literary history of the Protestant parsonage, Goethe not only identifies in a precise manner the mechanism by which the literary imaginary co-creates cultural myths but also cautions at the same time against a simplistic and realistic reading of literary portrayals of life in the rectory as if these were mirroring lived reality.

When Goethe wrote *Dichtung und Wahrheit* in 1811, the German answer to Goldsmith's Wakefield was the idyll *Luise* (1795) by a friend of Goethe, Klopstock and Lessing, the classicist, poet and translator of Homer's *Odyssey* and *Iliad* Johann Heinrich Voß. The work was widely known and well on its way to becoming one of the household texts for the idyllic portrayal of pastoral life for the whole of the nineteenth century. Composed in hexameters, the three-part idyll, which is identified as *Ein ländliches Gedicht* in the subtitle, revived the idyll as an artistic genre, as it transposed it from a distant antique arcadia to a realistic and contemporary rural setting, where a simple, bourgeois, patriarchal life was imbued by the ideals of the German Enlightenment. It describes the family life of the pastor of Grünau around the eighteenth birthday of his daughter Luise Blume, the visit of her fiancé, who is also a pastor, and the private wedding ceremony undertaken by the father in his own house on the eve of the official church wedding. Picking up the contrast between hectic and immoral city life and the tranquillity and righteousness of rural life which had characterised the idyll genre since antiquity, the rural setting serves to guarantee peace, contentedness and stability, with the patriarchal figure of the pastor at the centre of a set of harmonious domestic and social relations. The first part, 'Das Fest im Walde', presents a cheerful and opulent picnic at the lakeside, in which closeness to nature and education (*Bildung*) are not conflictive contrasts but formative forces that complement and enhance each other. Enlightenment ideals are far more important than religion and are promoted in many ways, such as in allusions to Lessing's parable of the ring and the ideal of a brotherhood of all, or admiration for Moses Mendelssohn, the chief proponent of the Haskalah, the Jewish Enlightenment. These allusions link the tiny village of Grünau to the great questions of its time and thus work against the solipsistic and complacent isolation that can characterise idylls. Educational aspirations and practices are prominent throughout. In the morning the pastor's wife encourages her husband:

> 'Liesest du erst ein wenig im Bett? ein Kapitel der Bibel;
> Dort auf der kleinen Riole zur Seite dir; oder ein Leibbuch
> Jener Zeit, da noch Menschen wie Washington lebten und Franklin;
> Oder den alten Homer, der so natürlich und gut ist?
> Daß du es warm mittheilst bei dem Frühstück? …'[13]

Voß's idyll, although forgotten today, is a key text, not just because of its omnipresence in nineteenth-century anthologies and school textbooks but because it demonstrates in an archetypal manner how closely Protestantism, the Enlightenment and the formation of a bourgeois identity were linked in the German lands at that time, and the formative role the classical tradition played in this context. As Fritz Martini has observed, the antique metre employed by Voß serves to instil a sense of timelessness, dignity and authority into the proceedings in Grünau, and to counteract the flare of self-sufficient and philistine narrowness that the depictions of rural idylls so easily possess.[14]

The other canonical and even better-known idyll in verse is Eduard Mörike's doggerel poem *Der Alte Turmhahn* (1852), which became the archetypical *Biedermeier* expression of the cultural myth of the Protestant vicarage, especially after it was republished in 1855 with Ludwig Richter's homely woodcuts in the series 'Beschauliches und Erbauliches' (something tranquil and edifying). The lyrical voice in the poem is that of an old weathercock which, after 100 years of faithful service at the top of the church tower, overlooking the entire parish and weathering many storms, is demounted and removed. To save him from ending up with the scrap dealer, the pastor takes him in and allows him a dignified retirement on the top of the oven in his study. From this position the weathercock muses about the passing of time and longs for his old position in the middle of things, but he also witnesses the pastor's daily routines and rituals and takes stock of the inventory that makes up and signifies the spirit of the rectory.

> 'Hier wohnt der Frieden auf der Schwell!
> In den geweißten Wänden hell
> Sogleich empfing mich sondre Luft,
> Bücher- und Gelahrtenduft,
> Gerani- und Resedaschmack,
> Auch ein Rüchlein Rauchtabak.
> [...]
> Die Sonne sich ins Fenster schleicht,
> Zwischen die Kaktusstöck' hinstreicht
> Zum kleinen Pult von Nußbaumholz,
> Eines alten Schreinermeisters Stolz;
> Beschaut sich was da liegt umher,
> Konkordanz und Kinderlehr',
> Oblatenschachtel, Amtssigill,
> Im Tintenfaß sich spiegeln will,
> [...]
> Und gleitet übern Armstuhl frank
> Hinüber an den Bücherschrank.
> Da stehn in Pergament und Leder
> Vornan die frommen Schwabenväter.'[15]

The weathercock is an astute and affectionate observer for whom the pastor's study becomes a microcosm of parish and church life; this also gives his musings their specific idyllic quality. It is impossible, however, to overlook the distinct melancholic tone of the poem, the atmosphere of nostalgia and farewell. The weathercock has, after all, seen better days and lost his prominent position in the midst of things, and he perceives the noises of the outside world largely as a threat. While it might be going too far to read this as a diagnosis of a church in decline or under threat, the immediate biographical context can explain this air of melancholy. Mörike wrote the first unpublished version of the poem after he took the old weathercock of his church in Cleversulzbach into his possession in 1840. His nine years as pastor at Cleversulzbach between 1834 and 1843, before his retirement from the clerical life at the age of only 39, were all but idyllic: Mörike suffered greatly from serious and prolonged periods of ill health, from debts and financial insecurity, from the narrow-mindedness of his surroundings and complaints of parishioners about him, and from serious doubts and scruples about his vocation, which long pre-date the Cleversulzbach years. As he confessed to his friend Johannes Mährlen as early as 1829: 'Du hast keinen Begriff von meinem Zustand. Mit Knirschen und Weinen kau ich an der alten Speise, die mich aufreiben muß. Ich sage Dir, der allein begeht die Sünde wider den heiligen Geist, der mit einem Herzen wie ich der Kirche dient.'[16] Yet in 1852 he wrote to Theodor Storm about the poem: 'Das Ganze entstand unter Sehnsucht nach dem ländlichpfarrlichen Leben'.[17] Such pronounced ambivalence, in this case firmly rooted in personal experience, is not untypical of many of the literary portrayals of life in the rectory and will characterise the remaining three examples, all taken from pastors' sons.

Jakob Michael Reinhold Lenz is an early case of a rebel in the rectory who, like Lessing, refuses to follow in his father's footsteps, aborts the study of theology and becomes a writer instead. Lenz made the frustrations and acts of despair of a candidate for theology the topic of his most famous literary work, the provocative tragicomedy *Der Hofmeister* (1774). His protagonist, Läuffer, has to wait years and years, as so many had to, for a vicarage, and instead has to sell his services as a private tutor to a noble family who treat him with arrogance, exploit him and humiliate him. It opens with a monologue in which Läuffer complains about his lack of prospects and the lack of support from his father figures, which, like all figures of power and authority in the novel, are overbearing and condescending. 'Mein Vater sagt: ich sei nicht tauglich zum Adjunkt. Ich glaube, der Fehler liegt in seinem Beutel; er will keinen bezahlen. Zum Pfaffen bin ich auch zu jung, zu gut gewachsen, habe zu viel Welt gesehn, und bei der Stadtschule hat mich der Geheime Rat nicht annehmen wollen.'[18] The play is governed by a stifling atmosphere of control and oppression, and all attempts to improve the situation or to break free are frustrated or end in catastrophe. Despite its rather forced happy ending, the play is a radical anti-idyll, oscillating between a sarcastic realism and grim exaggeration. It thus serves as a corrective to the idylls discussed so far, giving a vivid sense of the precarious economic and social situation often endured by the Protestant clergy at that time and the heavy toll this took on their happiness, sense of fulfilment and sense of identity. An almost unknown text by Lenz, his novella *Der Landprediger* (1777), is his more positive counter-narrative, which presents a veritable social utopia. Its protagonist, Johannes Mannheim, is more interested in agrarian reform and in softening the stark class divisions of the time than in theology, and uses his position to relieve poverty and improve the harsh living conditions of his flock. His vicarage also becomes 'in gewisser Art eine Akademie der Künste und Wissenschaften, weil sich Künstler und Gelehrte zu ihm flüchteten'.[19] Familiar motifs and topics discussed above resonate here, crystallising into a kind of bourgeois model biography of what a pastor's life ideally could look like—an idyll of agency and of educational, social and economic reform, informed by a radical enlightened spirit.

If these two texts by Lenz in their contrast serve as an example of an enlightened perspective on the distinctly double-edged reality of life in the vicarage, then the prolific Romantic writer Johann Paul Friedrich Richter, alias Jean Paul, masterfully manages to present such ambiguities within one and the same satirical portrayal. In three of his texts he sketches life at the pastorate as a drab prosaic existence full of deprivation on the one hand and with elements of idealistic and poetic elevation on the other. The satire *Das Leben des Quintus Fixlein* (1795), moving back and forth between idyll and grotesque, depicts the difficulties experienced by its protagonist in lifting himself from the waiting position of humble schoolteacher to the acquisition of a wife and a proper parish, which at the end he only attains because of a mix-up and some illegible handwriting. His *Jubelsenior* (1797) thematises the widespread practice of passing on a parish from father to son, and stresses intellectual and spiritual freedom as the central ingredient of the dignity and professional identity of the Protestant clergyman and as the one which can lift him above material and social problems. In his rich and vivid autobiographical *Selberlebensbeschreibung* (1829), Jean Paul describes his youth in his father's vicarages in Jodlitz and Schwarzenbach on the River Saale—from abject poverty and seven hours of daily instruction in Latin and the catechism with his siblings by their strict and unforgiving father to more rewarding hours of joyful discovery in his father's library of more exciting reading, such as *Robinson Crusoe* and Gottsched's *Weltweisheit*. Jean Paul highlights the stark contrast between the narrowness and isolation of village life and the limitless worlds which the adventures of reading and imagination were opening up to him: 'Man erwäge nur, in einem volkleeren Dorfe, in einem einsamen Pfarrhause mußten für so eine hörbegierige Seele Bücher sprechende Menschen, die reichsten ausländischen Gäste, Mäzene, durchreisende Fürsten und erste Amerikaner oder Neuweltlinge für einen Europäer sein'.[20] What Jean Paul conveys here is an experience quite characteristic of an upbringing in a Protestant rectory, and it also provides a scene of origin for the boundless literary cosmos that he would later create as a writer.

The very incomplete selection presented here of course has to leave out many important names and texts which would have deserved more than a mere mention, among them Friedrich Nicolai's *Leben und Meinungen des Sebaldus Nothanker* (1773–6), Karl Philipp Moritz's *Andreas Hartknopf* (1786; 1790), Hermann Kurz's *Die beiden Tubus* (1850), Ottilie Wildermuth's *Schwäbische Pfarrhäuser* (1852), Wilhelm Raabe's *Der Hungerpastor* (1864) and *Horacker* (1876), Theodor Fontane's *Stechlin* (1889), with its vivid portrayal of the progressive pastor Lorenzen, or Ina Seidel's *Lennacker* (1937), to name only some of the best known.

The last word, however, is reserved for the greatest critic and most influential adversary of Christianity ever to come from a Protestant pastorate, Friedrich Nietzsche. This most famous 'lost son' from a long line of pastors, who relentlessly polemicised against Christian 'slave morality' and whose rallying cry 'God is dead' rang in European scepticism and nihilism, can demonstrate better than anyone how deeply the formative influence of the Protestant vicarage goes, even—or perhaps especially—when its thought systems and doctrines are rejected and contested. Reminiscing in 1881 about his youth in the pastorate, Nietzsche contends: 'Es ist aber doch das beste Stück idealen Lebens, welches ich wirklich kennengelernt habe; von Kindesbeinen an bin ich ihm nachgegangen, in viele Winkel, und ich glaube, ich bin nie in meinem Herzen gegen dasselbe gemein gewesen. Zuletzt bin ich der Nachkomme ganzer Geschlechter von christlichen Geistlichen—vergeben sie mir diese Beschränktheit!'[21] While such an idealising and nostalgic statement might elicit surprise, the lasting influence of the Christian heritage on Nietzsche in a blend of cultural imprint, opposition and transformation is undeniable. Richard Friedenthal, among others, has argued that Nietzsche's poetic diction and his vivid imagery owe a lot to the Bible, and that his writings breathe the spirit of the preacher much more than that of the scholar. Furthermore, he sees in Nietzsche's 'Bejahung des Schmerzes, als zu heroischer Haltung aufrufend ... nichts anderes als die Abwandlung der christlichen Leidenserfahrung'.[22] In the preface to *Jenseits von Gut und Böse*, Nietzsche himself articulated the psychological and cultural dynamic at work here, of which the lasting legacy of the Protestant vicarage—the subject of the present article—was a crucial facet: 'Der Kampf gegen den christlich-kirchlichen Druck von Jahrtausenden ... hat in Europa eine prachtvolle Spannung des Geistes geschaffen, wie sie auf Erden noch nicht da war: mit einem so gespannten Bogen kann man nunmehr nach den fernsten Zielen schiessen.'[23]

Notes

1. Two important articles discuss the Protestant rectory as *lieu de mémoire*: Oliver Janz, 'Das evangelische Pfarrhaus', in Etienne François and Hagen Schulze (eds), *Deutsche Erinnerungsorte*, vol. 3 (Munich, 2001), 221–38, 704–6; Siegfried Weichlein, 'Pfarrhaus', in Christoph Markschies and Hubert Wolf with Barbara Schüler (eds), *Erinnerungsorte des Christentums* (Munich, 2010), 642–53. See also the earlier Richard Friedenthal, 'Das evangelische Pfarrhaus im deutschen Kulturleben', *Lutherische Zeitschrift der Luther-Gesellschaft* 1 (1971), 1–15. It is indicative of the importance of the subject for Lutheranism that this academic journal opens its first volume with this article by the famous Luther biographer. An excellent and richly illustrated source is the catalogue of an exhibition which the Deutsche Historische Museum displayed between October 2013 and March 2014 and which toured Germany between 2014 and 2018: *Leben nach Luther. Eine Kulturgeschichte des evangelischen Pfarrhauses* (Bönen, 2013). The best contextualisation of the topic in English is Nicholas Hope, *German and Scandinavian Protestantism 1700–1910* (Oxford, 1995).
2. Franz A. Schmitt, *Beruf und Arbeit in deutscher Erzählung. Ein literarisches Lexikon* (Stuttgart, 1952), 210–27. Schmitt lists under the entry 'Geistlicher (evangelisch)' more than 350 prose titles written between 1769 and 1951 that fictionalise the lives of Protestant clergy. The subsequent Hans-Martin Plesske, *Beruf und Arbeit in deutschsprachiger Prosa seit 1945. Ein biographisches Lexikon* (Stuttgart, 1997), 231–54, lists under the entry 'Geistlicher' for the period 180 memoirs and diaries of clergy, and almost as many fictional treatments. Unfortunately for our purpose it no longer differentiates between Catholic and Protestant clergy.
3. Two survey articles on literature which thematise the Protestant vicarage present a more comprehensive overview: Robert Minder, 'Das Bild des Pfarrhauses in der deutschen Literatur von Jean Paul bis Gottfried Benn', in *Kultur und Literatur in Deutschland und Frankreich. Fünf Essays* (Frankfurt, 1962), 44–72; Fritz Martini, 'Pfarrer und Pfarrhaus. Eine nicht nur literarische Reihe und Geschichte', in Martin Greiffenhagen (ed.), *Das evangelische Pfarrhaus. Eine Kultur- und Sozialgeschichte* (Stuttgart, 1984), 127–48. Christine Eichel, *Das deutsche Pfarrhaus. Hort des Geistes und der Macht* (Berlin, 2012), 159–99 and 231–4, also discusses literature in some detail. This book by a journalist and author who is herself a pastor's daughter is an excellent overview, well written, with fascinating insight and a wealth of material. It contains an extensive bibliography, but unfortunately quotations are not referenced. The most recent volume, *Pfarrhausbilder*, edited by Christian Albrecht, Eberhard Hauschildt and Ursula Roth (Tübingen, 2017), contains chapters on important authors not discussed here, none of whom were pastors' sons, namely Gottfried Keller, Theodor Fontane, Wilhelm Raabe, Thomas Mann, Lion Feuchtwanger and Uwe Johnson, and also one on 21st-century novels on the topic.
4. See Janz, 'Das evangelische Pfarrhaus', 232f.
5. Martin Greiffenhagen, 'Einleitung', in Greiffenhagen, *Pfarrhaus*, 7–22.
6. Heinz Schlaffer, *Eine kurze Geschichte der deutschen Literatur* (München, 2002), 55f.
7. See Walter Schulz, *Der Gott der neuzeitlichen Metaphsyik* (3rd edn, Pfullingen, 1963).
8. Janz, 'Das evangelische Pfarrhaus', 228.
9. Ernst Kretschmer, *Geniale Menschen* (Berlin, 1929), 64ff; 'cultivation of genius' in the 'caste-like sharply formed social group' of the 'old families of learned men and pastors'

in which the 'one-sided selection based on exam results and the predominantly corporate marriage' resulted in a 'uniform and precise formation of exquisite verbal and logical capacities'. Unless otherwise indicated, English translations in the footnotes are by the author.

[10] Johann Wolfgang von Goethe, *Aus meinem Leben. Dichtung und Wahrheit. Zweiter Teil. Goethes Werke. Hamburger Ausgabe*, vol. 9 (ed. Erich Trunz) (Munich, 1974), 427. 'A Protestant country clergyman is perhaps the most beautiful subject of a modern idyll; he appears, like Melchizedek, as priest and king in one person. To the most innocent situation that can be imagined on earth, to that of a husband-man [*sic*—*recte* 'farmer'], he is, for the most part, united by similarity of occupation, as well as by equality of family relationships; he is a father, a master of a family, an agriculturist, and thus perfectly a member of the community. On this pure, beautiful, earthly foundation rests his higher calling; to him it is given to guide humans through life, to take care of their spiritual education, to bless them in all the leading epochs of their existence, to instruct, to strengthen, to console them …', *The autobiography of Goethe. Truth and fiction: relating to my life*, vol. 2 (trans. John Oxenford) (New York, 1882), 34.

[11] *Ibid.*: '… grant him good-nature, placability, resolution, and everything else praiseworthy that springs from a dedicated character, and over all this a cheerful spirit of compliance, and a smiling toleration of his own failings and those of others,—then you will have put together pretty well the image of our excellent Wakefield.' *Ibid*.

[12] *Ibid.*, 434. 'My astonishment at finding myself so actually in the Wakefield family was beyond all expression' (*ibid.*, 40).

[13] Johann Heinrich Voß, *Luise. Ein ländliches Gedicht in drei Idyllen*, in Adrian Hummel (ed.), *Ausgewählte Werke* (Göttingen, 1996), 40–93, at 58. 'Do you read a little in bed? A chapter from the Bible; / there at your side on the small shelf; or a favourite book / from those times, when still men like Washington and Franklin lived; / or old Homer, who is so natural and good / so that you convey it warmly over breakfast.'

[14] See Martini, 'Pfarrer und Pfarrhaus', 130.

[15] Eduard Mörike, *Der Alte Turmhahn. Idylle,* in Herbert G. Göpfert (ed.), *Werke in einem Band* (Munich/Vienna, 1977), 141–9, at 143f., 148. 'Here peace reigns at the threshold! / Within those brightly whitened walls / At once I sensed a special aura, / The smell of books and garden, / Geranium and mignonette, / Even a faint tobacco scent. / […] The sun peeks in through the window / A strip of light between the cactus plants / Over to a small walnut table it glides, / One of old Stolz's, the cabinet-maker; [*sic*—*recte* the pride of an old cabinet-maker] / It inspects objects lying about, / A concordance, a catechism, / A wafer box, an official seal, / Tries to reflect itself on the ink vase, […] Glides across the armchair unhampered / To the bookcase. / There in parchment and leather mainly / The pious Swabian fathers are kept' (trans. Charles Cingolani, accessed 12 October 2018, http://www.cingolani.com/131em.html).

[16] Letter to Johannes Mährlen, 26 March 1829, in Hans-Henrik Krummacher, Herbert Meyer and Bernhard Zeller (eds), *Werke und Briefe. Historisch-Kritische Gesamtausgabe*, vol. 11, *Briefe 1829–1832* (ed. Hans-Ulrich Simon) (Stuttgart, 1985), 21. 'You have no idea of my state, with gnashing and weeping I chew the old fare, which is working me into the ground. I tell you, thou alone commits a sin against the Holy Spirit, who serves the church with a heart like mine.'

[17] Letter to Theodor Storm, 21 April 1854, in Krummacher, Meyer, Zeller. (eds), *Werke*

und Briefe. Historisch-Kritische Gesamtausgabe, vol. 16, *Briefe 1851–1856* (ed. Bernhard Thurn) (Stuttgart, 2000), 181. 'The whole thing originated under nostalgia for the rural clerical life.'

[18] Jakob Michael Reinhold Lenz, 'Der Hofmeister oder Vorteile der Privaterziehung', in Sigrid Damm (ed.), *Werke und Briefe in drei Bänden*, vol. 1 (Munich, 1987), 41–123, at 42. 'My father says I was not suited for an adjunct. I believe the problem lies with his purse; he doesn't want to pay. I am too young for a cleric, and too handsome, have seen too much of the world, and the privy councillor did not want to employ me at the city school.'

[19] Jakob Michael Reinhold Lenz, 'Der Landprediger', in Sigrid Damm (ed.), *Werke und Briefe in drei Bänden*, vol. 2 (Munich, 1987), 413–63, at 439; '… in a certain way an academy of arts and sciences, as artists and scholars fled to him'.

[20] Jean Paul, 'Selberlebensbeschreibung', in Norbert Miller (ed.), *Sämtliche Werke. Abteilung I*, vol. 6, *Späte Erzählungen. Schriften* (Munich/Vienna, 1987), 1037–103, at 1056f. 'Please consider: in a village empty of people, in a lonely vicarage, books had to become eloquent people for a soul so eager to hear, like the richest foreign guests, patrons, rulers passing through, and first Americans or inhabitants of the New World for a European.'

[21] Letter to Heinrich Köselitz, 21 July 1881, in Friedrich Nietzsche, *Briefe Januar 1880– Dezember 1884. Nietzsche Briefwechsel. Kritische Gesamtausgabe. Dritte Abteilung. Erster Band* (ed. Giorgio Colli and Mazzino Montinari with Helga Anania-Hess) (Berlin/New York, 1981), 109. 'But it is the best element of an ideal life that I really got to know. From early on I traced it into many nooks and crannies, and I believe that in my heart I was never cruel against it. After all, I am the offspring of a whole lineage of Christian clergy—forgive me this limitation!'

[22] See Friedenthal, 'Das evangelische Pfarrhaus', 7.

[23] Friedrich Nietzsche, 'Jenseits von Gut und Böse. Vorspiel einer Philosophie der Zukunft', in Giorgio Colli and Mazzino Montinari (eds), *Nietzsche Werke. Kritische Gesamtausgabe. Sechste Abteilung*, vol. 2 (Berlin, 1968), 4. 'The struggle against the Christian-ecclesiastical pressure of millennia […] has created a magnificent tension of spirit in Europe, the likes of which the earth has never known: with such a tension in our bow we can now shoot at the furthest goals.' *Beyond Good and Evil. Prelude to a Philosophy of the Future* (ed. Peter Horstmann and Judith Norman, trans. Judith Norman) (Cambridge, 2002), 3.

10
Marking the Reformation 500 years on—
Quo vadis ecclesia semper reformanda?

Martin Sauter

We live in times of momentous centenaries on this island. Since the beginning of this decade we have been looking back over the last century at the formative years that shaped the social and political contexts on the island of Ireland. Most recently we were exposed to the interlinked events of the year 1916, which became the fork in the Irish road that 'has made all the difference'.[1] The civic, academic and cultural commemorative events were very inclusive on the whole, and they have hopefully left us a little wiser and with a richer understanding of what the choices of that generation were, and what lay outside their grasp.

A few months on, we have entered another cluster of commemorations, this time intimately connected with our Christian faith: 500 years ago, the German Augustinian monk and priest Martin Luther published his *Ninety-Five Theses (Disputation on the power of indulgences)* at the University of Wittenberg in Saxony, where he was Professor of New Testament Studies. With this publication he had intended to stir up a critical debate among theologians and the church leadership on the practice of paying for papal letters of indulgence, which were popularly perceived as a way to pay for the forgiveness of sins—an understanding that was not very strongly denounced by the church of the day. Indeed, church leaders were deeply implicated, particularly since the sale of these letters was a lucrative income for a church that was busy transforming Rome into Renaissance splendour, such as we still marvel at when we visit the Eternal City today. The income from these sales also helped to finance the extravagant lifestyle of the pope and the princes of the church. This situation had been widely criticised inside and outside the church since the late fifteenth century.

Such was the sentiment of spiritual discontent and widespread anti-clericalism—especially in urban settings in the Holy Roman Empire in central Europe—that the *Theses* spread far and wide as they were translated into the vernacular. With this grass-roots call for transformation of the church, which spread like wildfire from town to town, began what historians call the Reformation period. Within a few decades the unity of the western Latin church was broken and the Protestant denominations emerged, and Christianity in western Europe was profoundly transformed forever. The process of church reform also led to far-reaching religious, social and political strife, often crushed by military means and much violence. As a result, not only the religious but also the political landscape changed beyond recognition.

However, the brave stand of the Reformers gave rise to a new energy in faith and a re-dedication to Jesus Christ as the head of the church. First and foremost this was the fruit of Martin Luther's fearless and tireless stand against the abuses in the old church. But he was not alone; across the Continent there were theologians and scholars of other disciplines whose passionate concern for the well-being of the church as the Body of Christ, as much as for the commonwealth of the body politic, energised them to give leadership to the widespread desire of people across the entire social spectrum for an authentic expression of faith and social justice.

Pre-eminent in the lasting legacy of the Lutheran Reformation is Luther's insistence on individual faith which was the fruit of intensive study of the Scriptures. Indeed, Luther's reorientation towards Jesus Christ as God's most precious and only gift for the salvation of all humankind is inextricably dependent on the believers' knowledge of Scripture. As the faithful study and take to heart the message of the Gospel and the New Testament, they discover that their salvation is a total and irreversible gift from God, who in infinite love and through pure grace lifts all humans out of their bondage to sin—the Bible's term for our distance or disconnection from God and his intentions for human well-being. Such grace can only be discovered in the light of Scripture and it can only be received in faith, the Bible's term for trust. For Luther, having faith meant daring to put one's trust in the God of whom the Bible gives testimony. Such a life of faith in the light of grace as it is proclaimed in the Gospel of Jesus Christ brings about freedom, which in turn is freely dedicated to serving others. For such a faith to grow, it is a necessary condition that all believers receive an education that enables them to read the Scriptures and make sense of them. Indeed, the Reformers everywhere immediately began to set up an education system with schools for all, both boys and girls.

The communal worship of the faithful is shaped by their equal empowerment through grace: the old categorical distinction beween clergy and laity has been levelled; the priesthood of all believers through baptism, of which 1 Peter 2:9 speaks, becomes a cornerstone of Luther's ecclesiology. Devotions, images, decoration of churches, music and liturgy, although no longer in themselves necessary to establish the believers' relationship with God, nevertheless remain spiritual and aesthetic forms of human expression of faith and praise of God and are cherished as such.

The Reformers did not agree on everything. In fact, within a couple of years an unbridgeable gap emerged between the Swiss Reformers in the south, under the leadership of Huldrych Zwingli and later Jean Calvin, and the circle around Luther in Wittenberg, in the north. Besides this gulf more radical positions arose, most prominently in the movement of the Anabaptists, whose insistence on conscious adult (re-)baptism brought them into opposition to all other Christian groupings. Their Gospel-based practice of freedom of association made them the target of persecution by the institutional churches of all persuasions, Roman Catholic, Lutheran and Reformed. Those who survived did so only because they fled to the New World and found there the first opportunity to practise their faith in liberty.

Looking back on those tumultuous years five centuries ago, and looking at them from across the Irish Sea and the English Channel, what remains? Is there inspiration to be gleaned from this legacy that will help us to walk on down the road of faith? As a 21st-century Lutheran I would cautiously but firmly like to say 'Yes'. As Christians in our age we need to continue to insist on thorough and inspired education that empowers our children and our young adults with wisdom that will shape their hearts and minds and strengthen their resolve to stand up for justice and for peace. We need to insist that questions be freely asked and answers freely given, both in society and by those in authority, but also by us as believers when asked to give an account of our faith and practice. We need to insist that men and women are equal before the law as much as before God, with all that that entails for ministry. We need to insist that each and every Christian, but also those looking in from the outside, can develop a mature faith, not as a means for escaping the world—a temptation only too understandable as we scan the horizon with its ever-darkening clouds—but in order to learn to bear witness in our age to the message of God's overflowing love for all of creation without exception. We need to continue to expose our own fearful hearts to Luther's discovery of the freedom and joy gained through Jesus Christ, which made him fearless in the face of adversity and adversaries of all kinds.

We need to hold on to our freedom to give expression to our faith in art, music and poetry, our freedom to engage science and the knowledge it uncovers: a source of spiritual wonder. But we are also called to remain alert to the developments in our civilisation as a result of technological advances and blindly held economic assumptions. We are called to stand for truth, for speaking out for those on the margins, be they hidden under our very noses or in the forgotten niches of global society; and we are called to tirelessly seek forms and words by which those who walk through life with us can taste and see how good God is.

In this fifth-centenary year commemorating the European Reformation one thing has profoundly changed, and this is the greatest source of encouragement: we no longer look back statically entrenched in our divisions. Since the last centenary, the landscape of the Christian church has been transformed. With accelerating momentum, the ecumenical movement has taken hold and has brought us one-time enemies and quarrelling siblings in the Christian family into a dance of ever more trust and fellowship with one another. At this stage this is true of intra-Protestant relations, which produced agreements such as the Anglican–Methodist Covenant or the Leuenberg Agreement and the Community of Protestant Churches in Europe. It is indeed also true of the relationships which were so deeply wounded in the sixteenth century, i.e. between the Roman Catholic Church and the Lutheran churches, and the relationship between the mainstream Protestant churches and the Mennonites, the descendants of the Anabaptists. In 1999 the Lutheran World Federation and the Roman Catholic Church signed the Joint Declaration on the Doctrine of Justification, which has opened up completely new ways for the building of relationships between the centuries-old antagonists. It is a special joy that in 2006 the Methodist World Council, too, signed this ground-breaking document, and, as recently as in the summer of 2017, the World Communion of Reformed Churches also joined in. In the last couple of years exciting new steps have been taken on the road *from conflict to communion*,[2] which for now have culminated in Pope Francis's very moving visit and active participation in the Lutheran opening service for the centenary year on 31 October 2016 in Lund Cathedral in Sweden.

Quo vadis ecclesia semper reformanda? In our age of twilight it is strong nourishment that we Christians of different denominations shall walk the road together, freely conceding to each other that Christ is indeed walking with each and every one of us, and with each of our churches, even if we do not agree on everything yet. Therefore we shall be walking side by side, patiently and freely giving friendship, trusting that the Holy Spirit is out in front, always with us, continually inspiring each and every one of us with love, joy, peace, patience, kindness, goodness, faithfulness, humility and self-control. No doubt, then, that in this way the church will always be reforming and reformed.

Notes

[1] Robert Frost, 'The road not taken', first published in his poetry collection *Mountain Interval* (1916).

[2] *From Conflict to Communion: Lutheran/Catholic Common Commemoration of the Reformation in 2017. Report of the Roman Catholic–Lutheran Commission on Unity* (2014). At the time of writing this was the latest and most forward-looking document arising out of Protestant–Roman Catholic dialogues. It contains an extensive reflection on the role of the healing of memories, as well as on ways forward towards visible unity.

THE NEXT 500 YEARS HAVE BEGUN

Epilogue 1

Stephan Arras

An important anniversary celebration of a historical event sometimes evokes an expectation that a similar change, or even progress, might happen in the present time. Many theologians, bishops, clergy and members of congregations who commemorated 500 years of Reformation combined the anniversary with the expectation of new impulses, new energy or even greater unity in Christianity. One can well understand that, as the number of Christians in western Europe is significantly declining. There was a special—indeed, an ecumenical—hope: in 2016 great expectations were attached to Pope Francis's visit to Lund, Sweden. He was invited by the Lutheran World Federation, which was founded in Lund in 1947. Would this be the time and place to announce the long-expected breakthrough concerning Eucharistic hospitality on the way to a newly united church? Not only Protestant Christians approached the anniversary year 2017 with much anticipation in many European countries, including Ireland.

It was a great pleasure and an honour studying and reflecting on the Reformation and its impact while living and working as a German Lutheran pastor in Ireland. There is a huge interest in the history of the Reformation and in Martin Luther, even though (or because?) the church's history in Ireland has been quite different when compared to the European continent, and the Lutheran Church in Ireland is one of the smallest churches on the island. The Theological Symposium, which gave reason to publish this book, discussed some of the most important themes of the Reformation. For example, the participants learned how Martin Luther's theology was not unique but was embedded in the theological and spiritual contexts of his time. Further, a keynote about the Lutheran Church in Sweden revealed that not long ago it controlled, as a State church, the daily lives of families, with strict laws combined with a system of supervision quite different to the freedom of the Christian which Luther had rediscovered. Or, as the lecture on the Reformation in Ireland showed, it became clear that it is to be understood as an opposite phenomenon to the Reformation on the Continent: in Ireland it was the Catholic priests who met the people in their daily lives and spoke their language, whereas the Anglican priests, coming from England and representing foreign rule over Ireland, insisted on using English in the services.

To learn from the time of the Reformation means to learn that changes in the churches and in Christianity take time. As Christianity trusts the work of the Holy Spirit there is no possibility to 'make' a new Reformation. Nevertheless, when we consider our own times and our churches today, it is obvious that there is a change and a sort of reformation to come. But what direction will it take? Are the growing Pentecostal churches and 'free churches' a hint of a renewed Christianity? And what needs renewal?

As this book is a special Irish contribution to the commemoration of the Reformation, some observations from the Irish perspective are significant. Not long ago 93% of the population were Catholic. In the 2011 census 84% were identified as Catholic, in 2016 78%. Indeed, other religious groups and Christian denominations in Ireland are growing, such as the Muslim community (63,400 in 2016, an increase of 28.9% compared to 2011) and the Orthodox Christians (62,200 in 2016, an increase of 37.5% compared to 2011). But the fastest-growing 'religion' are those who were identified in the 2016 census as 'without any religion': 468,421, an increase of 73.6% compared to the 2011 census (for all statistical figures see the official census report, www.cso.ie).

Leaving those figures aside, from personal conversations I have had with families at baptisms, confirmations, weddings and funerals it is obvious that younger people see themselves as Catholic or Protestant in cultural terms, with little or no adherence to their faith tradition. Indeed, some went so far as to say that religion is toxic, and they celebrated the 66.4% 'Yes' vote in the referendum on the Eighth Amendment (which took place on 25 May 2018 and concerned abortion) as a liberation from the power of the Catholic Church. Clearly, in modern Irish society (as in many other countries) church and religion now play a diminishing role. The place of science is also central today. 'Science tells us the truth, so we do not need any God', is a very common opinion held by students in schools. On the other hand, the stance of the so-called 'creationists', who deny any evolutionary theory and other scientific facts, certainly cannot be a Christian response to an overly positivistic view of science either.

So what do we learn from the history of Reformation and from these present circumstances for the future? Is there any line that can be drawn from 500 years ago into the future? While we do not know what the future will hold, I want to outline five fruits that might ripen in the years to come, forming and shaping Christianity.

Listening to the Word

According to the Global Scripture Access Report, the Bible is available in 674 languages today. This implies that 81% of the population worldwide are able to read the Bible in their own language. When we consider Europe, however, we realise that people may own a Bible but no longer read it, and in fact may never have spent even an hour glancing through its pages. In many parish centres, rooms are booked for well-attended entertainment or social activities, but Bible study groups get less attention and only a small number of people attend. Social and political issues and human reason are more important than the Bible for many clergy as a strategy for the future of their church.

This is in some ways similar to Luther's time. It was not entertainment and strategy but the church and the heavy weight of its tradition that had become more important than the Bible. The ordinary people received God's Word only through the authority of the church. In the early sixteenth century, Luther was one of the theologians who felt that there were gaps between the biblical stories and the teaching and dogma of the church. Luther listened to the Word and so he rediscovered that God grants grace through Jesus Christ without the 'grace-treasure' of the church.

Listening to the words of Holy Scripture means to hear it in its whole complexity. It needs both professional theology to dig into the deeper layers and a spiritual way of listening and waiting, the Word echoing in our souls. Maybe European Christianity is diminishing in numbers, but faith is never about numbers; it is about truth and God's love. This comes not through strategic plans; it comes first through listening to God's Word, the Bible.

Language and education

In modern times there are Christians who mistrust theological scholarship. In their understanding, scientific approaches to the Bible expel faith, but faith does not mean to stop thinking.

With his translation of the Bible into the vernacular, Luther significantly contributed to the formation of the German language. He also encouraged the development of education, because people should be able to read and understand God's Word for themselves. Holy Scripture is not a simple manual for how to become a faithful Christian; it is a book full of experiences with God. The long time of its formation includes different styles and genres. The complexity of this book and its old languages do not constitute a problem; rather they are an invitation to read, to discuss and to grow deeper in faith while exploring all facets of the biblical stories.

A fruit of the Reformation is the emphasis on a good education for all, including those who train for the priesthood. In times of a lack of young people studying theology, it would be wrong to decide on lowering the quality of the university degree and of the pastoral training of priests, deacons and others involved in church leadership.

Church and politics

The Reformation was successful because some of the local rulers adopted Luther's theology. No doubt there was a strong connection between throne and altar, between power and faith: '*Cuius regio, eius religio*' was the formula from 1555. The local ruler decided whether his people would become Protestant or remain Catholic.

This was to change, however, not only in Germany but also in Ireland and in many countries. We now have freedom of religion, and religion is separated from politics—more or less. In debates about religion in society, people usually hold that religion is a private matter. It is private, as faith comes through a personal relationship with God and Jesus Christ. Nevertheless, following the Gospel, a Christian cannot keep silent in cases of injustice, intolerance, environmental pollution and any kind of extremism. Even as a small number, Christians are called to be the salt of the earth (Mt 5:13); we are called to be involved in political and ethical discussions.

Fear and freedom

Most people in the western world do not fear God in the sense of being afraid of God. The mainstream trusts in the achievements of science and the freedom of living in democracies. On the other hand, however, there are new fears: 'Do I earn enough money? Does my life have any value? Will we live in peace in the future? What about all these strangers entering our countries?' Luther's rediscovery of freedom and justification by grace through faith is still a gift for us today. Believing in the living God means that we see our lives as a gift from God. Each day is a gift. So we can accept what happens and we should be free from fear because we are bound to God's love. Galatians 5:13: *For you were called to freedom, brothers and sisters; only do not use your freedom as an opportunity for self-indulgence, but through love become slaves to one another.* Fear is not a good adviser. It is up to Christians to share this understanding of life. Life without fear opens up for us to find the right answers to all daily, cultural and political challenges.

Churches and unity

Since the inception of the ecumenical movement (the World Council of Churches was founded in 1948 and had several precursors), there has been a longing for unity among the different Christian denominations. Instead of unity, however, we now witness an even greater variety of churches than a century ago, with a growing number of independent churches. A climax of this longing for unity, combined with lots of expectations, was Pope Francis's visit to Lund in 2016. But is it all about unity? And is an encompassing unity really necessary? What if it may have been God's will that different churches and denominations would emerge, as people are different? What if the great number of different churches and traditions is an echo of the fact that there are four Gospels in the New Testament and not only one? Indeed, each church, each tradition, brings out special ways of being Christian.

Further, in Ireland a huge change has happened: over the last few centuries the Catholic Church and the Anglican Church (Church of Ireland) stood face to face. But now there are a number of Christian churches in Ireland that are standing side by side, sharing the new challenges of secularism and declining numbers.

The vision of accepting the great variety of churches and traditions as a gift rather than as an accident already has a 'half'-solid ground: it is the fact that nearly all churches accept baptism received in other churches. The second part of that solid ground would be Eucharistic hospitality. If we see Jesus Christ as the one Who invites us to His table, and not a denomination which does so, this hospitality should not be as difficult to realise as it still seems to be. Reaching full Eucharistic hospitality might be one of the next steps in the ecumenical movement. Unfortunately, even the pope's visit to Lund for the inauguration of the 500th anniversary of the Reformation did not lead to this long-hoped-for realisation.

Conclusion

The year of celebrating 500 years of Reformation is now behind us. There is no great or obvious change in sight. This is no surprise. The future cannot be anticipated. Nevertheless, maybe the jubilee strengthened Christianity to move on humbly and full of trust in the living God. It may happen, then, that future generations, looking back at us, will recognise these fruits ripened for them over time.

Finally, I would like to mention the unique story of a wealthy tourist from Ethiopia in Acts 8. He was the treasurer of the Ethiopian queen who travelled to Jerusalem to visit the temple. A eunuch, he was not allowed to enter it, but he was impressed enough and bought a gift, as tourists do to this day. He bought an edition of the prophet Isaiah's writings. Suddenly Philip came to him into the chariot, helping him to understand the Scripture and telling him about

Jesus Christ. After a while the eunuch stopped the chariot, saying: 'What is to prevent me from being baptised?'

What is to prevent one from being baptised? Quite a lot, modern churches might say. First, one has to apply for membership. Some might ask for money. Others might ask for a proper faith-exam, like 'Did you learn the creed by heart?' Finally, there may be churches who won't allow individuals to be baptised because they are gay or lesbian. But, as Acts 8 tells us, Philip baptised him. There was nothing that would stop God's love in that special moment.

Maybe Christianity should trust more in those moments and less in paperwork. (Well, without paperwork churches cannot exist, but it is a question of priorities—of what matters essentially and what does not.) Maybe churches should trust in God's love instead of blaming people who are different.

After baptising the eunuch, Philip went away and the eunuch continued on his journey. He did not become a member of the first Christian community in Jerusalem. We do not know how and where his life journey went. This happens to many people in our time: they come into contact with the Gospel, without immediately becoming members of our churches. They knock at our church doors, asking for a prayer, for a sermon at a wedding, etc. Maybe we should trust in God working in them and accept that not all of them will stay for long.

Finally, it is said that the eunuch went on his way rejoicing. Being baptised brings out deep joy. This is said to all of us, to all of Christianity, 500 years after the Reformation: called to freedom, we are invited to continue our way rejoicing without fear.

Epilogue 2

Martin Sauter

In her 2008 book *The Great Emergence*,[1] the late American commentator on contemporary Christianity Phyllis Tickle argued that we are currently experiencing one of the periods of transformation to which the church in the West has had to adapt every 500 years or so, when, responding to epochal shifts in the economic, socio-cultural and political environment of the surrounding society, the foundations of Christian thought and praxis give way to epochal changes—changes which those living through such a period experience as deeply disorienting and troubling. Past transitions show, according to Tickle, that faith life which had come to feel very inadequate and old enters a painful period of transformation, when, as in a chrysalis, all taken-for-granted components of former communal faith life seem to dissolve. In the process of such a transition, a new Christianity emerges, reconfigured and revitalised. The result is a faith and a faith community that once more feel fresh and can respond effectively to human social reality. Earlier periods of transition were the collapse of the Western Roman Empire around AD 500 and the Great Schism between the Greek Church and the Latin Church of 1054. The most recent one happened 500 years ago, when the sixteenth century witnessed what Tickle calls *the Great Reformation*, which gave rise to our current faith reality and, of course, to the Lutheran Church.

The regained freshness of faith life has a price, so it seems. Back in the 1500s, the two church worlds newly emerging in the European West, Protestantism and Tridentine Roman Catholicism, gave fresh faith answers to the new conditions for life in the horizon of early modernity. But the price came in the form of mutual and violent antagonism that arose out of the confessionalist new theological and institutional arrangements of the emerging refurbished churches.

It is this last great transformation that we commemorated in 2017 in quincentenary commemorations and celebrations at every level of church organisation, from the local to the global. The Lutheran Church in Ireland marked the occasion with a number of memorable events and services that reflected not only on the theological and historical role of Martin Luther and other Lutheran reformers but also on the wider cultural and spiritual implications. The undoubted highlight of the year was the Symposium to which this book is a tribute and to which its participants bear witness in their very fine contributions collected here.

The foundations of the sixteenth-century faith dispensation, according to Tickle, lasted for more or less 500 years until our time, when we painfully observe many of them unravelling. Under conditions of post-modern culture and religious pluralism, of neoliberal global capitalism and the digital communication revolution, the mainstream churches in the West have been reeling from the loss of membership and from a generational rupture that has made the younger generation a minority in the churches, thus undermining their long-term viability. Moreover, the impact of this new cultural constellation has been compounded not only by the seemingly inadequate answers of the churches to the challenges of life in the 21st century in the West but even more detrimentally by the global exposure of the blatant contradictions between the life and teaching of Christianity's founder, Jesus of Nazareth, and the life and power practices of some of His most prominent followers, in particular when it comes to sexual abuse. Meanwhile, on the fringes of the old, new forms of worship and church life have emerged and grown, such as Pentecostalism, which is gaining exponential and rapid growth in membership, beginning in the global South but spreading rapidly North, creating a new and evolving Christian spiritual landscape.

The quincentenary year has been good for us Lutherans. Right around the globe it drew attention to the rich legacy of the Reformation: Martin Luther's struggles to find a gracious God; his discovery of the 'Freedom of a Christian', revitalising the old faith in thought and deed; the introduction of the entirety of the Good News to all people irrespective of class and through the dissemination of the Bible in the vernacular; and the great effort and emphasis on education so that truly all believers would gain access to God's message of grace, to name only a few. Thankfully, too, the commemorations did not hide the sad reality of sectarianism and intolerance in all faith communities back then towards all who did not embrace the new faith in the fashion that one's own group deemed to be the only true one.

It was good to dust down our complex cultural memories, to revisit our *lieux de mémoire* and refresh our convictions and connections to our spiritual and theological roots, and to do so for the first time in an ecumenical, mature and reconciling fashion, as both the global and local celebrations made evident. This was most pronounced in the great gathering of global church leaders of all denominations on 31 October 2016 together with Pope Francis in the

Lutheran Cathedral of Lund in Sweden, but also in Dublin, Ireland, where the commemorations by our tiny Lutheran Church in Ireland were graced with the truly joyful and joy-giving presence of Christians and church leaders of all parts of the Body of Christ. These were hope-inducing, relationship-deepening, faith-increasing moments, much cherished: food for the road ahead, no doubt.

And yet, as the centenary year vanishes beyond the horizon, we are confronted with new spiritual challenges arising from the rapidly evolving socio-economic and political situation in the context of the larger trends of our transition time. And it raises the question: what will remain, sustain and inspire as we confront this new world? What will emerge from the chrysalis of *our* moment, when so much of what was right previously seems no longer to provide adequate solid ground on which to stand?

I am writing these thoughts at the end of a fifteen-month stay in California, where I had the blessing of being received as pastor-in-residence into the community at the University Lutheran Chapel, Berkeley, as well as at the Pacific Lutheran Theological Seminary at the GTU (Graduate Theological Union, Berkeley). In 2018 two realities had a very strong and painful impact here. Because of their geographical and personal proximity to those affected directly, both had immediacy and were not just 'news'. I refer to the historically unprecedented ferocity of wild fires on the one hand and the arrival of the 'Caravan' in Tijuana, on the Californian–Mexican border, on the other. Both are manifestations of interdependent *global* realities, namely accelerating climate change and the uprooting of a great multitude of people in global migration flows and the Western world's increasingly hostile response to them.

According to official statistics, the 2018 Californian fire season has been the longest, geographically most widespread and most destructive ever recorded in this part of the world. The fire season also saw the occurrence of hitherto rare weather phenomena—fire tornados—and, again, where they occurred they were stronger, faster and more destructive than ever. More than 8,400 fires destroyed 1.9 million acres of vegetation in 2018 in the state of California and caused 3.5 billion dollars' worth of damage. They exterminated wild life, destroyed human livelihoods and brought death and destruction to countless communities, with 103 people killed, including six firefighters who lost their lives trying to rescue others. The all but total annihilation of the northern Californian town of Paradise with its approximately 26,000 inhabitants may stand as a chilling symbol for the loss experienced: 'Paradise Lost' gives a new harrowing subtext to the title of John Milton's much-revered and seminal book for Western religious imagination.

At the end of 2018 the 'Caravan' was the most recent headline-grabbing jigsaw piece of global migration as a result of the breakdown of social order, the lack of economic opportunity and environmental degradation. It started on 12 October 2018 in San Pedro Sula in Honduras, when, following the stolen presidential election there in 2017, approximately 160 people decided to leave their politically corrupt, crime- and drug-ridden and economically hopeless home city to seek asylum in the US. As they made their way through Guatemala and Mexico more and more people joined. On 15 November, a month after they began their trek north, the Caravan reached Tijuana on the Mexican side of the border with the US. By that time it had swollen to over 5,000, who joined some 2,600 people already waiting at the border crossing for their asylum case to be recorded by US Immigration. A couple of weeks before, in the final days of the US Congressional Midterm elections and in preparation for the approaching Caravan, US President Donald Trump had ordered some 5,000 personnel of the US Army to the border, an unprecedented and potentially unconstitutional use of the US military for border control. In December the situation on the Mexican side of the border in the informal makeshift refugee camp was exacerbated by the arrival of torrential rain. The encampment, overflowing beyond all capacity, now sank in mud and its inhabitants could find no space that was not wet and dirty.

Both the ferocious wild fires and the Caravan are but snapshots, regional instances of the transnational global conditions of climate change and the overlapping global migration crisis. The mass exodus of refugees from the Middle East and parts of Africa in 2015, their trek through the Balkans and their very dangerous and often fatal attempts to cross the Mediterranean were realities strongly experienced in Europe and with ongoing political consequences. On the other hand, flooding, storm damage, wild fires, extreme summer heat and drought are increasingly also a reality in our part of the world.

Such events are a result of fossil-fuel-driven neoliberal globalisation and its exponentially uneven socio-economic effects, combined with severe environmental degradation, which leads to failing nation states, bogged down in corruption and gang violence, where desperate people, seduced by the all-pervasive visual presence on social media of the allures of Western affluence, uproot themselves from hopeless situations, hand themselves over to criminal trafficking gangs and begin their perilous journey north into an uncertain future—a future which, precarious as it is, is nevertheless preferable to the politically, economically and environmentally ever-deteriorating situation in which they find themselves in their home countries.

These two global developments pose challenges for our communal living out of our Christian calling. Even we, as a small and sheltered church community in Ireland, will need to prepare our faith response to both. As Lutherans we will want to do so in the light of the Gospel of salvation in Jesus Christ and equipped with the best of what the Lutheran legacy may bring to these challenges. But we will be well advised to do so in concert with our siblings in other parts of the Christian church, as well as with our neighbours of different faiths and none.

What would such a faith preparation entail?

Climate change

Our reflection will need to begin by acknowledging the condoning, if not actively legitimising, role of Western Christian thought and culture in the unfolding of the West's exploitative attitude towards the Earth and all its creatures, including non-white humans—from the colonial submission of the earth and all its peoples that was understood as divinely ordained under the fifteenth-century Doctrine of Discovery[2] to the mass extraction of the Earth's minerals as 'resources' for human (read Western) development that has underwritten industrialisation since the seventeenth century to this day. That, again, was understood to be divinely sanctioned through a utilitarian reading of Genesis 1:28. The Earth's contribution to human flourishing—indeed, its foundational life-giving—has been ignored, and this has created a systemic blindness to the environmental costs of the present-day global economy. As Western Lutherans we fully share in this collusion in a culture of death and *Un-Creation*.[3]

Under conditions of accelerating climate change, it is becoming apparent that this blindness could lead to extinction not only of the majority of non-human species of our time but also of humanity itself, as the Earth's web of life comes under terminal pressure. Our Christian, our Lutheran, practice will need to become a truly Earth-honouring faith. We will need to reorient very intentionally and very fast our entire faith praxis, our common liturgical and spiritual life as well as our ethics, both as a community and as individual believers in the various contexts of our different life vocations. How can we as a community reflect in our life and work the fact that, according to Genesis 1:24, the Earth is named as God's co-creator, generating all life-forms living in its eco-system, a fact that until very recently[4] was overlooked in Western theology? What does it mean to believe and profess that the Earth is part of creation, not a manufactured product that can be used and discarded at will? What does it mean in the light of this to give honour to the Creator? For Lutherans, the overemphasis on *individual* human redemption that arose out of Luther's rediscovery of the central soteriological role of Jesus Christ will need to be thought through anew. More space will have to be given to the role of the other two divine persons in the mystery of the Trinity: God the Creator and God the Holy Spirit, indwelling, sustaining and renewing all creation. In that way our Christology would expand the Christ event into its cosmic dimension. Such a refurbished understanding of God's relationship with the entirety of creation will prepare us for the necessity of turning away from our death-bringing culture of overconsumption—a new and wholistic understanding of *metanoia*, repentance.

Migration and globalisation

In a world where, defended by globally operating security systems, political and economic power, wealth and opportunity are redistributed from the bottom and the middle to the top in a process of accelerating speed, the systemic nature of injustice is analogous to that of empire in bygone ages, including the empire of the Romans around the Mediterranean at the time of Jesus in Palestine. When we reflect on the Gospel in the light of empire a number of things stick out: the emphasis in the synoptic Gospels on Jesus' proclamation of Good News to the *poor*, οι φτωχοί [*oi ptochoi*]; Matthew's account of Jesus' parents plight as refugees in Egypt in the face of royal infanticide, together with Luke's setting of the nativity story in the context of imperial manifestation of power; God's proclamation of the birth of the Christ to the shepherds, those on the margins of society; and, finally, Luke's insistence on Jesus' blessing of the *physically poor* as the inheritors of the kingdom of God in the Sermon on the Field (Lk 6), in contrast to Matthew's *spiritually poor* in the Sermon on the Mount (Mt 5). This is, of course, not new; all these points have been made over decades by various proponents of liberation theology. Today, however, when in the West secularisation has brought an end to Christendom, the churches' calling to stand in alignment with those on the margins will need to include the migrant masses fleeing destitution and seeking refuge in the affluent North.

Climate change/climate justice and the upholding of human dignity in the face of globalisation are two components of what faces us. The task that our time seems to demand of us seems nothing short of another *great reformation*—indeed, a colossal reformation. To reorient our communal life and faith message in line with an earth-honouring practice that is attuned to the divinely ordained dignity of all creation and all creatures, as well as, following Jesus, to be in community with those most exploited in our global web of relations, will demand jointly focused intentionality and a revitalised return to the sources of our faith in order to once again drink in God's gift of grace freely available to all. In a culture of fear, such as has arisen all over the Western world, there are no easy answers; the realities hinted at here are vastly complex.

Putting into practice what we become compelled to see as true will face strong opposition and rejection. Nevertheless, if we wish to remain true to our calling, we need to step out of our religious comfort zone. In this we need not be anxious about having perfect answers straight away. We can willingly—indeed, joyfully—accept the provisional nature of our answers at any given moment along the way, just as Martin Luther and the reformers 500 years ago did not set out to build a new church structure set in stone for all times but responded to the newly perceived call of the Gospel with an energetic freshness and fearlessness, adapting to the necessities of every moment in that tumultuous phase of history when the old world became unhinged. In doing so, they made decisions. In hindsight a number turned out to be mistaken and of grave consequence, but many more were life-giving, energising and reorienting ones.

Like the reformers back then, so do we set out. In the light of all available wisdom of the moment and to the best of our ability and capacities, we dare to take one step at a time, ordering and reordering for the current moment our understanding of the reality of the Gospel. The ground on which we stand has been dislocated, the sands of time are shifting, we are in a chrysalis and we do not know the shape of the church to be, but we are called to get up and start moving.

We have a Lutheran compass—immersed in the reality of undeserved grace, testified and rediscovered in the freshness of the Gospel, and beheld in faith. And, like our ancestors before us, we, too, will discover that the Spirit guides us, Pillar of Fire by night and Pillar of Cloud by day: Exodus once more! Martin Luther would approve.

Notes

[1] Phyllis Tickle, *The Great Emergence—How Christianity is Changing and Why* (Ada, MI, 2008), cf. Chapter 1.

[2] Sanctioned by Pope Alexander VI's papal bull of 1493, the 1494 Treaty of Tordesillas divided up the world into two hemispheres: all lands *and* their inhabitants to be 'discovered' and which were not Christian would become the property of either the Portuguese or the Spanish empire. While subsequent imperial aspirations of other European kingdoms, among them Protestant England and later the USA, disregarded the Iberian claims to world domination, the legal principle of European, Western Christian *ownership* of non-Christian land and peoples remained firmly entrenched throughout the imperial era of European expansion.

[3] The terms *Un-Creation* and *Un-Creators* are used by Lutheran theologian and ethicist Cynthia Moe-Lobeda in her book on Earth ethics, *Resisting Structural Evil. Love as Ecological-Economic Vocation* (Minneapolis, MN, 2013).

[4] For a good example of a recent theological critique from an eco-feminist point of view see Grace Si-Sun Kim and Hilda P. Koster, *Planetary Solidarity. Global Women's Voices on Christian Doctrine and Climate Justice* (Minneapolis, MN, 2017).

Contributors

Pastor Stephan Arras studied church music in Frankfurt and theology in Mainz, Heidelberg, Jerusalem and Munich. He worked as Pastor in Beerfelden, Odenwald, and from 2000 until 2015 he was Dean of 25 parishes in the same region. He co-founded the interfaith committee 'Rat der Religionen' in the Odenwald region, was a member of the Synod of the Evangelische Kirche in Hessen und Nassau (EKHN) and was for six years a member of the Theological Steering Group of the EKHN. In 2015 he was elected Pastor of the Lutheran Church in Ireland, Dublin. He represents the Lutheran Church in the Irish Council of Churches, the Dublin Council of Churches, the Irish Council of Christians and Jews and the Dublin City Interfaith Forum. He is a member of the Iona Community, Scotland.

Jürgen Barkhoff, Dr phil., FTCD, is Professor of German (1776) in the Department of Germanic Studies in the School of Languages, Literatures and Cultural Studies at Trinity College Dublin. His main research areas are literature and medicine, science and psychology around 1800, questions of identity in the German-speaking world and Europe as reflected in literature and culture, and contemporary Swiss literature. He has published widely on these topics. From 2007 to 2011 he was Registrar of the University, from 2012 to 2015 Director of the Trinity Long Room Hub Arts & Humanities Research Institute and from 2015 to 2018 Head of School.

Markus Grimmeisen, Dr rer. pol., has been a member of the Church Council of the Lutheran Church in Ireland since 2011 and Chair of the Church Council since 2014. In 1997 he obtained his doctorate in Business Administration from the University of Stuttgart and joined the Robert Bosch Group in the same year. He is now Head of Resources at the European Foundation for the Improvement of Living and Working Conditions (Eurofound), an Agency of the European Union, located in Dublin, which is providing knowledge to assist in the development of better social, employment and work-related policies. He is also the Secretary to its Management Board and Executive Board and a member of the Internal Control Committee.

Revd Michael Jackson studied at Trinity College Dublin and at Cambridge University. He has been Church of Ireland Archbishop of Dublin and Bishop of Glendalough since 2011. He also serves as Co-chairman of the Anglican–Lutheran Porvoo Communion.

Revd Brendan Leahy is a prelate of the Catholic Church. Since 2013 he has been the Bishop of Limerick. He has served as Chair of the Irish Catholic Bishops Conference Committee on Ecumenism and Co-Chair of the Irish Inter-Church Meeting. From 2006 to 2013 he was Professor of Systematic Theology at St Patrick's College, Maynooth.

Volker Leppin, Dr theol. habil., studied theology in Marburg, Jerusalem and Heidelberg, where he also received his doctoral degree in 1994. In 1997 he was awarded his Habilitation. He was vicarious professor in Frankfurt from 1998 to 2000, and held the chair of Church History at Jena University from 2000 to 2010. Since 2010 he has held the same position at the Evangelische Fakultät at Tübingen University. He is a member of the Academies of Sciences of Saxonia and Heidelberg. His publications include *Wilhelm von Ockham: Gelehrter—Streiter—Bettelmönch* (Darmstadt, 2012), *Martin Luther: a late medieval life* (Grand Rapids, 2017) and *Franziskus von Assisi* (Darmstadt, 2018).

John McCafferty, Ph.D, is a Professor of History at University College Dublin. His work and publications are concerned with religious change in Ireland between 1500 and 1700. He is Director of the Mícheál Ó Cléirigh Institute, a collaboration between the Irish Franciscans (OFM) and UCD. He is currently Chair of the Irish Manuscripts Commission and *Praeses* of the *Consiglio Dei Reggenti* of the *Collegio San Bonaventura Frati Editori Quaracchi*, based at St Isidore's College, Rome.

Martin Meiser, Dr theol. habil., studied theology in Neuendettelsau, Hamburg, Tübingen and Munich. He has worked as a minister in Bavaria and has held academic positions in Erlangen, Mainz and Münster. Since 2007 he is Assistant Professor of New Testament Studies at Saarbrücken University. His research interests include Galatians, the Gospel of Mark, the Septuagint within the literature of ancient Judaism and ancient exegesis of the Bible.

Graeme Murdock, DPhil., is Associate Professor in European History and a Fellow of Trinity College Dublin. He was Director of Trinity's Centre for European Studies between 2014 and 2017. His research covers a range of topics concerning the religious, cultural and social history of early modern Europe. He has published studies on the Reformation in Central Europe and on Calvinism in sixteenth-century France.

Patrick Prendergast, Ph.D, was appointed to the Engineering Faculty in Trinity College Dublin in 1995 and has been Provost of the College since 2011. He is a Member of the Royal Irish Academy, a Fellow of the Irish Academy of Engineering and an International Fellow of the Royal Academy of Engineering in the UK. In 2016 he was awarded an Honorary Fellowship of the Anatomical Society in recognition of his contributions to bioengineering and anatomy.

Helga Robinson-Hammerstein, Dr phil., studied in the University of Mainz and subsequently in Marburg, where she wrote her doctoral dissertation, published as *Erzbischof Adam Loftus und die elisabethanische Reformationspolitik in Irland* (1976). She was a Fellow of Trinity College Dublin, where she lectured in Modern European History (1969–2008) and was also a long-serving Dean of Graduate Studies. She was co-editor of the *Bibliographie zur Thüringischen Geschichte* (1965) and co-author of *Bertholds und Bernolds Chroniken* (2002). She published *The Transmission of Ideas in the Lutheran Reformation* (1989) and *European Universities in the Age of Reformation and Counter-Reformation* (1998), together with many articles on the Lutheran Reformation and university history in early modern Europe. A regular contributor to the *Literatur-Bericht* of the *Archiv für Reformationsgeschichte*, she has also published many translations of early sixteenth-century German Reformation pamphlets with commentaries and facsimile reproductions. In addition, she served as General Secretary of the International Commission for the History of Universities (1995–2005).

Pastor (i.E.) Martin Sauter, MA, was born in Konstanz, Germany. A graduate in English and History from the University of Konstanz, he trained as a secondary teacher. On relocation to Ireland in 1990, he worked as a part-time lecturer in history, sociology and intercultural studies at Dublin City University. He has been active in the Lutheran Church in Ireland since 1991. In 2015 he was ordained as a non-stipendiary Pastor, the first Lutheran ordination in Ireland. He has been involved in ecumenical bodies at local, national and European level. In 2017/18 he was Pastor in Residence at the University Lutheran Chapel, Berkeley, USA.

Stephanie Springer, Dr jur., is a lawyer. Since 2013 she is President of the

Landeskirchenamt, Evangelisch-Lutherische Kirche, Hannover. She is a member of the Rat (Council) of the Evangelische Kirche Deutschland (EKD).

Gesa Thiessen, Ph.D, was awarded her doctorate in 1998 at Milltown Institute of Theology and Philosophy, where she lectured for many years. She is Adjunct Assistant Professor at Trinity College Dublin and Visiting Scholar at Sarum College, Salisbury. Her research interests have focused on theology and the visual arts and on ecumenical ecclesiology. She has published widely, including *Remembering the Reformation: Luther and Catholic Theology* (co-edited with Declan Marmion and Salvador Ryan) (Minneapolis, 2017), *Apostolic and Prophetic: Ecclesiological Perspectives* (Eugene, OG, 2011), *Ecumenical Ecclesiology: Unity, Diversity and Otherness in a Fragmented World* (London/New York, 2009), *Theological Aesthetics: A Reader* (London/Grand Rapids, MI, 2004) and *Theology and Modern Irish Art* (Dublin, 1999). She is a non-stipendiary minister in the Lutheran Church in Ireland.

Revd Donald Watts, Ph.D, was President of the Irish Council of Churches from 2015 to 2017. He was ordained in 1977 to the ministry of the Presbyterian Church in Ireland and served in Ballyholme Congregation from 1980 to 2001. He was then appointed Clerk of the General Assembly of the Presbyterian Church, a position which he held from 2003 until his retirement in 2014. He has served on a number of ecumenical bodies, including the then British Council of Churches, the Conference of European Churches' working groups on Human Rights and Peace and Reconciliation, and as secretary of the European Committee of the then World Alliance of Reformed Churches.

Gunda Werner, Dr theol. habil., was awarded the *Diplom* in Catholic Theology in 1998 at the University of Münster and her doctorate in 2005, also in Münster. She completed her Habilitation at Ruhr-University, Bochum, in 2015. She also holds a Diploma in Theme-Centered Interaction (2008). She was Assistant Professor in Bochum, Junior Professor in Tübingen and Interim Professor of Dogmatics in Bonn and Bochum. Since 2018 she has been Professor of Systematic Theology and head of the Institute of Dogmatic Theology at the Faculty of Catholic Theology at Karl-Franzens University, Graz, Austria.

Ruth Whelan, Ph.D, was a lecturer for thirteen years at Trinity College Dublin and has been Professor (chair) of French at Maynooth University since 1997. She has held Senior Visiting Fellowships at the Herzog August Bibliothek,

Wolfenbüttel, at Linacre College, Oxford, and at Archbishop Marsh's Library, Dublin. She was elected a Member of the Royal Irish Academy in 2000 and a Chevalier dans l'Ordre des Palmes Académiques in 2007. Her research specialises in the religious, political and intellectual culture of Huguenot refugees in Europe from 1680 to 1720. Her publications include *The Anatomy of Superstition: A Study of the Historical Theory and Practice of Pierre Bayle* (Oxford, 1982; 2nd edn 2013), *Toleration and Religious Identity: The Edict of Nantes and Its Implications in France, Britain and Ireland* (Dublin, 2003) and *Narrating the Self in Early Modern Europe* (Oxford, 2007).

Index

Abelard 75
Alen, J. 127
Anabaptists 11, 95, 160–1
Anglicanism 4, 10, 85–7, 121–2, 132, 161, 166, 169
   see also Church of Ireland, England, Ireland, Scotland
   Book of Common Prayer 9, 84, 121
   church interiors 47–8
   Forty-Two Articles 9
   Oxford Movement 9
   Prayer Book 9
Anna of Denmark 16
Antichrist 40, 55, 80, 84, 86, 130, 133
Anti-clericalism 27, 35, 41, 158
Archbold, N. 126
Aristotle, Aristotelianism 33, 41, 97, 99
Armagh 127, 131–2
Art 3, 47, 55, 61, 63, 145
   see also Cranach, Images, Luther
Augsburg Confession 22, 47, 60, 83
Augustine, St, Augustinian 1, 8, 68, 72, 95, 106, 158
Bale, J. 132
Baptism 11, 27 39, 160, 166, 169
Bartholomew's Day massacre 111, 116, 122–3
Basset, L. 105
Beckett, S. 13
Bedford-Strohm, H. 105
Bellarmine, R. 133
Benn, G. 143
Bernard of Clairvaux 2, 28, 40
Bildungsbürgertum 140
Bodmer, J.J. 142
Bora, Katharina von 16, 145
Bouhéreau, É. 118, 121
Brehm, A. 143
Brenz, J. 81

Briçonnet, G. 106
Broet, P. 135
Bruderschafften (brotherhoods) 34
Bucer, M. 8, 82
Büchner, G. 142
Bultmann, R. 97
Burckhardt, F. 82
Burckhardt, J. 143
Burton, S. 84–6
Caillard, G. 122
Calvin, J., Calvinism 8–9, 16, 47–8, 59, 63, 106–8, 126–130, 160
Canterbury 81–6, 127
Capuchins 126, 130–1
Carswell, J. 129
Catherine of Aragon 81, 126, 130
Catholicism 7, 9, 26, 86, 94–5, 114, 122, 131–2, 171
   see also Christianity, Church
   Catholic Church 26, 51, 59, 72, 75, 115, 136, 142, 161, 169
   Council of Trent 3, 26, 62, 67–75, 130, 133, 171
   curia 35, 39
   Decet Romanum Pontificem 40
   Decree on Justification 70–4
   Decree on Original Sin 71–2
   Decree on Penance 72–4
   Exsurge Domine 40, 73
   Laudabiliter 134
   Magisterium 66
   Second Vatican Council 15, 25, 48, 63, 75
   papacy, popes 8–9, 27, 35, 39–40, 58–60, 79–80, 86, 134–6, 158
   polemics against 2–3, 13, 24, 37, 41, 52–61, 132
   self-modernisation 75
   transubstantiation 8, 81
Céitinn, S. 128

Celibacy 8, 39, 141, 144, 147
Charles V 79, 81, 106
Chichester, A. 134
Christianity 5–8, 11–12, 15, 25, 78, 94, 133, 154, 158, 165–70, 171–2
  see also Catholicism, Church, Church of Ireland, Luther, Lutheran, Pentecostalism, Presbyterians, Reformation
  Christendom 11, 13, 26, 74, 176
  climate change 173–7
  congregation 41–2, 47, 60, 83, 93, 107–8, 129, 131, 133, 165
  Earth-honouring faith 175
  fear and freedom 168
  future of 5, 165–77
  globalisation 176–7
  language and education 167
  listening to the Word 167
  medieval church 24–7, 34, 58, 133, 136
  migration 173–7
  people of God 14
  post-modern culture 172
  religious pluralism 172
  universal 5, 27, 47
Church
  see also Catholicism, Christianity, Church of Ireland, Luther, Lutheran, Pentecostalism, Presbyterians, Reformation
  discipline 107
  life 2, 8, 10, 48, 151, 172
  and politics 168
  and state 11
  unity 5, 168–9
Church of Ireland (Anglican) 9–10, 128–37, 169
Claudius, M. 142
Clavairoly, F. 104
Cochlaeus, J. 13, 39, 57
Colonisation 7
Confession 22–3, 39, 60, 66–8
Cork 120–2, 136
Coverdale, M. 83
Cranach the Elder, L. 3, 38, 47–8, 51–61
Cranach the Younger, L. 3, 51–61
Cranmer, T. 9, 81–7

Cromwell, T. 82–3, 127
Crosses 38, 48
Crucifixes 47–50, 55, 60–1, 63
David, M. 118
Denifle, H.S. 25–6
Devil 34, 41, 49, 71
Devotio moderna 106
Diet of Worms 35, 41, 86
Dilthey, W. 143, 146
Dominicans 21, 131
Droysen, J.G. 143
Dublin 16–17, 80–1, 85, 87, 104, 118–22, 127, 129, 132, 135–6, 173
  see also Ireland
  Castle 121, 128, 130, 136
  Christ Church Cathedral 134
  parliament 126, 128
  St Patrick's Cathedral 121
Duffy, E. 51
Dunn, J.D.G. 92–4
Ecclesiology 2, 8, 39, 92, 121
Eck, J. 40
Eckhart, Meister 1–2, 21–2, 28
Ecumenism 2, 12, 14, 25
  ecumenical movement 4, 63, 161, 168–9
Edict of Fontainebleau 115
Edict of Nantes 105, 111–6
Edward VI 9, 83, 132
England 8–10, 78, 81–7, 111, 115–121, 126–37, 166
  Act of Uniformity 130
  King James Bible 130
  Supremacy Act 129
  Westminster 127
Enlightenment, the 3, 61, 74–5, 94, 140–5, 149–50
Erasmus 3, 23, 69–71, 106
Eugenius III 40
Euler, L. 142
Faith 1–16, 28–9, 38–43, 51–63, 68–9, 81, 94–6, 107, 159–60, 166–70, 171–6
  see also God, Jesus Christ, Holy Spirit, Redemption, Repentance, Salvation
Farel, G. 106
Fasting 43
Fitzgerald, S.T. Lord Offaly 127

185

Fontaine, J. 122
Fontane, T. 154
Foxe, J. 85
France 3–4, 9, 83, 104–25
Francis, Pope 11–15, 66, 161, 165, 169, 172
Franciscans, 126, 130–1
Frederick the Wise 40, 49
Freedom
   see also Erasmus, Luther
   of conscience 111–2
   divine and human 66–77
   religious 2, 123
Friedenthal, R. 154
Friedrich, C.D. 60
Gellert, C.F. 142
Germany 2, 4, 8–9, 16, 33, 41, 47, 58, 60, 105, 117, 132, 140–5
God
   see also Jesus Christ, Holy Spirit
   divine action 3, 66, 75
   and empire 7
   grace 1–2, 8, 14, 35, 49–54, 67–75, 79, 99, 145, 159, 167–8, 172–7
   in the soul of the believer 22, 28–9
   love 1, 3, 22–3, 52, 66–77, 79, 82, 94, 144, 159–61, 167–70
   Trinity, the 21–2, 49, 60, 176
   Word, the 32, 34, 36, 43, 79, 84, 129, 144–6
Goethe, J.W. v. 141–2, 148–9
Goldschmied, C. 24
Goldsmith, O. 148
Gospel, gospels, the 29, 42, 51–60, 67–8, 82–4, 95–9, 106, 133–4, 144, 159–60, 168–70, 175–7
   see also God, Scriptures
Gottsched, J.C. 142
Greiffenhagen, M. 144
Gryphius, A. 142
Guilt 66–77
   see also Penance, Repentance, Sin
Guise 66–77, 110
Haacker, K. 98
Hausmann, N. 42
Heaven 1, 8, 22, 52, 79
Henri IV 111–12
Herder, J.G. 148–9
Heresy 11–12, 21, 39, 80, 106, 111–13, 126–7
Hesse, H. 143
Holl, K. 25
Holland 111–21
Holy Communion, Eucharist 2, 8, 10, 29, 39, 48, 60, 80, 83, 165, 169
Holy Spirit 96, 161, 166, 176
   see also God, Jesus Christ
Homer 149–150
Huguenots 4, 104–25
   diaspora 116–22
   elimination 113–16
   France 104–16
   Ireland 118–24
Hus, J. 3, 39, 80–7
Iconoclasm 3, 8, 47, 49–50, 61–4, 111, 132
Iconodules 64
Idols 50
Idyll 142, 148–53
Images 2–3, 13, 38, 47–65, 79, 159
Ireland, Irish 2–5, 6–18, 78, 87, 104–25, 126–38, 158, 165–75
   see also Catholicism, Church of Ireland, Dublin, Huguenots
   Anglicisation 129–30
   anti-Catholic legislation 135
   Baltinglass rebels 136
   Catholicity 130
   Catholic reformation 11, 137
   census 2011 166
   clergy 4, 113, 132, 135
   Common Prayer Book 129
   Council of Churches 17
   evangelisation 127–31
   Foras feasa ar Éirinn 128
   friars 130
   Gaelic 127–36
   identity 127–37
   Inter-Church Meeting 17
   Non-Conformists 10
   Pale, the 127
   referendum on the Eighth Amendment 166
   religious change in sixteenth- and seventeenth-century 126–38
   religious choice 127
   seminaries in Europe 131
   Tiomna Nuadh ar Dtigherna 129

Index

Tudor reformations 126–32
Irish School of Ecumenics 12
Iserloh, E. 25–6
James II 120
Janz, O. 142
Jesuits 11, 130–1, 133–6
Jesus Christ 1–29 *passim*, 34–41 *passim*, 53, 56, 68, 73, 92–8, 104, 108, 159–60, 167–76
  see also God, Holy Spirit
John Paul II 136
Joint Declaration on the Doctrine of Justification 13, 161
Jones, T. 136
Judaism, Jews 13, 71, 92–6, 150
Junge, M. 12, 14
Justice 3, 66–77
Karlstadt, A.R. v. Bodenstein 29, 41, 49–50
Klopstock, F.G. 149
Koch, K. 12
Koerner, J.L. 60–1
Kretzschmer, E. 147
Kümmel, W.G. 95
Kurz, H. 154
Laity 1, 27–8, 34–5, 39, 80, 107
Lake, P. 9
Laudian Party 84
Lefèvre d'Etaples, J. 106
Lenz, J.M.R. 141–2, 152–3
Leo X 39–40
Lessing, G.E. 142, 149–52
Lichtenberg, G.C. 142
Lortz, J. 25–6
Luther, Martin
  see also Cranach, Melanchthon, Reformation, Scriptures, St Augustine, Staupitz, St Paul, Bora, Wittenberg
  Against the Bull of the Antichrist 40
  A Letter to Pope Leo X 40
  biblical scholar 3–4, 91–103
  Church Postil 28
  Commentary on Galatians 91–8
  Cranach 47–65
  Das alte Testament 79
  ecclesiology 2, 37, 39, 92, 159
  Epistolae quaedam piissimae et eruditissimae Iohannis Hus 3, 80–7

Eyn Enchiridion oder Handbuchlein 79
Eyn Freyheyt dess Sermons bebstlichen Ablass und Gnad belangend 78
good works 1–2, 25, 62, 99
Great Sermon on Usury 40
Ground and Reason for all the Articles wrongly condemned by the Roman Bull 40
Heidelberg Disputation 15
images 3, 47–65
indulgences 1, 21–8, 35, 38, 49, 56, 67, 78–9, 158, 168
Invocavit sermons 3, 42, 49
Judaism 94–5
justification 1, 8, 22, 28, 49, 52, 67, 70–5, 92–9, 161, 168
law and gospel 37, 51–3, 96–9
legacy for Pauline studies 91–103
mysticism 21, 28–9
New Testament translation 1, 158
On the avoidance of human teachings 41
On the Babylonian Captivity of the Church 39
One Hundred Theses against Scholastic Theology 33
polemics 2–3, 24, 37, 52–61
preacher 2, 32, 34
priesthood of all believers 28, 39, 159
printing press 32, 51
Psalms 33, 36–7
reform in L.'s sermons and pamphlets 32–46
Schwaermer (enthusiats) 29, 146
simul justus et peccator 68, 95
swan 81
The Adoration of the Sacrament 48
The Freedom of a Christian 1, 28, 104, 172
The Meaning of Two Gruesome Figures 58
The Ninety-Five Theses 1, 21–4, 35, 98, 129, 158
Theologia deutsch 24
To the Christian Nobility of the German nation 28

Trinity College library 78–88
vernacular 2, 32, 78, 80, 106–7, 128, 158, 167, 172
Wartburg 28, 39, 41, 49, 79
Zwei-Reiche Lehre (teaching of the two kingdoms) 143, 147
Lutheran
    Church 5, 17–18, 47–8, 55, 60, 63, 81, 161, 165, 171, 173
    clergy 4, 140–57
    compass for the future 177
    crucifix 47–50, 55, 61, 63
    differences between Lutherans and Calvinists 59
    European Road Map 2017 16
    Hausmusik 145
    Lutheran rectory in German culture and literature 140–57
    pastor 4, 59, 140–57, 165
    pastor's wife 141
    World Federation 12–14
MacCulloch, D. 85
Mährlen, J. 152
Marot, C. 106
Marriage 38, 42, 81, 83, 126
Martini, F. 150
Mary 29, 47, 50
Mary I 132
Mass, the 2, 21, 39–42, 81, 116, 129, 133–4
McGarry, P. 104
Melanchthon, P. 9, 33, 48, 51–60
    see also Luther
Mendelssohn, M. 150
Mercy 3, 14, 66-77, 99
Middle Ages, medieval 2–3, 21–8, 33–7, 42, 48, 58, 67, 78, 80, 132–7
Milton, J. 173
Moeller, B. 26
Mörike, E. 142, 150–2
Mommsen, C.M.T. 143
Monasticism, monastery 6, 8–9, 42, 98, 135, 145
    monks 1, 13, 21, 23–7, 40, 42, 52, 56–9, 97, 106, 111, 158
    nuns 21, 42, 58
Moritz, K.P. 154
Müntzer, T. 29
Myconius, F. 82–3

Mysticism, mystical theology
    see Luther
Nádasdy, T. 16
Nicolai, F. 154
Nietzsche, F. 141, 143, 154
Nordhausen, F.G. v. 33
Ó Cearnaigh, S. 129
Ó Cléirigh, M. 126
O'Devaney, C. 136
Ó Domhnuill, U. 133–4
O'Hely, P. 136
Ó hEodhasa, B. 131
O'Hurley, D. 136
Osiander, A. 81–2
Parsons, J. 123
Paul, J. 142, 153
Paul, St 1, 3, 8, 23, 39, 50, 52, 69, 71
    participationism 97–8
    Pauline studies 91–103
    New Perspective 91–103
Peace of Ryswick 116
Peasants' War 8
Pelagius 69
Penance 21–32, 38–9, 66–77
    see also Luther, Guilt and repentance 67-73
Perrissin, J. 107
Physicotheology 144
Piety 4, 7–8, 21, 25–8, 34–7, 42, 80, 85, 92, 142, 144, 148
Pilgrimages 38
Popular religion 38
Portarlington 120–1
Prayer 9, 14, 34, 43, 121, 129–30, 134, 145, 170
Presbyterians 18, 47, 121, 129, 132
Protestantism, Protestants 4, 11, 25, 28, 128, 132–3
    churches 17, 26, 135, 161
    clergy (in Germany) 140–55
    French 104–25
Providence 8
    see also Freedom, Will, Redemption, Salvation
Purgatory 1
Puritans 84
Raabe, W. 154
Redemption 5, 24, 67, 69, 175
    see also Penance, Repentance,

Salvation, Sin
Reformation, the
    see also Cranach, Germany, Ireland, Luther
    altarpiece in Wittenberg 60
    ecclesia semper reformanda 4, 15, 158, 161
    France 104–25
    freedom and democracy 4, 104–5
    German culture and literature 140–57
    images 47–65
    Kulturprotestantismus 140
    legacies of 91–177
    Lutheran rectories 140–57
    Quincentenary 1–2, 13, 16, 104, 171–2
    revocation 105–16
    women 16, 111, 115, 116, 146, 160
Rehmann, R. 143
Repentance 35, 67–77, 92, 98–9, 176
    see also Guilt, Penance, Redemption, Salvation, Sin
Reuchlin, J. 37
Rhau-Grunenberg, J. 32
Richter, J.P.F. 153
Richter, L. 150
Rogation Week 34
Romanticism (Germany) 60–1, 140, 142–5, 153
    Kunstreligion 145
Ruvigny, 2nd Marquis de (Henri de Massue) 120–1
Saints 38, 47–55, 60–3, 97
Salmeron, A. 135
Salvation 1–2, 8–9, 25, 27, 34–5, 41, 49, 52–6, 61, 69, 81, 92–9 *passim*, 145–6, 159, 175
    see also Penance, Redemption, Repentance, Sin
Sanders, E.P. 92–8
Schelling, F.W.J. 142
Scheurl, C. 33
Schiller, F. 142
Schinkel, K.F. 143
Schlaffer, H. 146
Schlegel, A.W. 142
Schlegel, F. 142
Schleiermacher, D.E.F. 60, 142, 146

Schliemann, H. 143
Schmalkaldic League 81–3, 126
Schulte, J. v. 142
Schulz, W. 146
Scotland, Scottish 9–10, 115, 129, 132–3
Scriptures 3, 8, 14, 37–42, 52, 68–9, 73, 79, 96, 98, 106, 159, 167, 169
    see also Gospels
Secularism 2, 11, 140, 144–5, 169, 176
Seidel, I. 154
Selwyn, D. 81–2, 85
Sin 3, 35, 51, 53–4, 92–9
    see also Guilt, Penance, Repentance, Salvation
    cupidity 68
    and divine action 67–77
    original 67, 70–4
    remission of 35, 38
Spenlein, G. 15
Spinks, J. 58
Staupitz, J. v. 22–4, 28, 36, 98
Stendahl, K. 92–3, 97
Storm, T. 152
Strype, J. 85
Sweden 8, 12–13, 118, 161, 165, 173
    Lund 11–14, 161, 165, 169, 173
    Malmö 11–12
Switzerland 4, 106, 111, 113–17, 120, 142
Talbot, R. 120
Tauler, J. 1–2, 21–8, 98
Todorov, T. 123
Torah 92–3, 97–8
Trant, P. 120
Treaty of Alès 112
Tudor 126–8, 132
Tyndale, W. 83
Ussher, J. 11, 132–3
Vallière, J. 106
Volf, M. 104–5, 123
Voss, J.H. 141, 149–50
Warham, W. 82
Wars of Rohan 112
Weber, M. 61
Wieland, C.M. 142
Wildermuth, O. 154
Will, the 3, 67, 69, 71–2
    see also Freedom

freedom of the will 3, 67, 69, 71–2
William III 120, 122
Williams, R. 18
Wittenberg 3, 4, 16, 22, 24, 33–42, 49–51, 59–62, 78–87passim, 126, 145, 158, 160
Wolfe, D. 136
Wohmann, G. 143
Woodcuts 3, 51, 55–6, 58, 80, 150
Wright, N.T. 92
Younan, Munib 12
Zell, K. 16
Zell, M. 16
Zwingli, H. 8, 16, 47, 59, 63, 160